West Academic Publishing's Law School Advisory Board

Trial Advocacy

Joseph C. Bodiford, J.D., LL.M.
Adjunct Professor of Law,
Stetson University College of Law

A SHORT & HAPPY GUIDE® SERIES

WEST
ACADEMIC

a short & happy guide series is a trademark registered in the U.S. Patent and Trademark Office.

© 2024 LEG, Inc. d/b/a West Academic
    860 Blue Gentian Road, Suite 350
    Eagan, MN 55121
    1-877-888-1330

Published in the United States of America

ISBN: 978-1-64708-761-6

Preface

If you have never seen a trial in real life, put this book down and run (not walk) to the courthouse and watch a trial. Or, for quicker results, watch one on YouTube or CourtTV. Even your law school will have mock trial classes with "full trials" as finals. Many law schools host competitions, and you can see the same case litigated by different people from all over the country. Whatever it is, the stuff in this book needs *context*.

The process of a trial is pretty much the same all over the country:

JURY SELECTION

Attorneys question potential jurors to pick the ones they like and eliminate the ones they don't

OPENING STATEMENTS BY BOTH SIDES

First chance to tell the story to the jury

WITNESSES TESTIFY AND ARE CROSS EXAMINED

The actual people involved tell their story

MID-TRIAL MOTIONS

OTHER SIDE'S WITNESSES TESTIFY AND ARE CROSSED

MORE MOTIONS, JURY INSTRUCTED

CLOSING ARGUMENT

Arguing about the testimony, asking for a particular verdict

FINAL JURY INSTRUCTIONS

DELIBERATION, VERDICT

POST-TRIAL MOTIONS; APPEAL(?)

All of these parts (save mid-trial motions and specific post-trial and appeal issues) will be touched on in this book. But to really understand the nuances of what goes on, you must watch real live trials. There is so much more that goes on—such as judges wanting the case to move faster, witnesses fighting on cross and slowing down the process, objections (and more objections and even more objections)—and jurors waiting unnecessarily in the hallways and jury rooms while the attorneys duke it out in the courtrooms. Understanding how the process works means understanding how the static impacts the proceedings.

Watch trials. Every lawyer and judge will teach you something, be it a "to do" or an "avoid".

Using this book.

Before moving on from this foundational section into the "nuts and bolts" of putting together a case for trial, let's look at what is coming up.

Trial Preparation	• Building a theory to use throughout the case • Analysis of facts and witnesses • Organizing your case for trial • Preparing yourself and your witnesses for the courtroom
***Voir dire* and Jury Selection**	• The processes of questioning and picking jurors • How you decide what type of juror you want and your case • Preparing for jury questioning and selection • The different types of questioning and selection • How to speak with jurors in a useful and helpful way • Objections and *Baston* (race) issues in the selection process
Opening Statements	• What an opening statement should be and should accomplish • How to prepare for opening statement • Developing the case theory, themes, and topics into "mini stories" • Delivering the opening statement
Direct Examination	• Identifying and understanding the purpose of direct examinations • Learn to analyze the facts and witness and their roles in the trial • Learn ideas of how to prepare for your direct examination

	• Learn best practices for structuring and organizing a direct examination • Explore tips for delivering direct examination • Understand how to handle and use evidence and demonstratives
Cross Examination	• Why cross examination is so important to our legal system • Preparing for and organizing cross examinations • How to get those golden "target facts" • Dealing with objections • Tools for controlling difficult witnesses
Closing Argument	• Preparing for closing argument • Ideas for structuring a closing argument • The importance of using the law (jury instructions) • The importance of "The Ask" • Techniques for delivering a persuasive closing argument
Evidence and Objections	• Authentication of evidence • Evidentiary objections to control the substance, the witness, and opposing counsel • When to make objections • The proper technique for making objections • Preserving the record if overruled
Post-trial Considerations	Final to-dos and considerations

At the outset of each chapter, you'll find a list of objectives—the key "takeaways" you should plan on getting out of that part of the book. After reading the chapter, review the objectives and think about what you might find most interesting, or what you think might need more study and practice.

Throughout this book, I will give you quick tips—kind of like what you would expect your trial advocacy skills professor or trial team coach to do after a practice trial. Those tips will be everything from stuff I have seen and thought was particularly good or bad, to style tips, and things to never, ever, ever do in a courtroom.

What this book is not. The law is becoming more and more specialized. Naturally, trials are becoming more and more specialized. The approach to a civil court trial on a defamation is different than from a criminal charge of burglary, for example. As such, specifics of the various causes of actions, damages, elements of crimes, and the like are largely left out. There are many sources (online and in print) for commentary on specific areas of law. This book is about the "nuts and bolts" of how to try *any* case in state or Federal court.

Thoughts and thanks.

Writing a book is hard. Writing a book on a live, in-person skill is even harder. After over 27 years as a trial lawyer, one might think it easier to write on the topic of trial advocacy. The truth is, it's incredibly difficult to corral all the thoughts, emotions, tactics, urges, instincts, and alchemy that go into trying a case. I hope that those who read this book feel my passion and love for courtroom advocacy, and that something in these pages helps them become better trial advocates.

Looking back at my career in the courtroom, there are so many people I owe a debt of gratitude to, that I would certainly miss some if I tried to list them all. Thank you to all my colleagues and friends in the legal community for all you do to make our system of justice work.

Special thanks go to the professors and staff at the Stetson University College of Law—for the wonderful advocacy education they gave me, and for allowing me the honor of teaching advocacy to future generations of trial lawyers.

My family has been most supportive, and always cheer me on. My sincerest appreciation goes to the love of my life, Diane, and our two wonderful daughters, Madeleine and Calista, for always believing in me. You three are my heart.

Joseph C. Bodiford
August 2023

Table of Contents

A Short & Happy Guide to Trial Advocacy

CHAPTER 1

Trial Preparation

OBJECTIVES: Preparing for trial is a long, long process. There are mundane tasks and intellectual struggles. There are things that are checked off a list, and there are issues that are discussed over and over. In this chapter, we will discuss:

- Building a theory to use throughout the case

- Analysis of facts and witnesses

- Organizing your case for trial

- Preparing yourself and your witnesses for the courtroom

1.1 Case Summary—*What's It All About?*

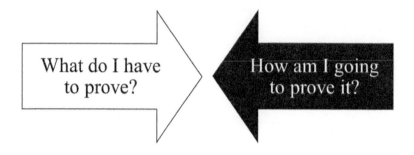

MY CASE IS SET FOR TRIAL—WHAT DO I DO? Simple: figure out what you have to prove, and how you are going to prove it!

 Learn the facts. Learn the law. Learn their relationship. Then tell your story.

By the time a case makes it to court, *something happened*. Seems simplistic, but that's the starting point—not just asking "what happened", but *determining* what happened and *the story* of what happened. Trial lawyers' roles are clearly defined in both civil and criminal cases. If you were to go in a courtroom and sit through an opening statement, and not know whether it is a civil or a criminal case, the lawyer has not figured out the case!

Everything we do in court must have a specific purpose. Calling witnesses in your case is not for the fun of it; calling witnesses is for the specific purpose of proving something. So, to start with, you must identify what it is you have to establish in your case.

In civil cases, the plaintiff's lawyer has determined that a wrong was done to her or his client, and has made the decision to seek relief in court by instituting the lawsuit. The civil defense attorney is tasked with proving the thing did not happen—if he or she determines that it in fact happened, then the case will settle, or at least not proceed to trial for a determination of liability. In either case, the advocate investigates the facts and decides how those facts fit the law that applies to the case.

In criminal cases, a law enforcement investigation has gone on, and an arrest made or an indictment filed. Sometimes the alleged illegality has happened a while in the past and the investigation has determined that a crime occurred. Other times that determination takes place in real time on the street, and an arrest is made on the spot. Either way, the prosecutor will confer with law enforcement and determine that a crime has occurred, and *if the facts prove that the applicable laws were broken,* proceed with prosecution. The criminal defense attorney will review the case, and if a determination is made that the defendant committed a crime, a plea will likely follow. If the determination is made that no crime was committed by her or his client, the case goes to trial.

The trial lawyer must conclude what happened, and develop a theory that explains the "who, what, when, why, and how" of what happened—all against the template of the elements of the cause of action or crime charged (the applicable law). For example, if a grocery store leaves a floor wet, and someone slips and falls, then the claim is for *negligence*. Recall from law school the elements of a negligence claim:

- Existence of a duty
- Breach of that duty
- Proximate cause by that breach
- Damages

Easy, right? Then the process of synthesizing the facts and the law begins. **What are the elements, and what facts prove or disprove them?**

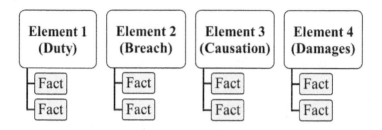

Also easy! Now you know the basics of what you have to prove and what you need to prove it. Time to get organized and dig deeper.

1.2 From Law to Facts: Developing a Case Theory, Themes, and Topics

Telling your story can be broken down into parts. You have the overall case theory. To prove that you have several themes, which are smaller "mini-stories". Within the themes, there are smaller topics, which are specific scenes that explain a theme. Finally, within each scene, there will be an important target fact.

To get there, you must first figure out the law, then apply the facts to the law, and finally you can structure your story at trial.

1.2.1 The Law

The best place to start in any case—civil or criminal—is the *jury instructions*. Jury instructions are the law—they contain the *elements* of the cause of action or crime charged. The "elements" are based on statutes and case law. Standard jury instructions are written by the courts and read to the jurors as guidance for what is the substance of the law upon which they should decide the case. The jurors must know the applicable law so they can apply the facts—as they understand them—to the laws and render a verdict.

There are instructions at the beginning of the trial, letting jurors know how the trial will be progressing. There are various instructions during the trial as to various issues, such as reminding jurors not to discuss the case on breaks, or as to certain evidentiary issues (such as limiting instructions on 404 (prior bad act) evidence, stipulations, experts, etc.).

 Always remember to check the jury instructions against the applicable statutes/laws, to make sure all elements are covered.

At the end of the trial, the final instructions on the law are given. It is in these instructions that the jurors are told what the "elements" of the cause of action or crime are, so they can apply the facts to those elements to decide the case. For example, consider the basic jury instructions for a misappropriation of a trade secret claim:

[Name of plaintiff] claims that [name of defendant] misappropriated a trade secret belonging to [name of plaintiff].

To prove [his/her/its] claim, [name of plaintiff] must prove the following facts by a preponderance of the evidence:

1:   [Name of plaintiff] owns a valid trade secret; and

2:   That trade secret relates to a product or service used in, or intended for use in, interstate or foreign commerce, that [name of plaintiff] calls [name of trade secret(s)]; and

3:   [Name of defendant] misappropriated that trade secret.

This forms the basics of what you must do at trial—prove, by a "preponderance of the evidence"—which is anything more that

50%—that (1) the plaintiff owns a trade secret, (2) that the identifiable trade secret was used in interstate commerce (to meet the requirement to be in Federal court), and (3) that it was "misappropriated."

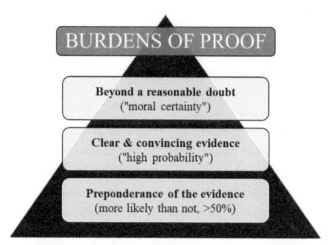

What does "misappropriated" mean and how do you prove it? The jury instructions hold the answer:

> *Misappropriation.* [Name of plaintiff] *claims that* [name of defendant] *acquired, disclosed, or used* [name of trade secret] *without the right to do so. This is called "misappropriation."*
>
> *For* [name of plaintiff] *to prove that* [name of defendant] *misappropriated* [name of trade secret], [name of plaintiff] *must prove the following by a preponderance of the evidence:*
>
> *1: [Name of defendant] acquired, disclosed, or used [name of trade secret] without [name of plaintiff]'s express or implied consent; and*
>
> *2: [Name of defendant] knew or should have known that [name of trade secret]*

i.   *was derived from or through a third person who used improper means to acquire the trade secret;*

ii.   *was acquired under circumstances giving rise to a duty to maintain the secrecy of [name of trade secret] or limit the use of [name of trade secret], or*

iii.   *was derived from or through a third person who was under a duty to maintain the secrecy of or limit the use of [name of trade secret].*

"Improper means" may include theft, bribery, misrepresentation, breach or inducement of a breach of duty to maintain secrecy, and espionage through electronic or other means.

 Use jury instructions throughout your trial prep, from start to finish.

There you go—what you have to prove, in black and white. Working backwards from the law to the facts, you will have insight into what you must prove, and then can set about proving it. It will be much easier to identify your ultimate issue and other target facts.

1.2.2   *The Facts*

Facts are stubborn things. Meting out the facts and getting to the bottom of what happened is critical. Think of facts as having one of three characteristics: (1) essential facts, (2) introductory, background, historical facts, and (3) impeachment/rebuttal facts. All those things go toward proving or disproving the elements of the cause of action or crime.

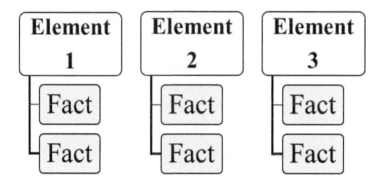

Factual analysis: categorizing your facts. You have to look at everything, down to the finest detail. Not every fact is important; whether the sky was cloudy or clear is not always important. Some facts are just inconsequential.

TYPES OF FACTS
Essential facts
Introductory, background, historical facts
Impeachment/rebuttal facts

Other facts go to either the ultimate issue or to a witness issue. Think about them—what do they mean for you? What do they mean for the other side? An easy way to do it is to apply a simple category to each fact: good (helps) or bad (hurts), and whether it's positive (for you) or negative (against you) (see section 1.2.3).

1.2.2.1   Essential Facts (*Ultimate Issue or Element Facts*)

Essential facts (aka *ultimate issue or element facts*). Without proving certain facts, you will not survive a mid-trial motion for acquittal or directed verdict. Proof of essential facts makes or breaks your case. As discussed above, the best way to define your essential facts is to go to the jury instructions:

1.   Look at the charging document (complaint, indictment, etc.)

2.   Pull the statutes or case law under which the case is pled

3.   Pull the jury instructions for each cause of action or crime—what are the *elements* to be proved?

4.   Look at your facts: which of your facts goes to proving the cause of action or crime?

5.   Once you have defined your essential facts, research case law for similar cases to see whether similar cases have gone through the courts—and what happened

6.   Adjust your essential facts as necessary

Look for identifiable facts in your favor—facts that help you win your case, facts that you need to make sure the jury hears. Remember, you may not have a witness to say what you need. You may have to use the other side's witness to get out a critical fact. And the other side may conveniently leave them out of a direct. You must be prepared to go get them on cross.

What is the ultimate issue? What is favorable to you? Who was involved, or was at a scene? What is one person saying happened as opposed to what someone else says happened (conflicts in the evidence)? When did something happen—the order, the day, the time? Why, perhaps getting into opinion, but still important—why someone went to a place at a particular time, or why someone was motivated to do something.

Once you have identified ultimate issue facts, you can build your story around them. Consider this witness list in a personal injury case you might be defending, where the ultimate issue is liability. If the issue is who caused or contributed to the injury, consider:

Witness	Role in case	Target fact
Amy Able	Mother of defendant teen driver, saw car crash from her front porch	Her son was a new driver; very little experience; been warned before about his speed in the neighborhood; will say husband was inside and did not see crash
Betty Baker	Neighbor, has known teen driver since he was a child; her child gets rids to high school with defendant	Her child stopped riding to school with defendant because she was scared to be in the car with him driving
Charlie Carter	Mailman in neighborhood; was walking, delivering mail and saw the crash	Almost to defendant's porch to deliver mail when heard crash; neither of defendant's parents were on the porch

And so on. The goal of this exercise, with every case, is to know who is going to say what. And more importantly, to know who is going to say *what you need them to say.*

1.2.2.2 Introductory, Background, Historical Facts

Setting the tone for the ultimate issue facts is important to telling your story. Just as with witnesses, some facts go not so much to the critical element of the cause of action or crime, but to the context.

Histories. Locations. Times. Back stories. Background facts are important to setting the tone and giving context. Tone and context allow your jurors to better visualize the case. When the jurors share your client's vision of what is going on, you are on the way to a favorable verdict. Never underestimate the power of background facts—but don't bog down in them, either. These facts include things like:

- Employment history

- History of a company

- How a product was researched and ultimately developed

- How someone came to know someone else

- Timeline of when a crime was discovered relative to when it was committed

- Expertise (including education, experience, publications, work history, etc.)

There is no specific list, but analyzing these facts help you build the setting for the important things in the trial.

1.2.2.3 Impeachment/Rebuttal Facts

 Know your predicates (impeachment, refreshing, etc.) so that you can get to impeachment facts smoothly.

Impeachment and *rebuttal facts* work oppositely of ultimate issue witness facts (ultimate issue facts). Impeachment facts break down the other side, to attack the credibility of the other side's witnesses and evidence. When credibility is critical, impeachments are crucial. For example, prior inconsistent statement witnesses are impeachment witnesses. So are witnesses who can testify as to prior bad acts, or acts/statements of the other side's witnesses that show bias and prejudice. Consider:

- Criminal record/prior convictions

- Ability to see/hear incident

- Prior inconsistent statements

- Lies and false statements

- Reason for testifying

- Interest in the outcome of the case (bias, prejudice)

- Memory issues

- Negative impeachments/omissions (what witness did *not* do that should have)

Credibility is built by showing the jury good witness facts. Witness facts should be scrutinized for possible bias and prejudice attacks.

Impeachment facts are like a quiver of arrows to destroy a witness' credibility. *Impeachment witnesses* are those who provide the impeachment facts.

Rebuttal facts are similar to impeachment witnesses, in that they are used to attack the other side. The difference is that while impeachment facts attack a witness' credibility, rebuttal facts explain, neutralize, or dispel the other side's evidence. Rebuttal facts go to the elements of the cause of action, crime, or defense.

1.2.3　Good Facts vs. Bad Facts

While some courts require a trial brief (see section 1.4), having your own running document with all the important facts, law, arguments, having a repository of your thoughts about the law and facts can be very helpful. It can be in the form of a fact analysis checklist (see 1.9.6).

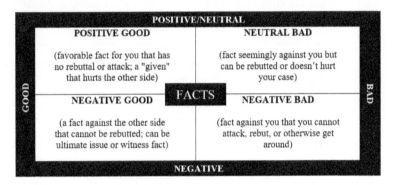

Positive good: Undisputed facts. A day of the week or a calendar date. A document, such as a contract or an insurance policy. A photo or video. A statement under oath. Any fact that is the strongest fact that supports your case—*essential element facts*.

Negative good: Undisputed facts that don't necessarily help you, but strike at the heart of the other side. These facts can be the same as "positive good" facts, but can also include rock solid impeachments. A fact from an objective witness who contradicts the other side is an example. Facts that directly contradict an element or defense is another—*impeachment/rebuttal facts*.

Neutral bad: Generally thought of as "I don't like that particular fact being out there, but we can deal with it" facts. Facts like insignificant, old prior convictions are bad but essentially neutral—especially if the witness has a more recent history of being honest and trustworthy. Easily rebutted comments that could be perceived as bias, but are mostly "throwing shade" at the witness, are seemingly bad but easily contradicted as just noise.

Negative bad: Negative bad facts are things so significant and damning that you should strongly urge your client to avoid trial. In a criminal case, undisputed confessions to the crime or DNA at the scene are negative bad facts. In a civil trial, a contract with breach with no legal defense is an example. These are *essential element facts* that need very close attention!

 "Take the wind out" of your opponent's "sails" by **dealing with bad facts on direct** and explaining them.

Dealing with bad facts. Bad facts are just bad facts. You didn't make the bad fact. You should not hide from the bad fact. You must *deal with it*, though. One tried a true method of dealing with bad facts is to be the first side to admit them, do your best to explain them, and move on. This is commonly called "taking the wind out of the sails" of the other side. If you have a bad fact, you can gain credibility with the jury for addressing and dealing with it. You also take away the other side's "sting" of being able to spring the bad fact on cross examination. Sure, the other side can cross on it, but you have already dealt with it. Your witness can simply say, "as I said before" and repeat the direct exam explanation. After that, if the other side pushes, you object to "asked and answered."

1.2.4   *Putting It All Together: Theory, Themes, and Topics*

Telling your story can be broken down into parts. You have the overall case theory. To prove that you have several themes, which are smaller "mini-stories". Within the themes, there are smaller topics, which are specific scenes that explain a theme. Finally, within each scene, there will be an important ***target fact***.

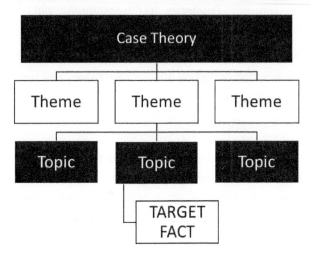

1.2.4.1   Case Theory

Your case theory is a concise statement of what happened and should be clearly based in fact, logic, and reasoning. Facts that are provable, that have emotional and other primal attachment, and are memorable are the best facts to focus on. But, as you will learn, there are several types of facts of significance. Identifying them is a good starting point.

Your case theory is the overall "what happened" that led to the reason you are in trial. It can be why, it can be how, who . . . or a combination of some or all those things. Consider these case theories:

BigCorp intentionally breached the contract to supply widgets to SmallCo because it found it could make more money supplying SmallCo's competitor, Big Bad Inc.

Vinnie Victim was robbed at gunpoint by Able and Baker.

Cosmetics LLC has always, and always will, put its customers first, and has the highest standards of testing for allergies and product control. Cosmetics LLC absolutely did not allow contaminated makeup to leave its factory. The contamination was the fault of the user, plaintiff Molly Model.

The emotion or feeling of your case theory will turn into your rivet phrase (see section 3.3).

1.2.4.2   Themes

With the overall theory of the case settled, you can begin to devise the storyboard and how the facts will be presented to tell your story. For example, in a negligence case, there are four elements: duty, breach, causation, and damages. Each of those have a "mini story": how was the duty created? How was the duty acknowledged by the defendant? What led up to the breach? How exactly did the breach happen? Who was responsible for the breach? What was the injury? How did it happen? And so on. Each part of the story can be clearly broken down.

More on this in sections 4.4 and 5.3.

1.2.4.3   Topics

Within each theme (or mini-story), there is a topic, or scene. That scene will play down to a final *target fact*. Using the negligence case and the theme of "breach", there could be a couple of topics or scenes that establish the target fact. For example, you might create topics for (1) safety protocols were set in place (by who, when, and how), and (2) protocols were not followed (who dropped the ball, and how). Continually drilling down into the story, just like in a Hollywood movie, you will be able to establish distinct scenes that illustrate important parts of your story.

Again, more on this in sections 4.4 and 5.3.

1.3 Witness Matrix

1.3.1 The Witness Matrix—*Who Are the Players?*

Careful preparation includes not only knowing exactly what each witness is going to say, but also what the role of the witness is in the story. One way to do that is to create a witness matrix. The witness matrix is a "at your fingertips" reference tool to keep everything organized and handy.

For your witness matrix, gather the following information. You may want to add biographical or contact information, such as addresses, phone numbers, and email addresses. There is no set format—whatever works for you, so long as you have this information centralized.

Who are the players? First, identify and categorize your witnesses.

TYPES OF WITNESSES	
Essential fact (element, ultimate issue) witnesses	Those who establish the elements and ultimate facts
Introductory, background, historical witnesses	Records custodians, people who had a small role in the over picture, people who can add context to the story but are not "essential fact" witnesses
Impeachment/rebuttal witnesses	Witnesses to prior bad acts (404), prior inconsistent statements, etc.; witnesses who have some "admissible,

	relevant dirt" that will attack the credibility of the witnesses
Experts	Qualified experts who add a degree of knowledge to the case that lay witnesses and jurors do not have.

Witnesses can play multiple roles in a case, depending on the facts. Just taking the time to analyze them and know how they can be used is integral to pretrial preparation and getting ready to tell your story.

1.4 Trial Order/Memo/Brief (Developing the Theory)

 Trial briefs are not always required by the courts but can be used internally for organizing and strategizing.

Many judges will require a memo or brief to be filed well in advance of the trial. Sometimes it is required to be filed jointly, with the agreement of the other side; other times, each side files their own version.

Going through the analysis of the facts and law is a great exercise to undertake *early* in trial preparation. You should do it whether the judge requires it or not.

The following is from an actual pretrial order, directing counsels to file a joint response. Note the content; you can use this information for your own prep whether or not you are required to file one with the court.

Contents of the Pretrial Order

The subjects discussed below should be addressed in separate, tabbed, and numbered sections of the Pretrial Order. The Pretrial Order either should be placed in a three-hole binder or clipped at the top left corner of the document, with tabs on the right side.

1.   Jurisdiction. A concise statement of the basis for federal subject matter jurisdiction, and if jurisdiction is disputed, the nature and basis of the dispute.

2.   Claims. A concise joint statement (1 or 2 short paragraphs) of the claim(s) of the plaintiff(s), defense(s) of defendant(s), and all counterclaims and cross claims and the defenses to them. In a jury trial, this statement will be read to the jury during voir dire.

3.   Relief sought. An itemization of the damages and other relief sought.

4.   Contested issues. A concise, numbered list of the contested issues of fact and/or law.

5.   Witnesses. A list of names and addresses of all witnesses including experts:

(a) who will be called; (b) who may be called; (c) whose deposition will be used. In a jury trial, this list will be read to the jury during voir dire. Any witness not listed in the Pretrial Order will be precluded from testifying absent a showing of very good cause, except that each party reserves the right to call such rebuttal witnesses (who are not presently identifiable as rebuttal witnesses) as may be necessary.

a.   Objections. A statement of any objections to the calling of any witness, including expert witnesses.

Objections not made in the Pretrial Order will be deemed waived absent a showing of good cause. If the objection is the subject of a motion in limine, the Pretrial Order may simply refer to the motion and need not repeat the grounds stated in the motion.

b.   Depositions. For each witness whose deposition will be used, the party that intends to call that witness shall submit the witness's deposition transcript with the testimony the party intends to read to the jury highlighted in yellow. The opposing party shall highlight its counter-depositions in pink. Any party that objects to the other party's designations shall submit a list of its objections by page and line number and the basis for the objection. The opposing party shall submit its response to such objections. This can be done in separate documents or in a side-by-side presentation in a Word table or Excel spreadsheet. The basis for an objection and the response shall be stated as succinctly as possible with appropriate citations to evidentiary rules or case law. Objections not made in the pretrial order will be deemed waived absent a showing of good cause. If the Court will be called upon to rule upon objections, a copy of the deposition is to be provided with the pretrial order.

6.   Exhibits. A schedule of all exhibits a party may introduce at trial, as well as any demonstrative exhibits or evidence, identified by trial exhibit number, with a brief description of each exhibit. Any exhibit not listed in the Pretrial Order will be excluded from evidence. Joint exhibits should be denominated "JX," plaintiff's exhibits, "PX" and defendant's exhibits, "DX." Copies of the exhibits should be included with the Pretrial Order, if practical, or submitted in a separate binder or folder.

a.   *Objections. A statement of any objections to each exhibit. Objections not made in the Pretrial Order will be deemed waived. The parties should follow a similar format for objections to exhibits as is outlined above for deposition designations.*

b.   *Exhibits to be displayed to jury. If an exhibit is to be displayed to the jury, the party intending to display the exhibit must make sufficient copies for all jurors or must use an enlargement or projection of the exhibit.*

This is just a sampling of what can be in a pretrial brief or memo. If permitted to actually brief out the story, be creative and persuasive. If you are not sure whether the judge would like one or not, *ask*. Just remember what you put in it—*the other side will get a copy!*

1.5 Pre-Trial Practice

This section is not intended to be a full "how to" of taking and defending depositions (which is very important!), or drafting pleadings and the like. But pre-trial preparation is directly proportional to success at trial. If you have investigated your witnesses, you will know who has impeachable prior convictions. If you have taken good depositions, you have locked in the witnesses and will be ready to cross examine them. If you know your case, you can direct how the story comes out at trial, as opposed to watching it unfold and trying to punch back after the damage has been done!

1.5.1   Depositions, Requests for Admissions and Production

Suffice it to say, depositions and pretrial production is where you will find your facts.

There are many written books on depositions and deposition skills. Taking thorough depositions will uncover facts of all types. However, you can't just go in blind and expect witnesses for the other side to simply hand things over. Do your homework. Investigate your case. Know the subjects you wish to inquire about. Question everything. Follow up on answers and ask for more. Do all of this with the basic facts in mind.

Similarly, you can get facts from admissions and production from the other side. The same rules apply—know where you are going and ask for the right stuff. Follow up. Ask the court for permission to ask for more if you think you need it.

The following West Academic books are highly recommended for further reading and study:

- Clary, Paulsen, and Vanselow's *Successful First Depositions*, 4th

- Moore, Binder, Bergman, and Light's *Depositions in a Nutshell*, 2d

- Scheindlin and The Sedona Conference's *Electronic Discovery and Digital Evidence in a Nutshell*, 2d

- Roen and Reich Paulsen's *Civil Litigation: Pretrial Case Development and Discovery*, 2d

1.5.2   Pre-Trial Motions

The importance of pre-trial motion practice and its impact on the case can be profound. A suppression of evidence will change the facts of the case; what was once there is now gone. Depriving the government of the use of your client's illegally-obtained confession makes the story a whole lot different. Suppression of drugs and guns will also change the narrative.

In both civil and criminal cases, motions *in limine* are fantastic tools to help you prepare the judge for trial. Motions *in limine* can also change what facts come out at trial. A really hurtful statement against your case can vanish if it is hearsay or in some other way inadmissible. Character evidence that is ruled prejudicial under 403 and precluded can even the playing field. Once you have mastered the facts, you can mount a pre-trial attack on them to change the story before the jury is even selected. Always check local rules, court rules/pretrial orders, and judge's preferences as to any filing deadlines.

As with books about depositions and admissions/production, there is a great deal to know about the proper practice for filing and litigation pretrial motions. The following West Academic books are highly recommended for further reading and study:

- Dessem's *Pretrial Litigation in a Nutshell*, 7th

- Roen and Reich Paulsen's *Civil Litigation: Pretrial Case Development and Discovery*, 2d

Renew, renew, renew. If you lose a pretrial motion, don't forget, *when the evidence comes up at trial, make your contemporaneous objection!* Too many attorneys spend time in pre-trial practice, litigating all sorts of motions to control the evidence—only to miss the objection at trial and lose the issue for appeal. Don't waste time and not preserve the issue for appeal!

1.6 Witness Preparation

Your witnesses are your teammates. Preparation is key to their and your success. Remember, most witnesses are not experts, and have never testified before. They need your help in understanding the process and preparing for direct and cross examination.

1.6.1   Preparing the Witness—the Star of the Show

Success on direct examination, like every other part of the trial, requires preparation. The difference on direct is that you have to coordinate with your witness so that there is a seamless and logical flow of information from the witness to the jury. Remember, at this point in the trial, *the witness is the star*. The story is coming from the witness and you cannot ever forget that.

It is absolutely fine for you to speak with and prepare your witnesses. In fact, not preparing witnesses to testify borders on (if it's not actually) malpractice. How would you feel if your attorney told you that he/she never prepared the witness? How much worse would it be if the witness flops and you lose your case?

1.6.2   Witness Dossier

 Never, ever speak to a witness in court without his or her dossier in your hand.

Every witness needs his or her own folder—a *dossier*, if you will. A dossier is simply a collection of documents about a particular person, event, or subject. Every witness should have his or her own file, whether paper or electronic. That file should have all info needed for the trial regarding the witness, such as reports, depositions, written or recorded statements, and the like.

The dossier should contain, at a minimum:

WITNESS DOSSIER CONTENTS	
Reports	Written reports of any sort
Statements	Written statements of any sort

Documents	Business records, summaries, etc.
Deposition transcript	Check local rules on the filing or providing copies of depositions to court and opposing counsel
Videos, audios, transcriptions of statements	If a recorded statement was given, have it transcribed and annotated with time stamps, for quick reference
Summaries of statements	YOUR summaries, for quick reference in trial
Related cases, issues	Certified copies of prior convictions; photos that may impeach, etc.
Attorney notes on the witness	YOUR notes, summaries of testimony, analysis of credibility, things to be ready for at trial

A word about recorded statements—have them transcribed for ease of use. You can use a traditional court reporter or stenographer, or easily and accurately have them transcribed via online services. Simply select a service, upload the audio/video, and select the quality of transcript. You can have simply "follow along" transcripts done by a machine for a few dollars. Or you can get an actual court reporter to give you a transcript via the online service. The difference is cost and turn-around time. The best part is that most of these services will provide the time stamp on the transcript. This is excellent for refreshing or impeaching in trial, and for preparation in general.

1.6.2.1   Documents/Reports/Statements

Any and all documents that pertain to the witness need to go into the dossier. Anything and everything. If there is a report that has multiple witnesses referenced in it, *make copies for each witness' dossier*. The reason for this is that you must have everything at your fingertips. If you have marked anything up with your own notes or comments, make sure to have clean, unmarked copies in the dossier as well. If you have to use them in trial, you don't want your notes (work product) becoming a part of the trial.

1.6.2.2   Photos, Diagrams, Demonstratives

As with documents, have all photos and diagrams in the dossier, with clean copies available. Diagrams and demonstratives are usually enlarged for the jury. Be sure to have the witness look at any enlargements before trial, so that the authentication is seamless.

1.6.3   *Meeting*

Always meet with your witnesses prior to trial, if at all possible. Lawyers are not only allowed to meet with witnesses before trial, but doing so is a part of effective representation. *Always* meet with your witnesses before putting them on the stand.

Some witnesses will refuse to meet, and you simply have to deal with that. In those cases, offer to provide reports, depositions, and the like and ask (in writing) that they review everything before trial. As a last-ditch effort, you can ask them to be at the courthouse early to go over things with you. You must at least make the effort, and document your file.

Some witnesses are going to be questionable as to their motives to testify for or possibly against you. If you suspect that the witness may have ulterior motives, have a third-party witness with you at the meeting. That third-party witness will be available later to discuss what was said in the meeting, and can confirm you covered certain things, or did not say certain things. The last thing you need is for a witness to say that you told them what to say (or worse, to lie) and you have no witness to say that you did not. And you cannot be a witness in the trial in case there is a need to impeach—that's when the third-party witness comes in.

1.6.3.1   What the Witness Might Expect

Most witnesses will not have ever been in a courtroom, much less have testified in a trial. Testifying can be nerve-wracking. Nerves can cause problems. Problems can neutralize your witness and sink your case.

If you have a chance, take your witness to see a different trial. Let them know going in what they will see and talk with them after about it. Ask them what they picked up on, and what they gleaned from the experience. Most will appreciate the concern you have for them and will reciprocate with excellent trial prep and testimony.

Don't tell them what to say. You cannot put words in the witness' mouth. Give them their prior statements, discuss with them what the truth is, and insist that they stick to the truth and nothing but the truth. Our system of justice is based on truth. Suborning perjury is unethical and contrary to the very concept of justice. It infects the function of the courts and the administration of justice.

What you *can* do is discuss with witnesses how to say things and prepare them for the foreign and adversarial nature of the courtroom. You can discuss with them proper wording, speaking clearly and concisely, using proper English, how to wait for the question to finish before answering, and how to maintain their composure and position on cross.

Sights and sounds. Explain the courtroom layout and visit the courtroom with the witness if you have a chance. Let him or her know where they will be sitting, and where the jurors will be. Tell your witness where the other party will be, so they know in advance. Talk to the witness about the judge—what the judge is like, personality-wise, and what to expect from the judge. Tell the witness a story about the judge to put the witness at ease (or forewarn him or her). The more information the witness has, the more comfortable he or she will be when entering the courtroom to testify.

Cues. Witnesses have to know they are not alone. Let him or her know that you will help them while they are on the stand. Explain what cues you may use to help them. For instance, tell the witness that if he/she is looking too much at you and not telling the story to the jury, *you* will look at the jury as a reminder. Let them know if your hand comes up, to stop talking. Remind them that certain phrases you may use will redirect them back to the question, such as "let me stop you there for a moment . . .". They will appreciate the help. Remember, you cannot tell them what to say other than the truth.

What's happening around them. Explain to your witnesses the courtroom dynamics that are in play while they are testifying. Let them know your thoughts about what the jurors may be thinking, and what certain body language may be saying. Finally, make sure your witness knows to stop talking when an objection is made, and to listen to the judge's ruling.

1.6.3.2   Preparation for Testimony

Practice sessions. In your meetings with witnesses, it is a great idea to turn them into practice sessions. If you have access to a courtroom or a mock courtroom, take the witness there so they get the feel of the process. You can then help them learn to and practice important things like where to look, the tone of voice to use, and how to handle evidence or use demonstratives. *Make sure your witnesses know they are important to telling the story to the jury—and to connect with the jury while they are on the stand.*

Direct examination. You can give them a list of questions to think about, and go over that with them in the practice session. Be careful about providing actual answers, as while it could be considered work product, it could turn into something that has to be produced to the other side. So, give them ONLY the questions— no pre-fab answers, and do NOT put any of your own notes or thoughts on the list.

Cross examination. Mock cross examinations are most helpful. One of the best practice sessions you could have is to conduct a mock cross examination. Have a fellow attorney come in and cross examine the witness. The more comfortable a witness is with being able to understand the back-and-forth of cross, the better they will be with sticking to their testimony. Be sure to train the witness on statements such as, "that is not what I said", "I have previously told you . . ." and "you are misunderstanding what I said, counselor". Those phrases are very handy in fending off aggressive crosses. Make sure the witness knows that it is perfectly OK to ask you or the cross examining attorney to repeat a question or rephrase a question the witness does not understand.

1.6.4 Subpoenas

Subpoenas are critical to presenting your case. Be attentive to preparing and serving your witness well in advance of trial.

Unless you are absolutely sure that the witness will show up, get the witness served with a subpoena. Rules for service of process vary from jurisdiction to jurisdiction, so be sure to check the rules and get the subpoena out well in advance of the trial. As with service, rules regarding enforcement vary. Remember, you cannot compel a witness to show up, or make some accommodation to get the witness in court, unless you have served them in accordance with the law. Never be the advocate standing there with no witness when you had every chance to ensure his or her attendance.

1.7 Trial Notebook/Folders

Whether to use paper notebooks or folders, or to go paperless, is a personal choice.

Paper notebooks are traditional. They are comfortable. Paper is easy to pull out and use, say for an impeachment of refreshing recollection. Paper is essential in an older courtroom with little or no technology. And paper doesn't have a battery that can run out and need recharging.

However, paper does take up physical room. Paper can be heavy in bulk, and hard to transport to the courtroom, and can quickly become cluttered and disorganized in the heat of a trial or hearing.

Electronic notebooks are, quite simply, *easier*. Most jurisdictions mandate electronic filing, so pleadings are already in PDF format. PDF pleadings are easy to transport and take up virtually (pun intended) no room in the trial briefcase. PDF pleadings are easy to replicate—one can keep a clean copy and make copies to highlight and bookmark. The titles of PDF pleadings can easily be changed to alphabetize or numerically sorted for quick access.

	PROS	CONS
Paper file	• Easy to see • Tactile • "Write on" enabled in court	• Bulky • Visible to everyone • Can tie you down (less flexibility) • Can get cluttered and disorganized
Electronic file	• Easy to categorize • Searchable • Portable • Can be used with electronic display equipment in courtroom	• Harder to refresh, impeach depending on the platform • Still need copies to submit into evidence or as demonstratives

It's all personal preference. Many attorneys find it best to use a hybrid approach: you can have the entire case file in electronic format with you at trial. Perhaps even with multiple computers and tablets, and with backup. Then have the critical witness dossier contents printed for ease of use. This author uses electronic almost exclusively, with a MacBook for the entire file, and an iPad to use for refreshing and impeaching. An Apple TV is used to connect to the courtroom projection equipment. Some important documents and witness dossier's are printed, of course. It's up to whatever you are comfortable with and makes you most prepared and effective.

Contact the judicial assistant or court administrator to get in the courtroom in advance of trial to see what technology is available, what cords/connectors are needed, and to make sure your equipment is compatible. And practice with it if you need to!

Contents of the trial notebook/folder. *Everything, organized.* Who in his or her right mind decides NOT to take every part of the case file to court for the trial? Narrow-issued hearings, maybe. Not for trial. Take it ALL.

Organizing the notebook, whether paper or electronic, is largely personal. Whether the folder is analog or digital, be specific in naming the file. Indexes are too easy to compile to not have and use them.

At a minimum, have in your trial notebook:

TRIAL NOTEBOOK/FOLDER CONTENTS	
General pleadings	All pleadings, with index (who filed, date)
Important pleadings	Critical things like indictment, complaint, etc.
Pre-trial motions/orders	Important pre-trial motions on critical issues, with orders
Voir dire and jury selection Opening statement	Jury selection questions, venire lists, juror profile, juror checklists
Witness and evidence list	Lists that will be provided to the court and counsel

Center Sheet (See section 1.8)	Sheet that keeps you in line (STAYS ON TABLE!)
Witness dossiers (one per witness, whether yours or the opposition's)	See above; all the info on the witness in once place; have it with you any time you are addressing the witness; have your CROSS SHEETS included
Exhibits	Indexed and pre-marked for identification
Research (case law, statutes, etc.)	One folder per issue; if providing case law, have copies for court and counsel highlighted to pertinent parts
Closing argument	Basic outline (or script) of your closing; notate it during the course of trial
Notes (**work product)	Notes from witnesses, objections and rulings; interesting points that come out; notes about your own performance

Just remember to have everything where it can be accessed quickly, so there are no lulls in the presentation.

1.8 Center Sheet

A *center sheet,* also known as an *order of proof,* is the "anchor chart" which acts as the roadmap of the case at trial. There is no specific format for your center sheet. Simple trials have less information, complicated trials have much more information. The author's basic sheet looks like this:

TRIAL CENTER SHEET

CASE: _____ [ ] PROS/P [ ] DEF   Page 1 of 2

JUDGE	
Opposing Counsel	

SUMMARY (CASE THEORY): _____

_____

MOTIONS IN LIMINE		
PMIL1		G D
PMIL2		G D
PMIL3		G D
DMIL1		G D
DMIL2		G D
DMIL3		G D

WITNESSES	
DIRECT	CROSS
[ ] ID / [ ] VENUE	
[ ] ID / [ ] VENUE	

EVIDENCE				
DESCRIPTION	WITNESS	ID #	EVID #	PUB'D?

TRIAL CENTER SHEET

CASE: _____ [ ] PROS/P [ ] DEF   Page 2 of 2

Directed Verdict/Judgment of Acquittal:

_____

_____

_____

[ ] Renewed at end of trial

Affirmative Defenses/counterarguments:

_____

_____

_____

Closing (*Plaintiff/Prosecution* – [ ] *reserve rebuttal* – *amount of time:* ____ *minutes*)

ADMISSIBILITY	Rule	Common hearsay Uses:	Rule
Best evidence		Not offered for truth of matter asserted	
Authentic		Show bias	
Relevant		Explain witness' actions	
Not hearsay (or exception applies)		Help jury understand the witnesses actions	
Not opinion		Effect on the listener	
Not privileged		Excited/spontaneous utterance	

MISC:

POST-TRIAL/APPEAL ISSUES:

_____

_____

Case info. Many times, there are two lawyers on one side, one as lead and the other as a second-chair for an "extra set of eyes", or simply to learn and take on a few small parts of the trial. To avoid forgetting names and being embarrassed later—write all of that on your sheet, along with the case number, the name of the judge (and courtroom clerk and bailiff!), and other "biographical" data.

Pretrial motions that need to be argued. There are preliminary matters, such as last-minute motions *in limine*, and other things that may pop up right before trial. For instance, you may get a call that a witness' flight into town was delayed, and the order of your witnesses may change. Anything that you need to let the judge know *before* things get started, note here.

Witness list. All of the witnesses anticipated at trial. You don't want to forget to call someone and have to ask to re-open your case. Include anticipated length of their testimony.

Evidence list. All of your evidence. Make sure everything is pre-marked for identification and shown to opposing counsel. Then note when it is admitted, and its number "in evidence." Note when the item is published (shown to the jury).

Mid-trial motions. Making contemporaneous and timely motions is important "in case" you have to take an appeal. Note your arguments, and the rulings.

Affirmative defenses and arguments. List what you think the other side is going to argue. If there are things they have to prove (i.e., certain specific elements), list them and tick them off as the trial progresses. It makes it easier to argue against them later.

Closing (time issue). This is not the place for your outline. It is simply a place for you to remember or remind yourself to reserve time with the judge. Most judges will limit your time; if you are a party that has a rebuttal, make sure to ask to reserve a few minutes. Otherwise, if you do not, the judge may stick it to you if you use all your time on first closing!

Evidence quick reference chart. Everyone should have a list of trial objections handy (as are found at elexpublishers.com, published by the author). At a minimum, you can have the basics for admissibility on your Center Sheet. That way, you can follow along as your opponent tries to admit evidence. Then you can make quick and concise objections if they fail to lay the proper predicate for authentication.

Post-trial and appeal issues. Things happen in trial. Write them down, along with the day of trial and the time. When preparing post-trial motions or preparing for appeal, you have a list of errors to work from.

Always remember your Center Sheet and you will reduce the chances of "oh, no, we forgot . . .!"

1.9 Checklists

1.9.1 What to Do in Pretrial

INVESTIGATION AND DISCOVERY		
NEEDED?	**ITEM**	**COMPLETED**
Y	Pull jury instructions	Y
	Visit to scene to photograph and inspect	
	Evidence viewing (if in custody of police or opposing party)	
	Reports, statements of witnesses	
	Medical records	
	Business records	
	Photos, videos, diagrams, recordings	
	Insurance information	
	Damages information (medical records and bills, lost wage reports, etc.)	
	Depositions	

	Experts	
	Disclosures to opposing side	
	Transcripts	
	Witness matrix *(the contents of this list become a dossier for each witness)*	
	File (electronic or paper)	

1.9.2 Final Trial Preparation Checklist

FINAL TRIAL PREP CHECKLIST		
PRELIMINARY CONSIDERATIONS		
Needed?	**Client Meetings, generally**	**Completed**
	All resolutions (settlements/pleas) discussed, file notated	
	Discuss resolution goals vis-a-vis possible/potential outcomes	
	Develop a "BATNA" (best alternative to a negotiated agreement)	
	Set deadline for negotiations, decisions	
	Alert client to any court-/rule-imposed deadlines for resolutions	
"Skull session" meeting (separate from resolution discussion)		
	Theories of the case, from both sides	
	"Good facts" vs. "bad facts"	
	Discuss how jury selection and trial will proceed (what to expect)	

	Discuss the witness, who they are and their role in the case	
	Discuss other side's proof and how judge/jurors may process and respond to it	
	Discuss client's testimony	
	Discuss need for additional discovery	
Discovery issues		
	All discovery in from other side	
	All discovery disclosed to the other side	
	Timeline for additional discovery needed	
	Hearing time needed for discovery issues?	
Prepare the trial notebook		
	Copies of all important pleadings accessible and in notebook	
	Research file indexed and organized	
	Witness "dossier" ready and indexed, annotated	
	Research file (general)	
	Jury instructions file	
	Evidentiary issue research file	
	Element-specific research file	
	Direct questions prepared	
	Cross sheets prepared	

	Outline of opening	
	Outline of closing	
	Pre-, mid-, and post-trial motions	
	WITNESSES	
	Witnesses subpoenaed	
	Witness meetings set, witnesses prepared to testify (direct AND cross)	
	Witnesses reviewed reports, statements, depositions, etc.	
	Discuss and prepare for "bad" witness facts (impeachments, bias, etc.)	
	Experts: CV updated, all reports reviewed and disclosed, all opinions closely vetted	
	Experts prepared (incl travel, fees, etc.)	
	Direct: prepare questions, review with witness	
	Cross: practice cross exam, engage other attorneys for practice crosses	
	Review exhibits with witness, have them practice foundation questions/ process and handling/using the exhibits	
	Review demonstratives with witness, practice testimony using demos	
	EXHIBITS	
	Disclosed	

	Prepared (copies, enlargements, electronic versions for courtroom technology)	
	Pre-marked and numbered	
	Admissibility issues researched and case law ready	
	Foundation/predicate questions ready	
	Demonstratives: prepared well before trial, timely disclosed to other side	
	GENERAL	
	Center Sheet prepared	
	Order court reporter, if necessary	
	Pre-trial motions filed, heard, ruled upon	
	Mid-trial motions prepared, researched	
	"Pocket briefs" or mini-briefs prepared for potential issues	
	Stipulations reached, reduced to writing	
	Judicial notice requests filed	
	Admissions ready	
	Courtroom technology tested	
	TIMELINE/COUNTDOWN	
	Deadlines calendared based on pre-trial order, local rules, rules of court	

	Deadlines for ordering transcripts, venire panel info, interpreters, etc.	
	Deadlines for subpoenas to be served	
	Pre-trial motion deadlines	
	JURY INSTRUCTIONS	
	Jury instructions prepared	
	Requests for special jury instructions prepared and submitted	
	VOIR DIRE **AND JURY SELECTION**	
	Request for venire panel requested from clerk	
	Jury analysis completed	
	Jury expert engaged; mock trials completed	
	Jury questions prepared	
	Requested jury questions submitted to court (if judge-only *voir dire*)	

1.9.3 *Deposition Notes/Prep*

DEPO PREP CHECKLIST	
	Review of elements of COA/crime (use jury instructions)
	List of what witness will prove/disprove vis-a-vis the elements
	What to cover? • Issues that *must* be covered • Issues that *may* be covered if brought up • What to *avoid* discussing (strategy or trial tactic)

	Witness dosser items needed for deposition
	• Biographical info
	• CV for experts
	• Witness' reports, statements, interview audios/ videos
	• Maps, diagrams, etc.
	Style considerations:
	• Start with broad questions
	• Follow up with details (who, what, when, where, why, how
	• Confirm if details given are known, guesses, or assumptions based on some logic (and why witness is assuming)
	• Get agreements to uncontroverted facts
	• As to facts in issue, question regarding lack of memory, ability to see/hear, alternate sources of witness' information
	• LIES, LACK OF MEMORY: commit witness to the lie to set up impeachment at trial
	• Always conclude with "is there anything I have missed that you think I need to know" question— witness may have something important that you do not even know exits and therefore don't ask about
	• Certify questions the witness refuses to answer
	• NEVER talk with the witness "off the record"
	• DEFENDING DEPO: make record of objections; answer all questions possible before concluding, and note anything witness will not answer and why before concluding

1.9.4   *Witness Preparation Checklist*

WITNESS PREP CHECKLIST
Witness matrix • Name, address, telephone, email, social media • Role in case (i.e., testimony expected) • Tangible evidence associated with the witness • Whether to be deposed, and if so, noted once deposed

Witness dossier
• Name, address, telephone, email, social media
• Role in case (i.e., testimony expected)
• Tangible evidence associated with the witness (reports, statements, etc.)
• Deposition transcripts, notated
• CV and research summary for expert
• Whether to be deposed, and if so, noted once deposed
• Criminal record, if any
• Important info for each witness (other cases, other testimony given, etc.)
• Note whether needs trial subpoena, and if so, when sent/served
• Investigator to locate witness if necessary
• Note "positives" and "negatives", such as:
   • Credibility
   • Bias
   • Prior record
   • "Good facts" or "bad facts"

• Note "target facts" for each witness

1.9.5 Elements Checklist

ELEMENTS (PROOF) CHECKLIST
• List all pleadings (pull from online case docket to be sure you have everything)
• Include critical pleadings (complaint, answer, indictment, substantive motions) to your case file

ELEMENT 1:	PROOF:
ELEMENT 2:	PROOF:
ELEMENT 3:	PROOF:
DEFENSE 1:	PROOF:
DEFENSE 2:	PROOF:

*   Note, your case may have more or fewer elements—make sure all are covered, and you have your proof of each (facts) clearly listed for each.

1.9.6 Fact Analysis Checklist

FACT ANALYSIS CHECKLIST
• List ALL facts
• Categorize facts as essential, I/B/H, or impeach/rebuttal
• Categorize facts as disputed or undisputed
• Categorize facts as "good facts" (for your side) or "bad facts"
• Identify which witness(es) will supply what fact(s)

Good facts (element/ultimate issue facts)	
FACT	**PROVED BY (witness, evidence)**
Element/ultimate issue facts	
Introductory, background, historical facts	
Impeachment/rebuttal	
Bad facts (neutral or really bad)	
FACT	**PROVED/DISPROVED BY**
Element/ultimate issue facts	
Neutral facts	
Witness facts	
Credibility fact	
Bias/prejudice fact	
Impeachment fact	
Introduction, background, historical facts	
Witness related background	
Case history (non-witness specific)	

1.9.7   *Exhibit Checklist*

	Item disclosed in discovery
	Exhibit identified by
	Exhibit authenticated by

	Custodian(s) of exhibit subpoenaed and available
	Chain of custody witnesses:
	Enlargement made (if needed)

1.9.8 Witness Checklist

	Witness disclosed in discovery
	Witness deposed
	Subpoenaed for trial
	Contacted, notified
	Prepared for testimony
	Dossier complete and ready
	Impeachment defense prepared

1.9.9 Research Checklist

	Elements (statutes, jury instructions)
	Case law interpreting elements
	Evidentiary considerations
	Directed verdict/judgment of acquittal research

1.9.10 Jury Instructions Checklist

	Pulled standard instructions in jurisdiction
	SPECIAL instructions—look in other jurisdictions for JIs that may be clearer, etc.
	Research supporting request for instructions pulled
	Charge conference set or prepared

CHAPTER 2

Voir Dire and Jury Selection

OBJECTIVES: In this chapter, we will touch on the process of questioning prospective jurors (*voir dire*) and weeding out the jurors who aren't fit for the particular case (ironically called jury *selection*). There is a difference. The processes are different, and have their own techniques. As such, we will think about:

- The processes of questioning and picking jurors

- How you decide what type of juror you want and your case

- Preparing for jury questioning and selection

- The different types of questioning and selection

- How to speak with jurors in a useful and helpful way

- Objections and *Batson* (race) issues in the selection process

2.1 Purpose of *Voir Dire* and Jury Selection

While you are picking the jurors, the jurors are picking you. Always remember, the trial is about them—not about you. How *they* process your case theory and your story, how *they* understand your themes and topics, and how *they* feel about your client is what will drive the verdict. Will you be in the jury room during deliberations? No. *They* will be. Maybe they will remember and be guided by you and your words . . . maybe not. That depends on you.

 Remember, while you are picking the jurors, the jurors are picking *you*.

This chapter is not intended to be a full analysis of the psychology of questioning and selecting jurors. There are countless studies and many experts in this field. Entire books, such as the excellent work *Mastering Voir Dire and Jury Selection*, by Dr. Jeffrey T. Frederick, are dedicated to this topic. Dr. Frederick's book is especially highly recommended, as it comes from one of the foremost jury consultants in the world, who has spent decades in court working with juries in some of the country's most important cases.

However, there are some basics to know that will assist you in this very important part of the trial. This chapter will help you understand the most critical aspects of speaking with jurors, and what to look for in the jurors you want for your case.

Let's get really simplistic here, by asking the questions, *what is a juror?* and *what is a jury?* Knowing the answer to these questions will unlock greater communication and persuasion in your advocacy.

What is a juror? A juror is someone not unlike you. A juror is just a person from the community. Rarely is a juror a celebrity, or someone everyone already knows. Most of the time the jurors don't even know each other. But you can count on this: *each juror is like you in more ways that you know.*

Think about it. Jurors are people. People have feelings. They have emotions, and they have personalities. Just like you, jurors work their way through life by measuring each new thing against what they already know. Each encounter is compared, consciously or unconsciously, to some past experience in that person's life.

What is a jury? A jury is a little community that will only exist for a short, finite period of time. In that time, it will develop its own leaders and followers, and a set of unwritten rules on how to behave and interact with other jurors. It will find its own way to deal with the 6 or 12 different personalities it comprises. It will see relationships form and dissolve. There will be moments of harmony. There will be moments of adversity.

 Never think of a juror as anyone other than someone like you.

Who is the "ideal" juror? Remember that (1) jurors are people like you and me, (2) they bring their life experiences with them to court and will view the case through the lenses of their lives, and (3) they will undergo certain processes in absorbing the facts, forming a mental version of what happened, then looking for the proper resolution in the form their verdict. Then, the jury will process all of that together and make a joint decision. The ideal juror is someone who will be *fair and impartial.*

2.2 *Voir Dire* and Jury Selection: Two Different Parts and Processes

Think of picking a jury as having two distinct parts: *voir dire,* which is essentially interviewing the jurors, and *selection,* which is the process of striking and making final selections. However, it is common for the entire process to be referred to by one term or the other. Even then, there are two distinct parts—the questioning and the selecting/striking.

2.2.1   What Is Voir Dire, and What's Its Purpose?

This is when you question the jurors. The only time you can speak *with* the jurors is in *voir dire*. You will get to talk *to* them later. Speaking *with* them gets you to know a little about their personalities, backgrounds and histories, thoughts, and (most importantly) biases and prejudices.

The basic purpose of this questioning is to find ideal, i.e., fair and impartial, jurors. Most judges adhere to that purpose, but some can limit your questioning based on the philosophy that "fair and impartial" is something that is clearly obvious based on a potential juror's simple promise that they will be "fair and impartial." But there is more to it.

2.2.2   What Is Jury Selection, and What's Its Purpose?

The process of juror selection is considered by many to be juror *elimination*. In other words, identifying the venire persons who you think will *not* be good for your case. For instance, consider a criminal trial on the charge of assault or battery on a law enforcement officer. In that situation, a juror who may answer all the questions correctly about being fair and impartial may seem to be a decent candidate. However, if that juror also was a former law enforcement officer, or has close friends or family members who are police officers, that person may not be ideal for the defense. Why? There very well could be a predilection in favor of law enforcement. That juror may tend to believe a police officer simply because that witness is a police officer—even if he or she won't admit it, or doesn't even consciously believe that he or she thinks that way.

Generally, people who have some attachment or connection to the case to be tried are going to be struck (or challenged). That connection may be because they know someone involved, or are perhaps even some way themselves involved (that's pretty rare). The connection to the case may be more deeply rooted than just being a witness or participant. The connection may be through some deeply-rooted emotional impact the case may have on them because of some similar experience that juror may have had. That experience may so intimately connect them to the case that they cannot be fair and impartial.

2.3 What to Know About Potential Jurors

2.3.1 Jurors Are Just People

Recall from above, that jurors are just people . . . complicated, complex, intricate, mysterious people. They are like us in every way, and unlike us in every way. But we can all be sure that almost everyone shares the same basic human qualities. We all understand right and wrong, help and harm, justice and injustice (although this one can certainly have various meanings!). But everyone's life experiences are different, and drives how they perceive the world around them.

Looking at your case theory, who would best respond to what you are trying to convey?

2.3.2 "While You Are Picking the Jurors, the Jurors Are Picking You"

The most important ideal you can remember and employ is that *first impressions are the most important*. Being funny and pithy seems like something that can endear you to the jury, but that can backfire and ruin your rapport with the jurors. *Read the room.* Courtroom decorum . . . image . . . expectations . . . all of that goes to credibility, likability, and believability.

2.4 Preparing for *Voir Dire* and Jury Selection

Remember, this is the time when you get to question the jurors. You can inquire about their likes and dislikes, their backgrounds, what they do for a living. You can get all kinds of information about them. You can also test some case theories on them to see how they may react. This is more limited, as you will see below, but still a good time to talk with them about their feelings and what makes them tick.

You can get to know your jurors on a cursory basis. Unless you "know them" know them, you have to assume or guess certain things about the jurors. Those things, called "juror attributes", are fairly predictable based on demographics, jobs, etc. Borrowing from marketers, we know there are several basic readily-identifiable demographics applicable to any group:

Age

Gender

Income level

Employment

Geographic location

Religion and ethnicity

Occupation and education level

Family structure (including marital status)

To be sure, there are countless others (i.e., race, political affiliation, language, etc.). People do not stop being who they are when they show up for jury duty.

2.4.1 Case Related Issues and Demographics (Relating People to the Case)

Knowing your case theory and what you intend to prove or disprove, you can start to identify people who might be a good fit for your case. What emotions and feelings drive your themes and topics? Is it trust and betrayal? Fairness and cheating? Sanctity and degradation?

Using your facts and witnesses, think about what jurors will best relate to them. What about a person's background might make your facts resonate with that juror?

When you identify those, you can identify people who will themselves identify with your story. You can begin to develop a general profile of your ideal juror.

Some examples:

Your case/story is about . . .	. . .so you want jurors who are:
Money laundering	Good with numbers
Cheating someone out of a business deal (tortious interference)	Business owners and employees of small businesses
Defending against improper police action	People who have had a bad prior experience with police, even something as trivial as a speeding ticket they don't think they should have received
Prosecuting a case with a child victim	Parents

Defending a tax fraud allegation	Taxpayers or accountants OR someone who has experienced dealing with the IRS and how hard its rules are to understand
A financial crime	Accountants
A product liability	Engineers
A defamation case	People who use and understand social media
A circumstantial evidence case	People with lots of life experience

2.4.2 How to Talk About Issues Without "Pre-Trying" the Case

Preparing for jury selection involves thought about your case, your cause of action, your facts, with the goal of answering this question: *what type of juror do I want for my case?*

Framing issues as hypotheticals. One thing you absolutely cannot do in *voir dire*: give the jury the exact facts of your case and ask how they would decide. That is called *pre-trying the case*. It's improper mainly because no evidence has been heard and jurors are told not to begin to decide until ALL the evidence has been presented.

You can talk about certain things as hypotheticals. For example, take a case where you know that the other side's main witness has given several versions of "the truth" and very well could give yet another version during the trial. You cannot ask if, because of that, a juror would decide the case against the other side. You can explore how much lying and false statements would impact the juror's thoughts.

Q   Ms. Juror 1, good morning.

A   Good morning!

Q   I'd like to know your thoughts on something. If you are selected as a juror in this case, you will hear witnesses testify about certain things. Generally, what do you think about when you assess someone's credibility?

A   Oh, I don't know that I have ever actually thought about that. I can tell you that how they look and talk is important to me.

Q   As in their appearance?

A   Yes

Q   What else?

A   Well, if the person just sounds crazy or is saying crazy stuff, I wouldn't believe him.

Q   I understand, and I see your point. Let me ask you this . . . suppose someone told you one thing today, and what they are telling you seems to check out. Ok? But then you found out they told a different version yesterday. And a different version from that the day before. How then would you feel about that person?

A   I would start to doubt them. If it was something important, I would probably want to know why they told different versions.

Q   If there was no good reason for not telling the same version every time, what would you think of that person?

A   I would not believe them.

In this case, you do not have to put out what it is that the upcoming witness has said in your specific case. You have asked the juror her opinion about people *like* the witness. She has let you know that she would have serious doubts about that person's credibility. You would want that person on your jury.

Suppose the juror answered, *I wouldn't really be too concerned about it. As long as what he told me today turned out to be true, that's all that matters.* Is this a juror you would want on your case? No.

Just about any issue you have can be addressed in a roundabout way, by asking "tell me" or "help me understand" style of questions about *them*—their thoughts and feelings.

How would you feel about . . .

*If you heard [particular thing], **what would be your reaction?***

***Would it concern you** if you heard [fact, impeachment point, etc.]? Would it concern you so much that you couldn't be fair to both sides?*

*If it concerned you, how much would it concern you? Would you be able to put that aside and still render a fair verdict based on the facts and the law? **What about you makes you know that?***

***What is your opinion about** [issue, such as the police, "hired gun" expert witnesses, people with prior convictions, etc.]? If such a person were to be a witness in a case where you were a juror, what would be your reaction? Could you give that person the benefit of the doubt? Why or why not?*

Do you believe people can make mistakes? If you know someone has made a mistake, what do you look for in how they deal with that mistake?

In your daily life, tell me, **how do you** access/judge/gauge someone's credibility?

What would you think of someone who elected not to testify in his or her own case? Can you think of reasons why someone would not do that? Could you render a decision without hearing from the plaintiff or defendant?

What would you want to know about [fact, type of witness, issue]?

*REALLY IMPORTANT NOTE: this is a "short and happy" introduction to a very intense and important process. There are no formulaic questions, no complete list of questions, or any other exact list of things to ask. The list above is nowhere near complete or comprehensive. It is for you to consider how you ask questions to get jurors talking.

Discussing jury deliberation issues. How a juror might process and decide about something is good to know. You want to try to get folks on your jury who can make their own decision, stick to it, and also move others to see things their way. Some questions you may want to have ready are:

Once you decide something, how hard is it for someone to change your mind?

* * *

If you have a belief about the case, would you stick to your side? Do you think you might be persuaded to agree to a different outcome just to "get it over with?"

* * *

If all the other jurors vote for one verdict, and you do not agree with that verdict, will you stand your ground about your decision?

More on this in section 2.7.

2.4.3   *Preparing the Client for the Process*

For most litigants, this is the first time they have been in a courthouse, much less in a trial. Some have no idea that this part of the trial even exists. Not because they are dumb, but because they simply have not ever experienced it or even thought about it.

Make sure your client knows the basic gist of *voir dire* and jury selection: to find fair and unbiased jurors. Let them know that his or her input is important. Let the client know that they can give their opinions about jurors, and that you will listen and consider it. Be sure they know that the judge will ask if they are satisfied with the jurors that are ultimately selected—and this is the one shot. There are no do-overs.

2.4.4   *Jury Venire Lists*

In many jurisdictions, the lists of potential jurors are available by request (and perhaps a small fee) from the clerk of court. Obtaining those lists in advance are valuable tools in understanding who will be in your venire and potentially on your jury.

If you are able to get a list, you can do some limited background research on the jurors. You can look at social media, to see if and what they post about and "like." You can check criminal histories. Some states make voter registration publicly available— you can get an idea of the political demographics of the jurors without having to ask in open court.

*ANOTHER REALLY IMPORTANT NOTE: you CANNOT contact jurors. Period. Don't even think about it. You may see someone you know on the list—don't bring it up that he or she may be in your jury pool. They will know soon enough!

2.5 Juror Questionnaires & Proposed Questions

2.5.1 Juror Questionnaires

Purpose. Juror questionnaires are used in many jurisdictions, to give jurors time to list basic information "at a glance". An example is included at the end of the chapter (2.9.3).

Contents. Most standard questionnaires ask about things that every juror will answer. This is so that valuable time is not wasted with every juror standing and stumbling through his or her biographical information. Jurors are nervous and will forget what to say, or inadvertently leave something important out. Questionnaires ask about:

- Home ownership/residence
- Employment
- Marital status
- Spouse/significant other/adult children occupations
- Education
- Military service
- Prior jury experience
- Prior litigation experience (been a litigant or juror)
- Whether ever accused of a crime
- Hobbies, TV/reading habits

When to use them. Most courts have standard procedures for written questionnaires. Some send the questionnaires with the jury duty summons. Others send a link in the summons for potential jurors to fill out the questionnaire online. Yet other jurisdictions have the jurors fill them out when they show up. When the questionnaires are shared with counsel also varies from place to place.

> Contact the clerk of court to find out about using jury questionnaires in your jurisdiction.

For those that do not, file a motion with a proposed questionnaire and explain why asking these questions in advance would help expedite the process.

Remember, even if you don't get to use written questionnaires, you can ask the jurors all the same questions in your *voir dire*.

2.5.2   *Proposed* Voir Dire *Questions*

There are two times to submit questions in advance. First, when the court requires it (which is usually in Federal courts where judges do all the questioning of the jurors). Second, when there are sensitive questions that jurors may be reluctant to answer aloud in front of strangers.

Sometimes you are looking for answers to questions that most people just don't want to discuss. Usually, this is someone that has been in some prior legal trouble that has not disqualified him or her from jury service but is still embarrassing. This prior brush with the law could color how that juror may listen to the case, especially a criminal case. Another situation is when a potential juror has been the victim of a crime or cause of action, such as sexual battery or sexual harassment. Most folks do not want to talk about that aloud because doing so triggers anxiety, feelings of shame, or worse—and they will shut down and just not acknowledge it.

In these cases, a juror will be much more comfortable and forthright disclosing those issues in writing—especially when he or she knows that the written answer will only be seen by the judge and attorneys and will be destroyed later. Further assurance that any follow up questions will be done in chambers or outside the hearing of others will assuage that juror.

Questions to propose. What do you want to know about your jurors?

You have to be very case specific. Taking the example of a juror that may have experienced trauma as a sexual battery survivor. You do not want to victimize that person or humiliate him or her publicly, but you have to know their trauma exists. Proposed questions may look like this:

Have you or anyone close to you ever been the victim of a crime, whether it was reported to law enforcement authorities or not? No ☐ Yes ☐ (if yes, please explain:)

This case involves charges of sexual assault. Is there any experience that you or anyone close to you has had that may affect your ability to serve fairly as a juror in a case such as this? No ☐ Yes ☐ (if yes, please explain:)

Have you or anyone close to you, including a child, ever been the victim of any form of sexual assault? (This includes actual or attempted sexual assault or other unwanted sexual advance, including by a stranger, acquaintance, or family member.) No ☐ Yes ☐ (if yes, please explain:)

Have you, or anyone close to you ever felt in danger of being sexually assaulted by another person, including a stranger, acquaintance, or family member? ☐ No ☐ Yes (if yes, please explain:)

Have you or anyone close to you ever participated in a class or discussion group, or read books or articles concerning sexual assault, or sexual abuse? □ *No* □ *Yes (if yes, please explain:)*

Have you or anyone you know had any contact with, worked for, volunteered with, used the services of or contributed to a rape crisis center, rape hotline, rape prevention program, battered women/children's shelter, or similar program? □ *No* □ *Yes (if yes, please explain:)*

Please state any reason why you believe you could not or should not serve as a juror in this case:

Think about your issues and develop questions to timely propose to the court before trial.

2.6 Procedure and Scope of *Voir Dire* and Selection

2.6.1   Questioning (Voir Dire) Process

There are two main methods of questioning jurors: questioning by the attorneys and questioning by the court only. All of the jurors are seated and usually are given a number (Juror 1, Juror 2, etc.). Every court is different, but all will have everyone in the room together for the questions and answers. The jurors may be seated in a configuration similar to this:

13	14	15	16	17	18	19	20	21	22	23	24
1	2	3	4	5	6	7	8	9	10	11	12

2.6.1.1 Attorney Questioning

The most common method of questioning, mainly found in state courts, is questioning by the attorneys who represent the parties at the trial. There are different methods for attorney questioning, discussed below.

Usually, the judge will do some basic instructions and questioning about availability for the trial, disabilities that may impact hearing, seeing, or sitting for long periods. Then it will be turned over to the attorneys for questioning.

2.6.1.2 Judge-Only Questioning

Some judges will conduct the questioning of jurors themselves. This is a practice mostly seen in Federal court, but some state judges employ the practice as well.

Opinions differ as to the efficacy of judge-only questioning, as most judges will stick to standard questions and not delve into thoughts, feelings, and the like.

Remember, you can always submit proposed questions in advance. The judge will review them, and there can be a discussion on the record as to which questions will and will not be asked, and why. Making a record can be important to appeal issues later, or a defense against claims that you did not attempt to make certain inquiries of the jurors.

2.6.2 Selection Process

As with the *voir dire* process, the selection process can take on many different iterations. There are, however, two main methods: *struck* and *sequential*. Before discussing how to speak with jurors, it's helpful to understand the format in which you may be questioning them.

2.6.2.1   Struck Method

This is the most common type of attorney questioning. If the jurors are all in the box and the questioning is addressed to all the jurors at once, the court is using the *struck method*. The court selects a certain number of prospective jurors from the venire (or even the entire venire) for *voir dire*. Typically, the number of jurors selected is equal to or greater than the number of jurors required for a viable jury in that court (6 or 12), plus the total number of peremptory challenges allowed to the parties. For example, if a jury of six is required and each side has three peremptory challenges under the applicable rules, the court will call at least 12 individuals for questioning.

Under the struck method, a judge often determines before seating the strike panel whether any of the prospective jurors should be excused for hardship (for example, because the individual suffers from a medical condition or is a caregiver). During or after *voir dire* on the strike panel, the court decides any challenges for cause (see section 2.8). The attorneys then exercise their peremptory challenges against this group. The remaining individuals from the strike panel are then empaneled on the jury.

Jury panel as a whole. You can talk with every juror, starting with Juror 1 or whichever one you want. You can jump around, and talk to Juror 11 then ask a follow-up of Juror 18. Just be sure to speak to every juror if you have time. After both sides question the jurors, cause and peremptory strikes are made, and the remaining requisite number of jurors are seated.

One set of jurors at a time. In this format, you may be initially limited to speaking with Jurors 1, 2, 3, 4, 5, and 6 (or 1 through 12 if a 12-person jury). The idea is to try to get a jury out of the front people, and not waste time talking to Jurors 23 and 24 if there is no way they will get selected. Once both sides have finished questioning those jurors, cause and peremptory strikes are made. Depending on how many out of that mini-group are dismissed, jurors will be pulled from the venire and questioned, and strikes are made. The process repeats, narrowing until the requisite number of jurors are seated.

Individual questioning. Recall that there are times you will have jurors that cannot discuss their issue or situation in the group setting. Those jurors are questioned once everyone else is out of the room, or at a sidebar, or in chambers—then they are considered along with everyone else in the selection process.

Alternate jurors. In the seating chart example above, alternates might be selected from Jurors 15 and 16, or randomly from the remaining jurors. Some courts will seat the total needed plus two alternates, for a total of eight or fourteen jurors, then wait to decide the alternate right before deliberation (perhaps even by drawing numbers from a hat!). Alternates are usually *not* told they are in fact alternates, so they will pay close attention and not otherwise be inattentive, thinking they will not be a deliberating juror.

2.6.2.2 Sequential Method

The sequential method is when cause and peremptory challenges are exercised immediately after the questioning of the individual juror. Using the example above, both attorneys would limit questions to Juror 1. Then, usually at sidebar, the attorneys would exercise any strikes on Juror 1. Then Juror 2, and so on.

The major complaint with this method is that it creates a "walk of shame" situation, where the juror is immediately dismissed. So, the whole courtroom knows that the juror said something or is some type of person one of the sides does not like. It creates a really intimidating feeling in the room, and can severely impact how authentically the remaining jurors answer questions. No one wants to be singled out, and most folks will avoid doing anything that highlights them in a perceived negative way.

See section 2.8.1, below, for more about exercising challenges/strikes.

2.7 Asking Questions and Talking *with* Jurors

2.7.1 Engaging Jurors—Talking with Them, Not to Them

If you watch most jury selections, you will see a confused person asking odd questions of a large group of equally confused people. Translation: most attorneys are using canned "talking" questions and jurors have no idea what is being asked of them or why. The result? No one knows anything more about the process or the people after the *voir dire* than they did before it began.

Jurors are people, and you must treat them as such. Ask them how they *feel* about something. Ask them what they *think* about an issue. Ask them to tell you how they would *react* if they were to see certain types of evidence. But whatever you do, do not take all the time you have talking to them. Let them talk *to you.*

2.7.2 Asking Questions That Call for Discussion

Following up on section 2.4.2, consider this question: *can we all agree that the government has to prove its case beyond a reasonable doubt?*

Uh, yes. You will get immediate "yes" responses, then others will join in because of group dynamics and not wanting to be wrong or considered unknowledgeable. So, what do you learn from jurors by asking such a broad, stodgy, lawyer-ese boring question? Nothing!

How about this: *the Constitution of the United States (pointing to U.S. flag in the courtroom) guarantees to every citizen accused of a crime some very important rights. . . one of them is that the government—the accuser—has to prove its case to a high degree before a jury can convict. That's called "beyond and to the exclusion of every reasonable doubt". Who here recalls that from civics class? (jurors raise hands). Probably have not thought about that in a while, but that is the very thing that we do here in the criminal courts every day. Ms. Smith, do you remember earlier when the judge said there will be jury instructions for you all to consider and follow? Yes? One of those is the instruction about reasonable doubt. How important is it, in your opinion, for jurors to follow those instructions? How do you feel about the government having such a high burden? Is that good? OK? And if the constitution says that the defendant has to prove absolutely nothing, how do you feel about that? What do you think about the defendant having no duty to prove or disprove anything, Mr. Jones?*

The questions in the preceding paragraph are engaging—the idea is to introduce the topic, get the jurors thinking about a very important tenet of the law, and get them talking about it. From that you can get their own thoughts and ideas, as well as get them talking to and about each other's comments. And you just might educate them a bit!

When creating questions, think about how you would elicit a response. Try your questions out on friends and family. See if you can draw out comments from them. Even better, do it in a group setting where you can gauge the reaction of the crowd—does your question invite response, or shut it down?

Remember, use neutral and open-ended questions that signal to jurors that their opinion is important. Use phrases like

What is your feeling about . . .

What is your impression of . . .

What might your reaction be to . . .

What would your response be if you heard . . .

What is your sense of (or about) . . .

What would you think about (or if you heard). . .

What would you consider to be important (or not important, or to know, etc.) about . . .

Have you ever . . .

Would you want to know more if . . .

Why would you want to know more about . . .

Would it concern you if/that . . .

Always follow up with "why" or "tell me more" or "help me understand." That is where you will get more and better information, and also engage the juror. Connections can be made, or not. Either way, that will impact your selection of that juror.

Avoid "do you have a problem with . . ." That is a somewhat challenging statement. "Hey, buddy, you got a problem?" has proceeded many fistfights. Implying a problem connotes negativity and that you might take issue with the juror's response.

2.7.3   *Following Up*

Often times you will see attorneys ask a question, and while getting the answer, they are already looking for the next question to ask in their notes. So, they miss the juror's response—they may *hear* it, but they don't *listen* to it. That practice can result in a missed opportunity to find out more about the juror and her or his perceptions on the issue.

Thank you for your answer, Mr. Lynch. If I may, let me ask you a few things about that experience. When was it? Did you report it to the police? Was there a lawsuit filed?

Did it go to trial? How did that impact your feelings about the justice system?

* * *

Mr. Winchester, I understand from your earlier conversation with the judge that you have served on a jury before—did I get that right? When was your service? Where? Federal or state court? What type of case was it? What was the most memorable part of your jury service? Do you feel that experience would help you though service on this case, if you were selected? Do you want to serve on this or another jury again? Why?

* * *

Mr. Marshall, I understand that you once were in law school. Tell me about that—did you finish? Did you practice law? Are you currently practicing? Did you have any cases with a charge/cause of action like this one?

Have a conversation with the jurors. It's no different than any other conversation—show interest, ask questions that lead to more information, and make the jurors feel that you care about and are interested in them.

2.7.4   *Things to Do and to Avoid in* Voir Dire

There are many analogies and examples that you will hear in actual courtrooms that are simply silly, and can be annoying. In the words of Gen Z, "it's cringe!". Cringy is probably the best word to describe such antics.

Pithy analogies do not work. In the chapter of "this attorney has no idea why he or she is asking this question", comes the cringy analogy that is (1) stupid, (2) embarrassing, and (3) totally not helpful to understanding who your jurors might be, and their thoughts and feelings. The "elements of a crime are like ingredients in a cake—if you don't have eggs, you don't have a cake, right? So, if the government doesn't prove X, then they don't have a conviction, right?" line is just juvenile.

Remember, try not to look like an idiot in jury selection. That tag will stay with you through the whole trial.

Gratuitous friendliness does not work. Like the server at your favorite restaurant, trying to be your best friend in order to get a big tip, trying too hard is so cringy. Jurors can smell it a mile away. Most of them do not want to be there to start with, so pandering to them is only going to make things worse. Instead of being fake, be professional and courteous. That will get you so much further.

Avoid stupid questions. As discussed above, things like "can you follow the law?" are not helpful. Dig deeper, think about your questions, and ask something that will get you a response. If you want to see how quickly an undesigned, off-the-cuff question can get you in trouble, just do an online search for "stupid questions lawyers ask" and see what you get. Most of them are a product of simply not thinking.

Don't ask questions you have no idea why you are asking. We have already discussed it, but be sure to know why you are asking a question. Know what it is that you want to know about your juror and ask *that* question. Avoid lists of questions that someone gave you unless you review the list prior to questioning the jury and know the purpose of the question and have your follow up questions ready.

Don't be cute or funny. Court is serious. Cases are serious. People are on trial for their lives or for huge amounts of money. Jurors are taken away from their daily routine and forced into the cold and sterile courthouse. There is a time and place for everything. That is not to say that there are not some organically funny moments in even the most serious of cases. When they happen, it is ok to have that moment of levity. But don't try to create it by telling jokes or laughing inappropriately. Avoid clowning around or playing with the jurors in an effort to get them to like you. Jurors will appreciate and respect you if you have an approachable demeanor and are kind and professional to them.

Don't ask hypothetical questions that could be "pre-trying" the case. As discussed above, don't try to get all of your details before the panel to see who agrees with you. Judges will not let you pin down a juror and ask him or her to commit to a particular decision based on a set of facts. *See i.e. Graham v. All Am. Cargo Elevator,* 2013 WL 5604373, at *3 (S.D. Miss. Oct. 11, 2013) ("[q]uestioning which, in effect, asks prospective jurors to weigh evidence that they have not heard is improper because it seeks a commitment from the prospective jurors which may interfere with their ability to fairly consider the evidence"); *Sells v. Thaler,* 2012 WL 2562666, at *17 (W.D. Tex. June 28, 2012)).

Don't embarrass jurors. Asking personal questions in front of the group, or chiding a juror for not knowing what a "preponderance of the evidence" is will get you nowhere. The juror you do it to will resent it, and there will be other jurors that notice it and will hold it against you. If there is something personal you have to discuss with a juror, ask the judge to bring that juror in alone so that his or her business is not put out there. He or she will appreciate it. If a juror doesn't get something, reassure him or her that there are no right or wrong answers in the process, and move on.

Don't forget to follow up with important issues. One of the main points of this chapter—*follow up, follow up, follow up.* Your goal is to know a little about your jurors, whether they will be fair and impartial and good jurors for your case. Your job is to get them to talk to you about why they will be!

Don't miss an opportunity to speak with every potential juror. One of the worst feelings in the world is to get into jury selection and realize that you have to make a decision about someone to which no one has spoken! Every lawyer has been there, no matter how much experience he or she has. *Voir dire* is tough, and there are a lot of moving parts between listening and thinking ahead. Do you best to try to speak with each juror if you can. Try something as simple as asking them about their occupations, or if they heard something that day that they want to comment on or that made them think about something. You never know what someone may volunteer to you that can make a difference in your selection.

2.7.5   *Objections*

Objections can be made in *voir dire* questioning, usually to the form of the question. You should prepare questions in a way that you can ask them without inadvertently drawing an objection.

Common objections in *voir dire* include:

- Misstating the law

- Improper question

- Confusing the jury

- Pre-trying the case

Most of these are products of getting in the weeds with a confused juror and trying to bring him or her back, or educate them, or pull him or her to your side of thinking.

Misstating the law. Most judges don't want you talking too much about the elements of the case, as to avoid pre-trying the case. If you are going to talk about whether the jurors can abide by a certain burden of proof, or whether they have an issue with a law (typically the legalization of marijuana), ask generally their thoughts and if they can follow the law. And be accurate.

Improper question. Pre-trying the case, asking the jurors to commit to a particular verdict, is not proper. Remember, questions that ask prospective jurors to weigh evidence that they have not even heard is improper.

Confusing the jury. Usually this objection is made as "improper", but the point is that when getting into hypothetical questions about how a juror feels about an issue, you can get so far into the weeds that problems arise. Control the conversation and don't let the juror get lost or start talking about irrelevant things. Be especially careful about burdens of proof—you do not want to get the entire panel so confused that it gets stricken and you have to start over (want to see an angry judge?!?!).

Pre-trying the case. Again, be very careful to avoid asking for commitments to a particular verdict under a particular set of facts.

2.8 Jury Selection: Challenges and Strikes, *Batson* Issues

Now that we understand questioning techniques, let's get back to the process of selecting—or eliminating—jurors.

2.8.1 Challenging or Striking Jurors

Remember, selecting involves *eliminating*. Some attorneys believe the entire process, is, in fact, juror elimination. There are two "challenges" (or "strikes") available to you to remove a juror: a challenge for *cause*, and a *peremptory* challenge.

The *voir dire* examination plays a critical role in securing the right to an impartial jury in civil, as well as criminal, trials. The principal purpose of *voir dire* is to probe each prospective juror's state of mind to enable the trial judge to determine actual bias and to allow counsel to assess suspected bias or prejudice. Thus, a *voir dire* examination must be conducted in a manner that allows the parties to effectively and intelligently exercise their peremptory challenges and challenges for cause.

While the peremptory challenge and the challenge for cause serve the same end, that of securing an impartial jury, they offer the parties two distinct, although complementary, methods of challenging biased jurors. Both types of challenges are important to the effort to obtain a fair tribunal. The challenge for cause is narrowly confined to instances in which threats to impartiality are admitted or presumed from the relationships, pecuniary interests, or clear biases of a prospective juror. The peremptory challenge is considerably more extensive in scope. It serves to remove jurors who, in the opinion of counsel, have unacknowledged or unconscious bias. "While challenges for cause permit rejection of jurors on a narrowly specified, provable and legally cognizable basis of partiality, the peremptory permits rejection for a real or imagined partiality that is less easily designated or demonstrable."

. . . The two types of challenges, in combination, are designed to achieve two important objectives: first, that when a jury is finally chosen it will perform its duties in a fair and unbiased manner; and second, that the parties and the public will have confidence in the impartiality and integrity of the jury.

Darbin v. Nourse, 664 F.2d 1109, 1112-13 (9th Cir. 1981) (internal citations omitted).

2.8.1.1 Cause Challenges/Strikes

Some jurors will not be able to serve due to overwhelming biases, prejudices, or even hardships. Biases and prejudices must rise to the level of causing the juror not to be fair and impartial.

Rehabilitation can occur if done properly and save the juror from being dismissed for cause (the proponent of dismissing him or her can still use a peremptory challenge). Rehabilitation questions might sound like this:

Q   *Juror 2, you said earlier that your brother is a retired as a captain from the local sheriff's office. I'd like to ask you about that. I anticipate that you will hear from some law enforcement officers in this case. As you know, I am the prosecutor in this case. My question is: do you think that you would believe a law enforcement officer over a civilian witness?*

A   *I don't think so, but I might. It depends on who the civilian is.*

Q   *I understand. What if the civilian was a witness for the defendant?*

A   *Then I think I might.*

Q   *What if the civilian witness was the defendant herself?*

A   *Then I think I would believe the cops over her.*

Q   *Help me understand. Why is that? Remember, there are no right or wrong answers. We just want to be sure that we have the right folks for this case.*

A   *Well, the defendant has everything to lose.*

Q   *Sure, anyone on trial has a lot at stake. You're not saying that you would discredit the defendant entirely just because she is the defendant?*

A   *No, I'm not saying that.*

Q   *So you would give the defendant the same consideration as any other witness?*

A   *Of course.*

Q   *And for law enforcement, would you also listen to them fairly and consider everything they say?*

A   *Yes.*

Q   *Thank you. At the end of all of this, all we are looking for is fair and impartial jurors. If you were to hear from law enforcement, could you still be a fair and impartial juror in this case?*

A   *Yes, I can do that.*

Q   *Do you have any concerns that you may not? In other words, as you sit here right now, not having heard any evidence or testimony, is there any concern in your mind that you might just go with whatever a cop might say, and not consider anything else?*

A   *No, I will listen to everything and be fair.*

Once the attorney heard that there may be an issue, he sought a promise from the juror that he would be fair and impartial. The juror is rehabilitated from being challenged for cause. Anytime a juror equivocates, your job is to push them and get a commitment one way or the other. The questioning above could have ended like this, necessitating a cause challenge:

Q   *Thank you. At the end of all of this, all we are looking for is fair and impartial jurors. If you were*

*to hear from law enforcement, could you still be a
fair and impartial juror in this case?*

A   *Well, I don't know. I have been around my brother
and his fellow deputies my whole life. I trust them
and I could not imagine that I could just disregard
something they would say. After all, they were
sworn to uphold the law. So, I just don't think I
could get that out of my head.*

2.8.1.2   Peremptory Challenges/Strikes

Always consult local rules regarding selection of jurors. See,
for example, Federal Rule of Civil Procedure 47, which refers to 28
U.S.C. § 1870. That rule permits three peremptory challenges in
civil cases, and states that "all challenges to cause or favor,
whether to the array or panel or to individual jurors, shall be
determined by the court." There IS variation on this rule between
state and federal courts (for example, Arizona has completely
eliminated peremptory challenges, and between civil and criminal
cases—so *check your local rules.*

So, what is a peremptory challenge? It's based on *gut feeling,*
really. Did a juror not respond to your inquiries as he did to the
other attorney? Did a juror show some facial expression toward your
client that make the client uncomfortable or worried? Did the juror
say something that was close to being a cause challenge, but the
court didn't agree? Is there some friend or family relationship, or
prior work or life experience, that worries you about how a
particular juror may view your case? *Anything* that makes you and
your client feel as though that juror will not be fair to you is reason
enough to exercise a peremptory challenge.

You will only have a finite number of peremptory challenges.
Again, check your local rules. Use them wisely. Make sure you have
spoken to all the jurors. The last thing you want is to have to decide

to use your last peremptory on a juror, and not know anything about the juror behind him. Horror movies teach us that the monster you know is not nearly as scary as the monster you don't know. Taking an "almost" ideal juror is better than taking one you know nothing about

One thing to note: if you have asked for one or more jurors to be stricken for cause, and the court denies it, you may have to use your limited number of peremptory strikes on those jurors. If that happens, you burn strikes you may need for other jurors you don't want. If that happens, ask the court for more peremptory strikes, and explain why. If the court doesn't grant you more, make a record (in case of appeal) as to why you need them and move on.

2.8.1.3   How It Works: Exercising the Challenges/Strikes

Consider this example, in selecting a six-member jury:

- 24 jurors on venire

- Both sides have 3 peremptory strikes

- 2 cause challenges made

Going juror by juror, alternating between sides, the following strikes occur:

Judge: As to Juror 1, what says plaintiff?

Plaintiff: Accept.

Judge: Defense, Juror 1?

Defense: Accept.

Judge: Now the defense goes first. Defense, what do you say about Juror 2?

Defense: Accept.

Judge: Plaintiff, Juror 2?

Plaintiff: Strike.

Judge: Plaintiff, Juror 3?

Plaintiff: Accept.

Judge: Defense?

Defense: Accept.

And so on. Jurors 8 and 11 were struck for cause. The following strikes are made: Juror 4 (defense), Juror 5 (plaintiff), Juror 6 (defense), Juror 10 (defense), and Juror 13 (plaintiff).

13	14	15	16	17	18	19	20	21	22	23	24
1	2	3	4	5	6	7	8	9	10	11	12

The jurors for the trial are 1, 3, 7, 9, 12, and 14.

2.8.2 Backstrikes

Backstriking is the process of first accepting a juror, then later exercising a peremptory strike on the juror. Know this: some courts allow it, some don't. It is largely rule driven, so be sure you know what is permitted in your jurisdiction.

2.8.3 Batson Issues: Fighting Racially Motivated Strikes

In 1986, the United States Supreme Court decided *Batson v. Kentucky*, 476 U.S. 79 (1986), and held that peremptory strikes cannot be used solely on the prospective juror's race (this is in both civil and criminal cases). While the rule is simple in theory, *Batson* is difficult to enforce, and requires the trial court to actually judge the credibility of the attorney making the challenged strike. The process involves three steps:

1.   The party that opposes the peremptory challenge must establish a *prima facie* case that the strike was

race-based (and therefore discriminatory). The opponent of the strike must make the argument that the strike was based solely on the juror's race, and for no legitimate reason;

2. The party that has proposed the strike needs to provide a *race-neutral explanation* for their decision;

3. The judge has to find that the explanation is or is not in fact race-neutral.

In the event that you think your opponent is striking a potential juror simply because of race, you must object, and ask for a race-neutral reason. If you are defending a strike, you have to establish a legitimate reason for your proposed strike. It would sound something like this:

Judge: As to juror number 4, Ms. Beane, what says the government?

Prosecutor: The government will exercise a strike on Ms. Beane.

Defense: Objection, your Honor. I note for the record that Ms. Beane is African American. She indicated in my questioning of her that she would be fair and impartial in this case. I would ask the Court to inquire as to a race-neutral reason for the strike.

Judge: Ms. Prosecutor, what is the reason for your strike?

Prosecutor: Ms. Beane stated during voir dire that she has two sons, one of which has been prosecuted by my office and sent to prison, and another which is currently facing *charges being prosecuted by my office. In fact, I am the prosecutor on that case. Her son is facing the same charges as the defendant in this case. While she did state that she can be fair and impartial, it is the government's belief that her sons' cases may have an undue effect on her decision in this case, which would not be fair to the government.*

Judge: *I note that was in fact her testimony, and find that the government's response is genuine, and racially neutral. I will allow the strike. Defense, your objection is overruled, and your record is made.*

* * *

The bottom line: *listen carefully, study the jurors and their responses.* Ask them pointed questions during *voir dire* (how they feel, think, etc.) and get them talking. If someone hesitates about being fair, or somehow equivocates, ask them about it:

Q   *Ms. Rauh, you seemed to hesitate a little when you were asked about being a fair juror in this case. That is totally fine, and there are no right or wrong answers here. But maybe I misheard that, so let me follow up with you a bit . . . you understand this is an accusation of sexual battery, right?*

A   *I did not at first, but yes, now I do. I think I do.*

Q   *I can't get into the actual facts at this point, but I think I can safely say that the evidence in this case will not be pretty. It will not be nice. Is that what is bothering you?*

A   Yes. I don't want to hear about that stuff. I get really emotional.

Q   Now, I know you and everyone here promised to be fair and impartial. Do you worry that this may not be the right trial for you to serve on?

A   Yes. No. I don't know. I was fine until I heard the charge, and then my anxiety kicked in. I'm sorry . . .

Q   Don't be. This is real life, and tough stuff. Ms. Rauh, do you think that because of all that you may not be a fair and impartial juror for this particular charge?

A   I would try, but I can't promise.

Q   Do you think if this were a DWI charge, or a civil contract case, that might be a better fit for you?

A   Oh, heavens, yes. I could do that. I'm just not sure about this one. It would be hard to be fair.

This example could lead to a cause challenge, as Ms. Rauh would be a wonderful juror in any other case. This could be a good juror to ask the judge to permit private questioning, to get into why she has such anxiety about the charge. It could just be general nerves about the subject—or she may have been a victim of such a crime. And note the tone—the attorney was kind to Ms. Rauh, which she as well as the other jurors appreciate, and that approach got her talking.

The point: *follow up, follow up, follow up.* You don't want to be doomed from the beginning of the trial because you did not ask enough of the right questions!

2.9 Checklists

2.9.1 Ideal Juror Wish List (Juror Profile)

	What issues in my case are most important?
	Are there any people that immediately come to mind as good jurors, because of background, employment?
	What types of people would most likely embrace my client's story?
	Are there any demographics that would relate to those of my client (age, etc.)?

2.9.2 Issues Checklist

	Identify critical issues to discuss (elements or defenses, ex.: self-defense)
	Impeachment issues
	Hypotheticals well-prepared

2.9.3 Juror Questionnaire

What follows is a standard jury questionnaire used in Alabama state courts (found at https://judicial.alabama.gov/docs/library/rules/crsam56.pdf, last accessed May 2023). Note, the optional questions may or may not be usable in certain jurisdictions. If they are, consider the propriety of using them, and what even asking them might do to the environment in your courtroom.

Remember, even if you don't get to have jurors complete a written questionnaire before *voir dire*, you can still use the questions when speaking with them.

As you review these questions, think carefully about what the answers may tell you about your potential jurors.

SAMPLE FORM 56.

RECOMMENDED UNIFORM JUROR QUESTIONNAIRE

This questionnaire is for use only by the judge and lawyers in selecting a jury. It is not public information. If you need additional space to answer a question, attach additional sheets and number your answers to correspond to the questions.

Juror name/number:

Place of birth:　　Age:　　Sex: ( ) Male ( ) Female

Race: ( ) Caucasian/White ( ) African-American/Black ( ) Hispanic ( ) Other

Do you: ( ) Own home ( ) Rent home ( ) Rent apartment ( ) Live with friend or relatives ( ) Other

What cities/states have you lived in during the past five years?

Marital status: ( ) Single ( ) Married ( ) Divorced ( ) Separated ( ) Widowed.

If you are married: Spouse's employer:

Number of years your spouse has worked there:

Spouse's title and job responsibilities:

Educational background of your spouse, including any degrees or certificates earned:

Do you have children? ( ) Yes ( ) No If yes, please complete the following:

Age, Sex

School or occupation

Your level of education: Specify the highest grade you completed:

> *Elementary or high school (1-12)*

> *College (1-4 or 5+)*

>> *If college, what college, what degrees, and what was your major?*

Have you ever taken any courses in law, law enforcement, criminology, or criminal justice? ( ) Yes ( ) No If yes, what courses?

Your present employment status (check all that apply): ( ) Full-time ( ) Part-time ( ) Retired ( ) Unemployed ( ) Student ( ) Homemaker

Your current or most recent occupation:

Name of your current or most recent employer, or, if you are a student, your school and major:

How long have you been employed by your current or most recent employer?

What are/were your specific duties and responsibilities on the job?

Do/Did you supervise other employees? ( ) Yes ( ) No If yes, how many?

Do/Did you have responsibility for hiring and firing? ( ) Yes ( ) No

Please list all other occupations and employers you have had for the past 10 years:

Have you ever served in the military? ( ) Yes ( ) No

> *If yes, please complete the following:*

> *Branch: Rank: Dates: Duties: Type of discharge:*

What social, civic, professional, trade, union, or other organizations are you affiliated with?

Describe any offices you have held in the organizations listed?

Have you ever served on a jury before? ( ) Yes ( ) No How many times?

What type of jury: ( ) Grand jury ( ) Civil trial jury ( ) Criminal trial jury

If you have served on a <u>trial jury</u>, please state the following: Year served:

City and state where served:

What verdict was rendered? ( ) Yes   ( ) No

Civil case: ( ) For plaintiff ( ) For defendant

Criminal case: ( ) For state or federal government ( ) For defendant

Have you ever served as a <u>foreperson</u> on a grand jury or a trial jury? ( ) Yes   ( ) No

Have you testified as a <u>witness</u> in any court proceeding? ( ) Yes ( ) No

If yes, were you a witness for: ( ) Plaintiff ( ) State or federal government

( ) Defendant in a civil or criminal case

Have you or anyone close to you ever sued or been sued in any type of lawsuit? ( ) Yes ( ) No If yes, explain:

Have you ever been to court for any other reason (excluding divorce or traffic cases)? ( ) Yes ( ) No If yes, explain:

Have you ever been arrested? ( ) Yes ( ) No

Have you, a close relative, or a close friend ever been convicted of a crime? ( ) Yes ( ) No

What newspaper(s) do you read regularly?

What TV news programs do you watch frequently?

How many hours of TV do you watch per week?

What radio programs do you listen to most?

Which do you find more interesting? ( ) Local news ( ) National news

To what periodicals or magazines do you subscribe?

Of the books you have read, which three are your favorites?

Please list your hobbies, spare-time activities, and outside interests:

Are there bumper stickers on the vehicles that you drive or that your spouse/significant other drives? ( ) Yes ( ) No If yes, what do they say?

In a group situation, once you have formed an opinion, do you usually:

( ) Change your mind if a number of people have a different opinion?

( ) Stand by your original opinion despite what others believe?

Do you have relatives or close personal friends who are judges, attorneys, or court personnel? ( ) Yes ( ) No If yes, what are their names and relationship to you?

Based on your experience, what is your opinion of lawyers? ( ) Good ( ) Fair ( ) Poor

Do you have any medical problems (for example, problems with your vision or hearing) that may prevent you from serving as a juror? ( ) Yes ( ) No If yes, explain:

Do you have any ethical, religious, political, or other beliefs that may prevent you from serving as a juror? ( ) Yes ( ) No If yes, explain:

Is there any matter not covered by this questionnaire that could affect your ability to be a fair and impartial juror? ( ) Yes ( ) No If yes, explain:

List any reason why you do not wish to serve or why you should not serve:

Are you or is any member of your family in favor of limiting the rights of those accused of a crime so as to make it easier to convict? ( ) Yes ( ) No

In a criminal case, a defendant is presumed innocent until proven guilty based on the evidence. Do you agree with that principle? ( ) Yes ( ) No If no, why not?

Have you or a close relative ever been the victim of a crime? ( ) Yes ( ) No If yes, please describe:

Have you or a close relative ever worked in a law enforcement-related job such as police, sheriff, state trooper, prison guard, or military police? ( ) Yes ( ) No If yes, please describe:

Have you taken any courses or had any training in medicine or other health-care field? ( ) Yes ( ) No If yes, please explain:

ANSWERS TO THE FOLLOWING QUESTIONS ARE OPTIONAL

Do you belong to a church or otherwise have any religious affiliation? ( ) Yes ( ) No If yes, please specify:

How often do you attend religious services? ( ) Regularly ( ) Occasionally ( ) Never

Do you hold a special position in your religious organization? ( ) Yes ( ) No

What is your political party preference?

Are you or is any member of your family a member of any victims' rights organization? ( ) Yes ( ) No

Of any anti-crime group or other similar organization? ( ) Yes ( ) No

Of any anti-weapons or gun-control group? ( ) Yes ( ) No

Have you ever actively participated in a political campaign? ( ) Yes ( ) No If yes, ( ) Democrat? ( ) Republican? ( ) Other

CHAPTER 3

Opening Statement

OBJECTIVES: Opening statements are the first time you will tell your story to the jury, and it is an important time in which to grab and hold the interest and attention of the jurors AND to build your credibility. In this chapter, we will discuss:

- what an opening statement should be and should accomplish

- how to prepare for opening statement

- developing the case theory, themes, and topics into "mini stories"

- delivering the opening statement

"Incredibly critical" is perhaps the only way to describe the opening statement. It is the first time you get to actually tell your story to the jury. First impressions are critical, because the jurors immediately begin to build their own mental version of what happened. Also, whether consciously or subconsciously, they will start to judge whether to believe it or not. And thus the march to a verdict begins.

3.1 Purpose of Opening Statement

 Opening statement is where you *tell* and *sell*. Make it count.

Opening statement is the first time you get to really tell and sell your story to the jury. First impressions matter the most! A persuasive opening statement must tell your client's story, preview the law, and make an "ask" that you will come back to in closing.

3.1.1   Elements of a Good Opening

Maximum impact. That's what you need in your first seconds—*maximum impact*. Come out strong—grab the jurors' attention, engage their interest, and make them care. Sadly, too many times we see attorneys squander that precious opportunity.

ELEMENTS OF A GOOD OPENING
• Well-organized
• Strong "rivet phrase"
• Uses great facts
• Tells mini-stories
• Introduces the law
• Incorporates connects to common moral/ethical principles
• Clear "ask"

Consider the following two initial parts of an opening statement:

Bad opening

Hi, again, everyone. Thank you for being here. I know jury selection yesterday was long, but we all made it, right? Thank you all for doing your duty as jurors. We all appreciate it.

Now we are at opening statements, and that is when we attorneys get to talk to you about what we think the case is about. It's like a roadmap, kind of like what to expect as the trial progresses. I hope you will keep an open mind about the case.

On June 15 of last year, there was a burglary. Sarah Doe came home . . . Sarah Doe had gone out, then she came home. When she got home, I guess she didn't lock her door or something, but anyway later on she was upstairs folding clothes and she heard something downstairs. She went down and saw a man in her living room, looking in her things. She got a look at him and will come in and tell you it was the defendant, Willie McGee.

Great opening

The first scream was for help. The second is for justice.

Sarah Doe is a thirty-year old female who lives alone. She lives right here in Stetsonville, just a couple of blocks from the Town Mall. On June 15, Sarah experienced something she will never forget . . . a terrifying story that she will tell you today.

Sarah had gone out that morning to the mall, grabbed a few new summer blouses, and had made it back home to put her new wardrobe away, and to enjoy the rest of that sunny Saturday. Living alone, Sarah will tell you that she is very careful about her safety, and very conscious about locking her doors behind her. But, on this otherwise mundane Saturday, her excitement about trying on her new clothes, and juggling those oversized bags they use nowadays, she must have forgotten to throw that latch on the deadbolt.

While happily cutting off tags and making room in her closet for her new things, she heard a sound . . . a sound she immediately knew to be made by a person . . . footsteps . . . a cough . . . and the sound of drawers opening and closing. Sarah froze, goosebumps on her arms and her heart in her throat. Someone was in her house.

Sarah kicked off her shoes and tiptoed to the stairs and listened. It could have been her mom, but surely her mom would have called before popping over. She crept down the stairs, barely able to breathe, hardly being able to hear over the sound of her heart beating so fast. She peered around the wall of the stair landing and saw that man (pointing to the defendant) casually rifling through her entertainment system cabinet.

She screamed.

She screamed so loudly—the defendant turned and looked at her. Sarah will tell you that in that moment, she knew she would have to identify him one day, so she quickly studied every feature of his face. The defendant calmly walked to the door and out—but in those few seconds Sarah had memorized his face.

Her neighbors heard her scream, too. They called the police. Sarah gave that description to the police, and they were easily able to locate and capture the defendant down the street.

The first scream was for help. The second will be for justice.

You may know that "rivet phrase" as being the tag line from the movie *The Accused*. Which one is better? Just reading the words on the page you can tell which opening is going to grab and resonate with the jury. These are the first words of each attorney—who has captured the attention of the jury? Who does the jury want to believe? Why?

The second version is memorable, it sets the tone, and its shows the jury the way to the verdict.

An opening must be powerful. A powerful opening gets right to the point and grabs the jurors. Your opening must pique their interest, hold their attention. You must engage their desire to learn about your case. You must make them care about your client. Whether they ultimately decide for or against your client, you want him or her to be in the jurors' hearts and minds from the very start.

An opening must be compelling. A compelling opening is stronger and more memorable—it creates an impression and a situation that begs for resolution. To be compelling, you must tell the story in a way that moves the jurors to action in your favor. Using a "rivet phrase", mini-stories, vivid descriptions and creating a compelling and resonating story will engross your listeners.

An opening must use familiarity. A good opening uses places, activities, actions, and conditions that everyone knows or has experienced. This is especially true when using references to actual places, like the mall, and activities such as buying new clothes. It also grabs people. By using vivid descriptions, you will engage your jurors' own mental images of what they think happened. They literally put themselves in the situation.

An opening must have a degree of suspense—or at least tension that needs resolution. Once the jury is invested with what has happened to Sarah, they will need to resolve the problem. That's the whole reason they are there—to resolve the legal (perhaps moral, ethical, etc.) problem Sarah has. A great opening will set them on the path to do that.

3.1.2   *What the Jury Sees and Hears*

As we know, jurors are normal folks. They are curious. They want you to get to the point, and they want to start deciding. That is human nature. But they also want to be captivated and, to some degree, entertained—not in the comedy club or music concert sense, but in the sense of not being bored to tears. The more facts they hear, the more they learn. The more they learn, the more engaged they become. Once engaged, they become part of the story—the part that guides the resolution. What resolution they chose will depend on the strength of your story.

Jurors are looking at you. They are searching your face for signals. Are you confident? Are you prepared? Are you truthful? And they are probably wondering how old you are, if you are married, where you live, what car you drive, and the like. They are also looking to you for guidance as to how to resolve the legal or moral dilemma that the trial presents.

3.1.3   *Commitment and Conditional Acceptance*

In an opening statement, you have to accomplish one main goal, above all others: *get the jurors engaged.* Of course, you have to get out the facts, and the law, and "The Ask." But none of that matters if it is falling on deaf ears.

Think about a class that you took where you thought the information was good, but the teacher was boring, uninspiring, seemingly uninterested, and painful to listen to without your mind wandering. You likely read the materials but couldn't wait for the class to be over so you could get out of that mind-numbing situation.

Conversely, we have all had that class in high school that was taught by the football coach—who had to teach *something* to be able to be in his coaching position at all—and the fun we had in the class. The coach was not as much concerned with the materials as he was with telling stories, bending the rules a little (remember being able to have food in his class, and the little bond you had by him letting you and you not telling anyone about it?), and generally being thought of by the students as *cool*. Whether it was driver's ed, or "Physical Science" or some other low-level elective class, we have more memories of the times in that class than in geometry or world history.

Why? Because the teacher who engaged with us bought our commitment and our acceptance. The other simply floated out ideas with the hopes that someone, anyone, would latch on.

That concept is the same in classrooms as it is in boardrooms, political events, and Sunday morning church. And it is true of juries.

Jurors want to know you care. If you don't care, why should they? Conversely, if you care and show your passion (*pathos*), jurors will be obliged to take the case seriously and will be drawn into your story with you.

3.1.4   *Preparing for Opening Statement*

Theory of the case
Must be:
• Completely articulated
• Clearly explained
• Logical
• Persuasive

Having done your factual analysis, prepared your witness analysis and matrix, and knowing what you have to prove (elements), you are ready to prepare your opening statement.

As discussed, your opening should be powerful and should not only grab the jurors' attention, but it should get them liking you and ready to listen to what you have to say, i.e., prove your case. So, making sure you have all the right components is critical.

We have discussed how well you really need to know your case. "Knowing your case" means that you have complete command of every fact, every potential evidentiary issue, what the witnesses are going to (should) say, and the applicable laws. Too many times, attorneys are in trial thinking "why didn't I think of that?", or "how could I have missed that?" There is no excuse for being in a trial and not knowing *everything* about the case. Please refer back to chapter 1, "Trial Preparation" for more on how to get ready for trial.

Factual distillation. A great way to prepare for opening is to *distill your story.* Distillation is a process by which impurities are removed, and something is purified. In order to figure out how best to prove (or disprove/defend) your story, then write it out in story form, in two or three paragraphs. A summary, if you will—*what's the big story?* After that, take the case down further—set it out in two or three sentences. Think about the essence of the case, what the feeling is . . . what are the most important words and actions? What feeling do you want the jury to get about the problem your client has? Then, pick the one word that best summarizes your case. *That* is the purest emotion or feeling that you want to infuse in your case.

FACTUAL DISTILLATION PROCESS

THE BIG STORY

(2-3 paragraphs) Important facts, witnesses, and law; chrono or by witness

"FEELING" SENTENCES

(2-3 sentences) Like a movie "trailer" - most important of acts/words; the feeling of the case

EMOTION WORD

SINGLE WORD: The purest emotion of the case

The big story. Using the "who, what, when, where, why, and how" stratagem as a guide, you can craft a great story-summary of your case. A good rule of thumb is to pretend as if your grandmother or favorite aunt called and asked if you had any good cases coming up—your summary should be how you would explain the case to your Aunt Mildred.

Remember, no one (including Aunt Mildred, no matter how much she loves you) wants to be bored. No one wants to hear a jumble of facts, or a bland recitation of elements of causes of action. *People want to hear a story.* How would you incorporate both the facts and the law into a short story-summary?

Two or three "feeling" sentences. After you have the summary, distill it down even more. Can you explain your case in two or three sentences? How about in *one* sentence?

Those few sentences are the essence of the case, the overall "what happened" or "why we are here" that will guide you AND your jurors.

The emotion word. Finally, go for *one word*. If you can find the essence of your case in one word, you have hit gold. That one word can now help you move forward with finding themes, famous quotes, "hooks", one-liners, or other rhetorical devices that can make for great opening statement material. This one word will become the basis of your rivet phrase.

https___commons.wikimedia.org_wiki_File_Plutchiks-emotional-wheel-modified

This graphic, based on Professor Plutchik's famous "Wheel of Emotions", gives you a great starting spot. Forget the words for a moment—which of the reactions encapsulates the emotion of your story?

From that one word, you can work forward with similar words (use thesuarus.com), analogies, and powerful word choices that invoke feelings and emotions throughout your case presentation. You can work in reverse, building a "rivet phrase", mini-stories, and the full opening based on the emotion.

3.2 Structure of Opening Statement

So many advocates put very little effort into their trial presentations—and it shows. Perhaps it is a fear of public speaking, perhaps it is lack of advocacy education and training. But most likely it is because they do not think about *structure*.

While there are many ways you could approach opening statements, finding something that the jury can follow is your best bet. After all, this is the first time you have to be able to tell your client's story, and that first impression is incredibly important. So, bear in mind that you have to help your listeners follow so they get the maximum impact of your words.

A really good structure for your opening is to break it into four parts:

- **"RIVET PHRASE"**: a "power intro"; the one sentence that says it all—emotional, familiar, engaging; can follow with a preview or "movie trailer" what the evidence will be in story format—this is the 2-3 sentences that introduces the major dilemma to be solved

- **Setting up the "big story" with mini-stories**: the larger story, told in shorter form from whichever perspective best introduces the characters and the problem to be solved (chronological or witness by witness)

- **An introduction of the law**: sharing with the jury the law they will have to apply later

- **"The Ask"**: letting the jury know how to solve the dilemma; asking of them what you want them to do (verdict you want)

3.3 The *Rivet Phrase*—Grabbing the Jurors' Attention

Like a good movie or TV show, there is always some basic theme set out by an action or statement. Tag lines for movies grab you by describing the plot of the film, or the experience you will have watching it:

Just when you thought it was safe to go back in the water. (Jaws 2)

The true story of a real fake. (Catch Me If You Can)

A comedy of trial and error. (My Cousin Vinnie)

Hear the pictures. See the music. (Fantasia)

She brought a small town to its feet and a corporation to its knees. (Erin Brockovich)

The first casualty of war is innocence. (Platoon)

Family isn't a word. It's a sentence. (Royal Tenenbaums)

Think about the impact of the phrase. Even if you have not seen the movie, you totally get what the movie is about and can relate to the feelings and emotions conveyed.

<table>
<tr><td rowspan="2"></td><td>Rivet phrase:</td></tr>
<tr><td>

- Instantly sets the essence of the case
- Gains attention of jurors
- Holds jurors with emotional connect
- Makes jurors interested
- Can be a famous quote, saying, parable

</td></tr>
</table>

Often times, you will see attorneys squander a great opportunity to grab the jury and tell the story in a way that will have them interested, engaged, and wanting more. There is nothing worse than an attorney with great facts utterly failing to make a powerful and persuasive opening statement.

A very strong and persuasive technique is to start with an introduction as a stand-alone preview of the entire case. Think of movie trailers—Hollywood spends a lot of money producing 60 second trailers that give you just enough of a hint about the story that you will spend $10 on a ticket. It must work, because every movie has a trailer and Hollywood has been doing it for years.

For this technique, find a "phrase that pays". These are sometimes called a "hook" or a "theme"—that is too simplistic and trite. A rivet (noun) is a device that holds something together. To rivet (verb) means to hold someone's attention. Your rivet phrase should do just that—bind the facts to emotion/feeling and involve your jury. To find the rivet phrase, you have to really think about your case and what it is all about. That can be difficult, especially if your case doesn't have really interesting or shocking facts (think murder trial versus contract breach trial). Nonetheless, you can still find a good lead-off line.

Finding the rivet phrase. Think of common proverbs, idioms, and phrases that we have heard our whole lives. Our parents used them . . . we hear them in TV and internet commercials . . . we even drop them in everyday conversation. The familiarity of the rivet phrase immediately grabs your listener and focuses them in on where you are going. You can set the entire tone in a few words. Here are some examples:

- Where there's smoke, there's fire.

- It's a cover-up.

- Profit over safety.

- Easy come, easy go.

- Actions speak louder than words.
- It's all about money.
- Ignorance is bliss.
- Follow the money.
- Out of sight, out of mind.
- It's just common sense.
- Two wrongs don't make a right.
- Garbage in garbage out.
- Head in the sand.
- Money is the root of all evil.
- No one can serve two masters.

- You scratch my back, I'll scratch yours.
- A picture is worth a thousand words.
- Honesty is the best policy.
- If you can't beat 'em, join 'em.
- If you play with fire, you get burned.
- Keep your friends close, and your enemies even closer.
- Birds of a feather flock together.
- Lie down with dogs, wake up with fleas.
- Failing to plan is planning to fail.
- If you want something done right, do it yourself.
- There is no such thing as a free lunch.

If you don't know the meaning of some of these, look them up. A common phrase may have different meanings, depending on how you use it. Some you can use in the negative—to demonstrate that the actor did the opposite of what he or she should have done (ex: "ignorance is bliss" in a negligence case).

SOURCES FOR FINDING A GREAT RIVET PHRASE
Thesaurus.com
Wikiquotes.com
Goodreads.com
Litquotes.com
Bartleby.com
Quoteland.com

In a driving under the influence case (more on that in section 5.10), I represented a defendant who was captured on the officer's dashcam. She looked very, very good—did not exhibit any signs of being impaired by alcohol. Nonetheless, the arresting officer's approach was to try to convince the jurors that there were other things going on that were not captured on the video. Essentially, he was telling the jurors "don't believe your eyes." In my opening statement, I used several common phrases to remind jurors to *believe your own eyes*:

If it pleases the Court. Counsel. Members of the jury.

We have all heard these sayings before:

"The check is in the mail."

"We service what we sell."

"One size fits all."

"Your table will be ready in a minute."

"I'll start my diet tomorrow."

What do these saying have in common?

They are things that you are told, that when you see it, you can't believe it.

Because in this courtroom—just as in life—you have to believe your eyes, not what you are told.

Be creative, but stick to your theory of the case. Trying to shoe-horn a phrase that we all know means one thing into another set of facts can backfire.

Composing your own rivet phrase. Of course, you can fashion your own rivet phrase to fit the facts.

In a recent federal trial, my client was charged with being a conspirator in a scheme to steal money from people over the internet by using stolen personally identifying information (PII). The PII was used to access victims' accounts and take money, then buy computers at the local university bookstore and resell them. There were two clearly distinct tiers of the "bad guys": the masterminds who stole the money, and the college kids they paid to use their school ID to buy the computers at a student rate.

In the opening, I wanted to establish that there were the bad guys and there were some good people that got caught up in doing things innocently. The orientation of the story was "us" and "them." The goal was to move my client from the "them" (aka the criminals) to the "us" (victims and witnesses) side of the ledger. The core story was that my client was just deceived just as much as the people whose money was stolen—just in a different way. In doing so, I used a common term: *played*. Just about everyone knows that term, and its connotation: cheating, deceit, and harm. The emotions of the case were mistrust, loathing, and anger.

THE COURT: Mr. Bodiford.

MR. BODIFORD: If it pleases the Court, Your Honor, Counsel.

Members of the jury, there are players and then there are the played.

The players in this case, they bought. They are flashy. They have money. They attract attention. They are popular, but they also scheme. They scheme. They connive. They are careful. They calculate. And in this case they are criminals.

So we've got the played. We have the players, but then we have the played. The victims in this case; they are the chumps. They are the marks. They are the patsies. So in this case these folks are going to line up very clearly on one side of the ledger or the others, the players and the played. Now, the played—the victim, the prey, if you will—they come to us in two varieties. The first are these folks that are scattered across this country leading their lives oblivious to what is going on the Internet. In fact, Mr. Allen had been deceased for many, many years.

They have no idea that there is somebody out there crawling in the dark recesses of the dark web buying their information, buying their PII—their personal identifying information—buying the ability to sneak in the back door and steal their hard-earned money. Those are the victims; those are the patsies; those are the prey; those are the played.

And we cannot overlook in this case, members of the jury, that there were, in fact, some people right here in Tallahassee who were played. They were played for their naiveness, naivete, and naively being duped and being used by the players to accomplish the players' goals. We've heard their names so far today: Deshauan Sanders, Desiree Ferreira, Jacob Koller, Jessica Gallimore, Deshawn Taylor, Ki-Mani Ward, Lark Bailey, Voshon Howard, Jada Guzman, Jada Harris, and there is another Jada Barton.

Ms. Barton, stand please.

Again, my name is Joe Bodiford. Along with my associate Gannon Coens, we represent Ms. Barton here before the Court and before you all.

Thank you.

Now, Kh'lajuwon Murat put these students, these patsies, into his lie. He wove them into his web of deceit . . .

And so on. The idea was to use the word "player" (to instill anger) every time a "bag guy" was referenced, as in "Investigator, Mr. Murat was the main player in the scheme, right?" Similarly, when crossing the others similarly-situated to my client, the word "played" was incorporated, i.e., "when was it you knew you had been played?" or "you're here because you were played by Mr. Murat, isn't that right?" It worked; the defendant was acquitted.

3.4 Introducing the Story

3.4.1 Using "Mini Stories" to Introduce the Facts

Explanation of the Facts
Must be
• Completely articulated
• Clearly explained
• Effective organization of facts
• Evidence/facts effectively summarized
• Persuasive
• Theme consistently integrated

Where the rivet phrase gets the jurors engaged, previewing the facts is where you tell the story of the case. This is where you use the two or three (maybe four but not much longer) sentences to set the tone of the case.

In my example above, the second and third paragraphs you find the feelings of the case coming out—that there are evil people silently stalking innocent folks on the dark recesses of the internet. Jurors are constantly bombarded by TV and internet warnings about their personal information and cybersecurity. Everyone uses the internet. I was pretty sure that everyone could easily relate to that sentiment.

The "big story" comes during the testimony and introduction of evidence in your case-in-chief and other's sides rebuttal case.

Mini-stories give facts about the case without the minutia. In movie trailers, you will see various scenes from the movie, illustrating important and pivotal moments. When the trailer is over, you understand what the movie is about. You can decide if you want to see it. If the trailer was compelling, you will want to buy a ticket.

The trailer won't give you all the details. It may show you a battle scene, but it won't tell you all the details about the planning of the battle, and perhaps what alliances were made by who beforehand. It tells you there is an important battle. That's compelling—*why is there a battle?* Well, you have to watch the movie to find out.

Mini-stories should be compelling and draw the listener in. Be judicious with what facts you need *now* and what can be left for later. But even with brevity, be *accurate*.

3.4.2   *Telling the Story Chronologically*

The *chronological* approach to opening statement has the witnesses walking through the specific parts of the case facts, perhaps laying out things that will be linked up later. This is the story as it unfolds, the timeline as it encounters the various actors.

In my trial case, the story in chronological format would continue like this:

Now, Kh'lajuwon Murat put these students, these patsies, into his lie. He wove them into his web of deceit from the first day he arrived on campus.

Mr. Murat was part of a program for underprivileged students. All of these students were there on a scholarship, but they had been identified in the admission process as perhaps needed extra help. The program mission is to help students who are traditionally underrepresented in higher education enroll, persist, and graduate from college by providing them with the resources, tools, and network of support that will aid in their academic and personal development. In short, they help them transition into "real life"—scheduling, part-time jobs, money management, and the like.

Mr. Murat was well aware that the program was going to be full of needy students. He knew that they all could use more money. He saw an opportunity . . . he had a bigger project in mind.

University students can buy Apple products at the bookstore for a greatly reduced "student" price. They must use their student ID, and they only get the special deal one time. The university had a deal going: buy an Apple MacBook, and get a free pair of Beats headphones.

While most of the students did not yet have a part-time job, Mr. Murat was employed. He had his own business. His business was stealing personally identifying information from the web, or buying if off of the "dark

*web", and using other people's credit to buy things and
resell them. One hundred percent profit and untraceable
back to him.*

*A free-money source . . . computers at a reduced price
that could be resold for a profit . . . needy students . . .
free headphones. The scheme practically designed itself.*

*Mr. Murat's sales pitch to the students was super easy.
"Hey, want a free pair of Beats? I just need you to do
something for me."*

And so on. The story is unfolding by introducing the players and
the scheme. The perspective is not one individual witness, but
rather the circumstances and the setting. That perspective may
alternate between witnesses; you may end up calling witnesses
multiple times to tell the story on direct examination. There is not
any prohibition against re-calling a witness or calling a witness
multiple times. However, be sure that it is done in an efficient
manner as to not be seen as either unorganized or as a waste of
court time (or both). More on that in section 4.4.2.

Note, the nitty-gritty facts, such as whose information was
stolen on the web, or which students bought what on what date, are
left for later. The big story is the focus, all with the illegal scheme
as the main focus. The jurors know that, and can get verification of
that later during testimony.

3.4.3   Telling the Story Witness by Witness (Perspective)

The witness by witness, or *point of view*, approach to telling
the story is just that—you lay out what each witness' essential
testimony will be, from start to finish. This method gives the
perspective from the characters in the story. Depending on the case,
such as a sexual battery case or a defamation claim, the thoughts,

feelings, and emotions of the victim are essential to the tone of the story.

In the example above, we could lay out each witness in this type of manner:

> You will hear from Ms. Barton. She was the first person in her family to go to college. Excited and full of hope, she arrived at the university and got plugged in. Part of her scholarship was to participate in a program designed to assist first-time collegians, specifically those from families with hardships.

> In the program, she met all sorts of people from all over the country. She was introduced to people with diverse backgrounds . . . from different cultures . . . and with different goals. Many of her new friends were like here— looking forward to jumping into a new life with great things ahead. Some of her new friends were there for different reasons.

> Ms. Barton met Mr. Murat—and was immediately smitten with him. She never knew anyone so charismatic. He expressed interest in her, and would flirt with her whenever he saw her around the dorm. She was surprised that someone in the program dressed so well, and that he had a new red BMW. She didn't understand why he always had money. She watched him buy students food and coffee. Her interest in him grew each time he flashed that smile—the smile with golds and diamonds enameled to his teeth.

This sets the scene *from her perspective.* It shows her naivety, her innocence, and how she could be drawn into his web in the dizzying new environment in which she found herself. Each of the students in her position could be set out with the same story.

Whichever method you chose to employ in your opening, be sure to use clarity and concreteness to tell your story.

3.4.4 Additional Considerations for Your "Mini Stories"

Remember—facts are stubborn things. And opening is about *maximum impact*. Including, culling, and ordering your facts will create the most persuasive opening statement. Think about:

Proof facts (undisputed vs. disputed)	Will the facts you are using in opening get into evidence? If not, what can you do to "tease" it, or find another fact to use the same way? If in doubt, leave it out. You do not want to promise the jury something you cannot give them later.
Ultimate issue facts	Which facts are important to get out up front? Which can be left for later? Boring, unorganized, unprepared openings end up being just "fact. . .fact. . .fact. . .fact" with no emotion, feeling, or context. Avoid the temptation to overload the jury with *everything* in opening. *Use your best facts.*
Introductory, background, historical facts	Generally, there lots of I/B/H facts. You don't need them all in opening. Decide which are most important for maximum impact.
Impeachment/rebuttal facts	Perhaps not the most pressing of facts for opening—unless you have

	a huge whammy to reveal to set the tone *against* the other side.
Rebuttal (counterarguments)	How much do you need in opening? You don't want your opening to start you out on the defensive. Establish *your* case, perhaps mention something the jury may hear from the other side, but reference them back to your case "as you listen to the evidence."
Dealing with harmful facts (good facts vs. bad facts)	Depending on just how harmful the fact is, you may want to deal with it in opening. "You'll hear that my client made some differing statements about what happened. As you listen, consider when those statements were made, and under what circumstances." You can take the sting out a little by warning them of the bad fact, and helping them harmonize it with other evidence they may hear. NOTE: don't *argue* why it's not bad; just put it in context by asking the jurors to consider all the evidence.
Order/sequence of facts	Carefully lay out the chrono or witness perspectives. What should the jury hear first? What best tells the story? Do this exercise to (1) avoid missing a fact, and (2) to eliminate unnecessary facts, and (3) get maximum impact.

Primacy/recency (what's important??)	People remember what they hear first and what they hear last. Lots of stuff in the middle gets lost. But the "zinger" facts at the front and back of your opening for maximum impact.
Flow of info: big to small, small to big	Without getting too many facts in, and focusing on the power facts, think about how you want the story to flow. Do you start with the "a ha!" moment and work out to the overall scenario? Or you do start with the big picture and work down to the "a ha!" moments?

3.5 Introducing the Law

Introduction of the Law
Must be
• Completely articulated and accurate
• Clearly explained
• Legal issues appropriately framed
• Persuasive
• Theme consistently integrated

Jurors will look for a verdict that conforms with their understanding of and feelings about the facts. Once inside the jury room, the jurors will start the process of deciding a verdict they are comfortable with, and that comfort is based on them finding the verdict that most closely fits how they have processed the case and their own desired outcome. They will either work through the evidence and then look for a verdict, or they will establish a verdict and look for support for that verdict in the testimony and evidence.

Your job in opening is to give them an understanding of the *end result* before they begin the entire process. In other words, while the facts will continue to unfold, and the jurors' understanding of the facts will continue to evolve, their confirmation of certain facts and resolution of what happened will deepen—so giving them an understanding of the law and potential verdict from the outset will subconsciously guide their thinking through the trial.

> *Folks, as you know from Judge Smith earlier today, this case is a insider trading case. You are the finders of fact. Judge Smith is the keeper of the law. He will read you the law later in the case, and give you specific instructions that spell out the law. But going into this, you need to know what defamation is so you can listen for it as the case progresses.*
>
> *In order to prove defamation, we have to prove three things to prove insider trading.*
>
> *First, we have to prove that Mr. Defendant used an instrumentality of interstate commerce in connection with the purchase or sale of a security.*
>
> *Second, we have to prove that Mr. Defendant used a device, scheme, or artifice to defraud in connection with the purchase or sale of a security.*
>
> *And third, we must find that Mr. Defendant acted knowingly or with severe recklessness.*
>
> *As you listen to the evidence, you will learn that a stock is an "instrument of interstate commerce."*
>
> *Listen to the witnesses discuss late night meetings, emails, text messages, documents that will be proved to*

be falsified, and money missing from account. As you listen, see if you think that constitutes a "scheme" to defraud.

And listen to witnesses describe Mr. Defendant's statements about what he was doing. As you listen, consider whether Mr. Defendant's statements show he was acting knowingly.

And so forth. You are not "arguing" that any of the facts *are* violations of the law. You are simply telling the jury what you have to prove and where for them to look for that proof. Note, the elements in the above example come from Eleventh Circuit Pattern Jury Instruction 6.3.2.

Jurors need to know where they are going, and that it is OK for them to gravitate to a particular verdict. In fact, you want that verdict in their head as they listen to the case. If the jurors understand what law they have to apply, and they find your facts to align more with the law than does your opponent, you can motivate them to act and vote in your favor.

3.6 "The Ask"

Request for verdict
Must be
• Clear
• Concise
• Tied to the theory of the case
• An option the jurors will feel good about

Remember that jurors are not accustomed to the courtroom and its procedures. They need all the help they can get understanding everything from when the break is, to whether the case is civil or criminal. You have got to make it easy for them to follow you.

So there is no mistake, *be sure to clearly ask for the verdict you want*. This is tied to the intro of the law—the jury needs to understand where you want them to go, and have that goal in mind (or even in their subconscious) while they listen to the case unfold.

"At the conclusion of the case, based on the evidence you will hear, we ask that you find that the defendant is [liable] [not liable] [guilty] [not guilty]." For a little more personal feel, you could use ". . . Ms. Plaintiff asks that you find Mr. Defendant liable for defaming her." In my example earlier in the chapter, "Ms. Barton asks that you find her not guilty."

Never assume the jurors know what is going on. Always help them understand at each stage of the proceedings.

It's that simple, really. You have attached a conclusion to your story. You have given the jury a word to associate with your presentation and story. Once in deliberation, when the jurors begin to harmonize all the evidence and testimony, and to search for a verdict, your planted seed should already be growing.

Be careful with what you ask for—be reasonable, and if you ask big, be sure you can back it up. As my friend and Stetson Law professor Lee Coppock teaches, *a pig gets fat, but a hog gets slaughtered*. Don't overdo it and lose credibility. Save the "big ask" for closing, when all the evidence has come out and you have watched the jurors' reactions. But be sure to clearly let the jurors' know the verdict you want them to return.

3.7 Delivering the Opening Statement

3.7.1   *Commitment and Conditional Acceptance*

Once you have your structure defined, and all the facts and law ready to present, you are ready to work on your delivery. The most finely structured opening statement will fall flat if you fail to deliver it with conviction. If it is going to *resonate*, it has to be presented in a persuasive manner. This is where your *ethos* and *pathos* converge. First impressions count, so don't miss this change for *maximum impact*.

DELIVERING AN EFFECTIVE OPENING STATEMENT
• Maintain eye contact, talk *with* the jurors
• Use nonverbal communication (body language)
• Use conversational, inviting style
• Be poised and confident
• Articulate!
• Language clear, concise
• Use transitions to keep the jury organized
• Complete within time limit (set by judge, or what's reasonable)

There are numerous considerations for opening statements, and some are more critical to some cases and advocates than to they are to others. Some people are natural public speakers, and some struggle. Some people are predisposed to grandiosity and overselling, while others fail to strike a chord when the facts are ripe for it. Consider the following when shaping your style.

3.7.2   *Your Voice and Body Language*

Using *you* as an exhibit is a great way to start the case. First impressions count. How you stand and walk to the podium sets the tone for the rest of the case.

The best advice you can get about voice and body language is that you must be situationally aware and use courtroom decorum.

After that, use non-verbal communication, body language, and voice to credibly tell your story. A pause . . . a shrug . . . pursing the lips . . . there are many ways to telegraph the emotions of the case to the jury.

3.7.3   *Familiar Words, Simple Language*

"The evidence will show . . ."

"You will hear . . ."

Simple phrases. Good syntax. Rehearsed pronunciations. Easy words. These are the hallmarks of good public speaking. Remember, you are winning your case by conditional acceptance—the jurors will embrace your story if they can embrace you. They don't want to see unprepared lawyers wasting their time. They will be aggravated at disorganization. They will appreciate someone who knows the facts and can guide them through the case. And everyone would rather hear a compelling story. Make it simple and easy to listen along.

Be sure to tone down your lawyer vocabulary. Speak like the jurors do—in everyday language, using simple and familiar terms. Avoid swearing or cursing unless the facts require it.

Bad lawyer words	Great people words
Accrue	Gain, earn, add
By means of	By, with
Close proximity	Near, around
Determine	Figure out, decide
Encounter	Meet, found
Feasible	Can be done, doable
Females	Women*
Implement	Start, use
Monitor	Check, watch
Operate	Use, run
Purchase	Buy
Remain	Stay
Submit	Give *or* argue to

    *　*Be especially attentive to how you address genders, races, and pronouns. Do not alienate a juror from the start by insulting him or her.*

Another thing to remember—this is a *trial*. Trials are important. Jokes and glibness have no part of that. Moments of levity can naturally occur (I once had my Siri start talking to me during a closing argument in a murder trial). Don't be funny. Don't be cute. Take this seriously and the jury will repay the favor.

3.7.4　Memorization

Memorize your opening, but be careful not to sound robotic. Memorizing your opening allows you to focus your attention on the jurors. Watch their eyes, their movements, their non-verbal communication. Are they looking at you? Are they avoiding eye contact? Can you see some who are clearly with you, and some who are indecisive?

Memorization allows you the ability to adjust. Pay attention to the jurors' reactions as you speak. You may need to slow down or speed up. You may find that a word you used, or fact you stated, drew frowns. Figure out what that means and adjust during witness testimony.

It's OK to have your notes or outline nearby, just in case. If you have to refer to it, do so. But don't read from it—you'll lose the jury. No one wants to listen to someone read; people want to be wowed.

3.7.5 *Location in the Courtroom*

Depending on the jurisdiction and the judge, try to move around a bit. Don't be tied to the podium. Some judges have a rule of thumb—*don't get more than an arm's length away from the podium*. Not a bad policy.

Whatever you do, stay away from the jury box. Getting right up on the jurors can be uncomfortable and intimidating. It has the appearance of "invading the providence of the jury." You don't want to seem weird for running back and forth in front of them!

Moving with times pauses is effective. If you make a particular point about an important witness, move a little toward the witness stand and point it out. The jurors will imagine that person there, and later when you have that witness in that very spot saying exactly what you said he or she would say, you have fulfilled a promise. That gives you credibility.

As all courtrooms are set up differently and all judges' preferences are different, think ahead about where you want to move as you tell your story. Whatever you do, *don't wander around*. Refer to section 4.7 and understand the "no fly zone".

3.7.6   Tone and Tempo

Your tone reflects sincerity, belief, commitment, and respect. The right tone will let the jurors know how you feel about the case, and could impact how they feel about it. Conversely, the wrong tone can be off putting and even offensive. As will be discussed in later chapters, be sure to find the right tone with which to project your message.

Tempo is your speed. Tempo, along with cadence (the flow or rhythm of your words), are important to the sheer listenability of your opening statement. Too fast, people get lost and important points are glossed over. Too slow, people lose interest. And extreme of either can also have jurors ignoring *what* you are saying and simply focusing on *how* you are saying it. This is much like attorneys who use "and" at the beginning of every sentence or question, or say "uh" repeatedly—the jurors stop listening to content and simply listen to count how many times the offending word is said. It becomes a odd form of entertainment.

More on this in sections 4.7.2 and 5.6.

3.7.7   Avoiding Arguing in Opening

Remember these simple phrases from above: *"[t]he evidence will show. . . ."* and *"[y]ou will hear"*? What about *"[a]s you listen, listen for. . ."*? Those are all guiding statements. That's all. They don't explain evidence, they just point to evidence.

"Because . . ." Now, you are explaining. A good rule of thumb as to whether something is argument or not, is if whatever is being said is preceded with the word "because."

Argument: *John was nervous because he knew what he had done. He left the office in a frazzle because he knew the caper was up and he was about to be discovered.*

Not argument: *As you listen to the witnesses, ask yourself why John left the office early that day. Listen for what he said before he left. Listen to his assistant describe how anxious he appeared.*

The obvious use of "because" will draw an objection for arguing in opening. Stating what the facts will be from the witnesses is just that—pointing out the facts to focus on. The jurors can make their own decision from there. Remember, you give them "2 + 2", and they will get "4" all on their own.

Arguing is different from describing, reviewing, or summarizing.

There are some checks you can use to determine if something is an improper argument.

3.7.7.1   Testimony Check

If a witness will testify to something in court, you can point that out and it is not improper argument.

Argument: *If Mr. Witness was at the scene, and because he was there he must have seen and heard what was going on.*

Not argument: *Mr. Witness was in the Sack O' Suds convenience store that morning. He saw and heard what was going on. He will take the stand and tell you he saw that man (pointing at defendant) enter the store and point a pistol at the clerk.*

Here, you are simply describing what Mr. Witness will say happened. Easy.

3.7.7.2 Evidence Check

If you have an item of evidence, you can discuss it (assuming it will be admissible). You don't have to argue anything about it, because an item of tangible evidence or a photo/diagram/document speaks for itself.

> **Argument:** *The bank records are more important than witness testimony. Bank records don't lie. Witnesses lie. You should trust the bank records more than any person's words, because they're computer-generated and tamper-proof.*

> **Not argument:** *The bank records in this case show deposits and withdrawals. They show the history of the company. They will show you its financial health. You will be able to see just how much money was going in and coming out. And from where.*

The idea is to talk about the evidence without assessing its importance over another item. You can't argue its credibility versus a witness or other item of evidence. You can, of course, ask the jury to consider the source.

> *As you listen, you will hear about some employee records of the WidgetCo. These records, you will hear, have entries of work times, pay rates, and notes on employee performance. When you are listening to the testimony about these records, think about who made the records. Then listen to testimony about that person. As you listen, ask yourself why are somethings included in the file, and other things not.*

3.7.7.3 "Spin" Check

Some terms are not obvious argument, but enough "spin" on the facts that it becomes or constitutes impermissible argument. Once you leave describing, reviewing, or summarizing, and get into comparing/contrasting, evaluating, explaining, and asking for people to assess, you are arguing. Stick to telling the story.

"SPIN CHECK"—GOING PAST STATING FACTS	
They want you to think that [fact] is true, but . . .	Justifying why other side is wrong
They claim [fact], but . .	Evaluating
Mr. Plaintiff was right in thinking/ saying/doing . . .	Explaining
There will be no way you can believe . . .	Attacking credibility
That fact is not relevant . . .	Assessing
It seems clear that . . .	Discussing
You can conclude from that . . .	Asking jurors to assess
[Ultimate issue] will be shown by the fact that . . .	Explaining
[Fact] establishes/proves/shows/ indicates that . . .	Arguing proof
When you hear [fact], you will find/conclude that . . .	Asking jurors to assess

Most of these phrases can be cleared up with the "as you listen, consider for yourself the credibility of" or "it will be up to you to decide how you feel about the testimony of Mr. Plaintiff, but as you listen to him, listen for certain things. Was he able to see what happened? Was he able to hear what happened?" Those are much safer. Again, when in doubt, stick to just telling the story.

3.7.7.4   Objection Check

Will your evidence come in? If you know that something is not going to be admissible, then your statement is clearly only an argument. If it has no basis in the admissible facts of the trial, it serves no other purpose in your opening. It's just simply improper and unethical to talk about inadmissible evidence in opening.

Remember, if you have a question about the evidence, file a motion *in limine* to test the waters and get a ruling. If it's still undecided as to whether the evidence is coming in, perhaps best to make a blanket statement such as, "members of the jury, there will be other evidence of importance coming to you in this trial. Pay close attention to what you see and what you hear." Beyond that, leave it out of your opening.

3.7.8   *Conditional Acceptance, Revisited*

Finally, consider how all of this comes together.

 Get the jury liking you and you will get their *conditional acceptance*.

If your content is good, and your structure is logical and easy to follow, and you strike the right delivery, jurors will like you and you will win "conditional acceptance" from the jurors. In other words, if you do a good job on structure and delivery, the jurors will give you some credibility that will blend into the rest of the trial. In other words, a good opening statement will get you their attention and willingness to listen to you. A great opening statement could also earn you a place as the jurors' main source of information and authority about the facts and the law!

3.8 Using Exhibits/Demonstratives in Opening

3.8.1 Using Demonstratives

Demonstratives are always a good way to assist the jury in understanding the case. Anything from a PowerPoint-style presentation to a poster can enhance the jurors' understanding of your case.

Photos. A picture is worth a thousand words. Again—be sure it is admissible. Some photos are so gory that they may be best saved for later, when the jury has had some conditioning about what lies ahead. On the other hand, maybe the emotion of the case is *shock* and that photo will instill it.

Maps. People like maps. They like to be oriented. Using maps can help the jury know where things are. It will assist in their mental image of what happened by giving some real orientation.

Documents, etc. If it is coming in at trial, show it in opening. Why not? *This, members of the jury, you will learn this is the starting point of this entire case: the contract.*

Summaries. Summaries of huge amounts of evidence are admissible in the trial. Why not use them in opening? Work with your summary witness to prepare a precise demonstrative.

Be sure to show the other side the demonstrative, and alert the judge that you intend on using it. Every jurisdiction is a little different on how the judges feel about using demonstratives in opening statements—find out before you start your opening!

3.8.2   Jury Instructions

As mentioned above, you have to introduce the jurors to the law. They have to have some idea of what to listen for, and why they are even there. It's asinine to expect that a jury can listen to and properly process the facts with no idea what it is anyone has to prove.

In introducing the law, you can use a demonstrative of the jury instructions to help them visualize and remember their mission. If you have the ultimate issue instructions done, simply blow them up on a poster or use the courtroom overhead.

ELEMENTS OF DEFAMATION CLAIM
1. Defendant used an instrumentality of interstate commerce in connection with the purchase or sale of a security.

2. Defendant used a device, scheme, or artifice to defraud in connection with the purchase or sale of a security.

3. Defendant acted knowingly or with severe recklessness.

If the final instructions are not ready—which often times they are not until the evidentiary part of the case is over—then you can use the standard instructions. Most jurisdictions have standard instructions online. If not, look at the statutes and case law. You knew early on what you had to prove—condense that into a nice chart.

Using the defamation example from above, your chart could look as simple as the graphic here. Remember to alert the court and opposing counsel to the demonstrative before you begin you opening statement, to resolve any objections. In the event the court does not allow you to use it, you want to know that in advance—you do not want to get shut down in the middle of your presentation!

3.9 Example of Opening Statement

Here is the actual opening from the trial discussed above.

	(Following is an excerpt of the jury trial held on the 10th day of May, 2021, at 1:35 PM.)
	THE COURT: Mr. Bodiford.
Classic opening	MR. BODIFORD: If it pleases the Court, Your Honor, Counsel.
Main emotion: cheating, betrayal (superimposed over trust, innocence)	Members of the jury, there are players and then there are the played. The players in this case, they bought. They are flashy. They have money. They attract attention. They are popular, but they also scheme. They scheme. They connive.
The innocent financial victims	They are careful. They calculate. And in this case they are criminals.
	So we've got the played. We have the players, but then we have the played. The victims in this case; they are the chumps. They are the marks. They are the patsies.
Invokes feelings that the jury can relate to	So in this case these folks are going to line up very clearly on one side of the ledger or the others, the players and the played. Now, the played—the

	victim, the prey, if you will—they come to us in two varieties. The first are these folks that are scattered across this country leading their lives oblivious to what is going on the Internet. In fact, Mr. Allen had been deceased for many, many years.
Summoning the monster lurking in the dark	They have no idea that there is somebody out there crawling in the dark recesses of the dark web buying their information, buying their PII— their personal identifying information— buying the ability to sneak in the back door and steal their hard-earned money. Those are the victims; those are the patsies; those are the prey; those are the played.
Identifying my client with others—the financial victims as well as the uncharged co-conspirators	And we cannot overlook in this case, members of the jury, that there were, in fact, some people right here in Tallahassee who were played. They were played for their naiveness, naivete, and naively being duped and being used by the players to accomplish the players' goals.
Lining client up with those who were played but not charged	We've heard their names so far today: Deshauan Sanders, Desiree Ferreira, Jacob Koller, Jessica Gallimore, Deshawn Taylor, Ki-Mani Ward, Lark Bailey, Voshon Howard, Jada Guzman, Jada Harris, and there is another—Jada Barton.

Personalizing my client's introduction	Ms. Barton, stand please.
	Again, my name is Joe Bodiford. Along with my associate Gannon Coens, we represent Ms. Barton here before the Court and before you all.
	Thank you.
MINI STORY: the main player's scheme	Now, Kh'lajuwon Murat put these students, these patsies, into his lie. He wove them into his web of deceit. He wove them into his own selfish goals and into his criminal activities.
	See, he had a scheme. He made it simple. "Do me a favor." You've already seen the texts—"Do me a favor"—seemingly innocent, seemingly simple. He didn't ask any of his patsies or his marks or his dupes here in Tallahassee to go create a fake account, or go create a fake credit card in somebody else's name, or, Hey, I need you to pretend to be somebody else and go do this, that, and the other.
	No, he did this in a manner not to raise any alarms.
Personification of the simple, familiar phrase as evil	"Do me a favor." And it was a rouse that he used over and over, as we can see.
MINI STORY: main player's assumed persona	Now, he made it clear on his social media account that he had money. Remember the last image that we saw

	in Mr. Keen's presentation of all the dollars, all the money fanned out? And remember the testimony that you are going to hear about Mr. Koller who got $500? $500, a mint to a college student from Mr. Murat, just because.
	So he wanted the world to know, you'll hear, that he had money to spend, that he was generous, that he was the guy.
	So he preyed on these students' situation.
	Now, the CARES [sic] Program at Florida State University is the Center for Academic Retention and Enhancement.
MINI STORY: the setting—the university	And this is a program that Florida State University has for students, who, for the most part, are the first in their family to go to college and they have very unique educational and economic situations.
MINI STORY: poor college kids who became the played	Now, of course, we all know that college kids struggle. We expect them to struggle. That's part of being in college. But these students really struggled and Florida State University knows that and they provide for them. These students are essentially paid to go to school. So they receive tuition money from the University. They receive housing money from the

	University. They receive money for food and for clothes and for books and supplies. Basically, they exist on money that is not theirs. That's what the CARES program is.
MINI STORY: how the money moved around	Now, FSU disburses this money to these students on what is called this FSUCard. It's really not a credit card per say. It's almost like an electronic wallet. And as you heard, there will be testimony that there is guest log-ins where people can put money on this, essentially, virtual wallet for students. So it's very common, you'll hear, for students to have money coming in on their cards.
Resonating with the jury—explaining something unfamiliar in familiar terms	So, of course, Mr. Murat will choose to have the funds sent to these student cards. First, apparently, these students don't mind sharing their card number, FSUCard numbers, back and forth. Apparently they do it without thinking about it. And, again, that's probably, you'll hear, because it's not like the bank cards or credit cards that probably most of the folks in this room have in their pocket right now. It's very different.
Not argument, but a rhetorical question	So as the case progresses, you'll hear these students testify and you will maybe hear how the scheme worked. What would raise suspicion about

	putting money on a card that the University monitors?
Recalling that shady phrase	And Mr. Murat had that perfect excuse you'll hear—you'll hear from the students and you'll see these text message—"Do me a favor. Buy me an Apple product. Go to the bookstore and get me an Apple product."
MINI STORY: what it was main player needed his marks to do	You'll also hear at the time the policy of the University was to limit the number of Apple products any one student could buy. So, again, his scheme, Hey, I need you to go get an Apple product. It's simple. It's seemingly innocent and it's perfect for Mr. Murat to use to constrict his patsies and his dupes and his marks and sophisticated enough to get them in without raising an alarm.
Characterizing the played and what they did as seemingly innocent	What is a college freshman or a college sophomore—maybe 17, 18, 19, years old—really going to be concerned about? That they are going to get in trouble for violating the University policy? That somehow they are going to get in trouble for buying one too many Apple products beyond what they are supposed to be able to?
	So he played on their struggle. You'll hear that he played on their ignorance. And you'll hear that he played on their situation.

What they are going to hear (previewing the facts)	Now, you are going to hear from a lot of people in this trial, both the players and the played. Remember, you are going to hear from Mr. Telfort in a minute. You are going to see a lot of records, bank records, FSU records, texts, social media, and the like. And you are going to hear a lot of testimony from these students about the play, about the scheme, how it was designed and how it was executed.
	And so you will see a great—a great, great deal of information and in great, great detail that—a lot of stuff that will lead you to conclude that Kh'lajuwon Murat was the organizer and the puppet master. He's the player.
INTRODUCTION OF THE LAW	Now, there are some important words for you to consider as you listen, and I believe that you will see them and hear them in the instructions that Judge Hinkle will give you towards the end of this trial. Now, those instructions are the law. What he will tell you is: This is the law. And that will help you then be able to apply the facts that you are going to hear to that law to make a determination.
Pointing the jury where to focus as they listen to the trial	And I believe that you will hear these words at the end, so I ask you to bear them in mind as you listen to this case: Knowingly, intended, agreed, unlawful,

	knew—k-n-e-w—and join. Some very important words, because to prove bank fraud, the government is going to have to prove that Ms. Barton over here knowingly carried out or attempted to carry out a scheme to defraud and that she intended to defraud the banks.
	And to prove conspiracy—
	MR. KEEN: Objection, Your Honor.
Some prosecutors can't stand defense attorneys talking about the law—THE WHOLE REASON WE ARE IN COURT!	THE COURT: Overruled. Let's go on. I'll give you detailed instructions at the end of the case about just exactly what has to be proved. In openings the lawyers can talk about the issues and give you a shorthand version. Nobody is trying to give you the whole thing, and, of course, you'll take that from me at the end of the case in any event.
Judge agrees that it's fair to discuss	I don't know exactly how Mr. Bodiford phrased it. Mr. Keen obviously took some exception to it. Look, we are just talking about general issues here. Don't pay too much attention to the exact phrasing; we'll get to that later.
	MR. BODIFORD: Yes, Your Honor.
Back to what to listen for as the trial progresses	And without reading my learned friend's mind, I think what he's—what he ultimately says is there's four things he has to prove to prove bank fraud. The two that are concerning that you

	listen to contain the words "knowingly" and the words "intended." Knowingly and intended, keep those in mind.
	And the conspiracy to commit mail fraud, which is the other count—Ms. Barton is only charged with the two counts.
Laying it out the law in more detail	One is the conspiracy that everybody is in and then the one count of the mail fraud. But in that one, the government would have to prove two things: That two persons agreed to accomplish a common and unlawful—agreed to commit an unlawful mail fraud, and they have to prove that she knew the unlawful plan and willfully joined it.
Reinforcing the important words that I know they will not be able to prove— guiding the jury where to focus, knowing they won't find it	So there's a lot of important words I ask you to bear in mind as you listen to this case and listen to the evidence unfold: Knowingly, intended, agreed, unlawful, knew, and joined. So we talk about everything that you are going to hear regarding Mr. Murat. What you will not hear in this case is that Jada Barton knowingly carried out a scheme to defraud. You will not hear any direct evidence at all that she intended to defraud anyone. You will not hear that she knew of the unlawful purpose behind Mr. Murat's seemingly innocent "Do me a favor," and that she did not knowingly join any unlawful plan.

Referring to co-defendant's counsel's opening	As Mr. Collins talked about the proof in this case, the proof, the burden of proving, somebody has got to carry the burden in this. Somebody has got to be vested with hitting the ball out of the park. And that burden rests on the government's desk over here. The government has to prove all of these— we talk about four in one and two elements in the other. They have to prove all of those things beyond a reasonable doubt.
Reminding the jury of the burden of proof and how high it is. . . . . . and what it is not	Now, as you listen, you may hear things that bring to mind errors in judgment, carelessness, mistake, negligence, or even foolishness. But that is not proof beyond a reasonable doubt of intent to defraud or agreeing to join an unlawful plan.
Knowing client won't take the stand, reminding the jury of her Constitutional right (invoking patriotism, importance of following the law)	The law presumes that every defendant is innocent. And as the Judge has discussed with you this morning, Ms. Barton doesn't have to prove anything. She doesn't have to prove her innocence nor does she have to present any evidence. We believe that what you will see on the government's presentation, what very minuscule evidence that they have against her— that they claim to have against her will convince you that she's not guilty.

"The Ask"—clear, concise	So at the end of this case, we believe it will be clear to you who was the player and who was played; played for a fool as a dupe, as a mark, as a target. It was clear she was played and she is, in fact, not guilty.
	Thank you.

3.10   Checklists

3.10.1 Opening Statement Checklist (Elements, Witnesses, Etc.)

	"Rivet phrase" perfected to grab and engage the jurors
	2-3 sentence introduction of the case (introduces the story)
	Mini-stories OR witness-by-witness
	Introduction of the law • Burdens of proof correct • Correct law used • Precise and concise statement of the part of the law to which you are introducing the jury
	"The Ask" clear, concise, and tied to the facts and the law

3.10.2 General Rules for Openings

- Don't promise something you cannot prove later on
- Don't misstate a fact or incorrectly quote a witness
- Have a strong "rivet phrase" and a clear, easy to follow story

- Always introduce the law so they jury knows where you want them to go

- Avoid arguing! Use the checks to make sure you are not arguing or "spinning"

- Finish strong by concisely structuring and strongly delivering "The Ask"

3.10.3 Basic Structure: Chrono

Use as many mini-stories as you need to tell the story (you are not limited to three, this is just an checklist template).

	"Rivet statement"
	2-3 sentence introduction of the case
	Mini-story 1:
	Mini-story 2:
	Mini-story 3:
	Intro the law
	"The Ask"

3.10.4 Basic Structure: By Witness

Use as many witnesses as you need to tell the story (you are not limited to three, this is just a checklist template).

	"Rivet statement"
	2-3 sentence introduction of the case
	Witness 1:
	Witness 2:
	Witness 3:

	Intro the law
	"The Ask"

Direct Examination

OBJECTIVES: In this chapter, we will discuss the best practices for direct exams. We will cover not only the purpose of direct, and the philosophy behind it, but the technical aspects of conducting a solid direct. In this chapter, we want to:

- Identify and understand the purpose of direct examinations

- Learn to analyze the facts and witness and their roles in the trial

- Learn ideas of how to prepare for your direct examination

- Learn best practices for structuring and organizing a direct examination

- Explore tips for delivering direct examination

- Understand how to handle and use evidence and demonstratives

4.1 Purpose of Direct Examination: *Telling the Big Story*

Direct examination is more than just "and then what happened? . . . and then what happened? . . .". It is *the big story*, told in real time by real people. This is real-life drama and the most important part of our justice system—this is when people get their day in court. Too many attorneys put witnesses on the stand without thought of structuring the *story* of the direct, anticipating objections, handling and admitting evidence, and preparation of witnesses.

Direct examination is usually the first time the story is fully told. Direct examination is when the jurors get to do several things: (1) hear the evidence and witnesses, and (2) form their own mental version of that happened, (3) start forming opinions about the evidence and witnesses, and (4) start a search for the resolution (what happened and the right verdict). Direct examination is the time their version of the story, which they formed when listening to opening statements, and the actual story (told by the witnesses) begin to either converge—or diverge.

Telling the story in a logical and persuasive way is the key to success. For direct examination, that means thinking of the best way for the jury to hear the story (*structure*) and making sure it "lands" or resonates with the jurors (*delivery*).

Opening is only a preview. While we don't want to tell jurors that the opening statement is "just a preview", it really is just that, albeit a *powerful* one. You will hear attorneys say to juries, "opening statement is just a road map of where the case is going . . .", which only serves to diminish its importance. Many attorneys miss the chance to grab the attention of the jurors in a powerful opening by overtly diminishing its importance with the qualifier of "road map" or "overview."

The "big story" comes in direct examination. This is when the aggrieved plaintiff gets to discuss the accident, the medical treatment, and the impact on his or her life. This is when law enforcement officers get to lay out their case against a criminal defendant. Not only is this the point in our system that is designed for maximum impact, it is the time that jurors expect to hear the story from *the source*.

Keep the jury on point & following the story. As will be discussed below, direct examination should be so easy to listen to and follow, that every juror understands everything and is with you the whole time. It is when the jury will be learning about the case, developing opinions about the witnesses and evidence, and searching for validation about their feelings (comparing and contrasting witness' testimony, etc.).

If you design all your direct examinations to be logical and easy to follow, then your entire case will be persuasive and undeniable.

Build credibility through building credible witnesses. Good structure (below) and solid witness presentation (through thorough preparation) builds a believable story that juror can accept as fact and rely on in negotiating with other jurors and deciding the verdict.

While you don't really know the jurors (other than what you learn in jury selection), you can know your case and help them know your case. You control the flow of the story, of the information, and how your witnesses present themselves and the facts.

Thus, the credibility of your directs will be directly reflected in the credibility of your witnesses, tangible evidence, demonstratives, and how well they tell your story.

4.1.1   Introduce Witnesses and Target Facts

Direct examination serves to introduce your witnesses are characters in the story. Their histories, their involvement, their importance all emerge and support the credibility and believability of your target facts.

4.1.2   Establish Credibility

Your case—i.e. your story, must be believable. Believability is established through credibility. Credibility of witnesses is established through preparation, details, and personality. Your items of evidence take on their own personality (personification) and credibility by how the witness establishes their authentication and explains their importance.

4.1.3   Establish Liking

Your witness must be liked. Not to the point that the jurors want to have dinner with them, but at least to a minimum threshold of not finding them offensive. Disliked witnesses are hard to believe. Liking is established by how the witness speaks, explains, and responds to questions. Preparation is the key to ensuring the witness presents him-/herself well, knows the facts, has a clear thought process, and is familiar with the evidence and any demonstratives.

4.2 Preparing for Direct Examination

We cannot overlook how important preparation is to success at trial. For direct examinations, there are several components you have to prepare for and accomplish—get the witness to be liked and believed, establish the elements of the cause of action (or defense, or crime or defense), and tell the big story of the case.

4.2.1   What Do You Have to Prove/Establish?

Recall from Chapter 1, Trial Preparation, the discussion of what you have to prove. You have done the factual analysis and categorized the facts, and done the witness analysis and created a witness matrix. You have analyzed the law, and know what ultimate facts will prove the elements of your cause of action. You created a powerful opening, using a rivet phrase, mini-stories, and the introduction of the law.

Your witnesses and items of evidence will now give the jurors *all* of the facts. The "big story". Consistency is critical. You gained conditional acceptance with your opening statement. The jurors have a mental image of what the story is, and now they look for details to support their initial impressions.

Direct examinations should be anything but boring—now is the time for it to all come together for the jurors.

4.2.2   *Preparing the Witness*

Prepared witnesses are successful witnesses. They speak well, they make eye-contact, they know where the questions are leading and follow along. The flow is good and there are no stumbles.

Unprepared witnesses are difficult to listen to, and can even make jurors tune out. If your witness doesn't sound like he or she cares, why should the jurors?

Make sure you meet with the witness in advance of trial. Go over all the items in the witness dossier. Go over the structure of the testimony, and the subject to be covered. Make sure the witness understands his or her role (see below). Go over questions and answers with the witness. Do not tell the witness *what* to say (unless you need to remind them of a prior statement, etc.), but discuss with them *how* to say it. Be sure that any impeachment areas are identified and explanations prepared (and how to deliver the explanation).

4.3 The Role of the Witness

As we know from Chapter 1, different witnesses play different roles. Some witnesses can play multiple roles. It is up to you to define the witness' role and employ them appropriately in telling the story of your case. Let's look at a negligence fact pattern:

Paula Plaintiff went to GroceryCo on Saturday, June 15, to do her weekly grocery shopping. She arrived around 8:00am, hoping to get in early and beat the weekend rush. The store opened at 7am, but it would be filling up by mid-morning. She got out of her car, walked across the parking lot, entered the store, and got her shopping cart. She then went on in to the main part of the store and began shopping. She loved to shop at GroceryCo. She had shopped there her whole life, from when she would go with her mother and ride in the cart while they shopped.

GroceryCo is a nationwide chain that began as a "mom and pop" sundry store in 1930. It grew over the years into a Fortune 500 company and one of the most recognized brands in the country. The annual sales top over one hundred and forty billion dollars. GroceryCo has stores in 40 states, totaling over 2500 individual locations. GroceryCo has over 450,000 employees, making it one of the largest employers in the country.

GroceryCo has a specific protocol for its daily operations, which are codified in the Store Operations Manual. Each employee is trained on the manual, and given regular testing and refresher training on the standard operating procedures for his or her specific job or jobs. There are also special safety training programs each must complete.

One of GroceryCo's main sales center and marketing tool is its produce section. GroceryCo dedicates more square footage in its stores to produce than any other chain. Its huge variety of fruits and vegetables attracts customers from all over, and is usually the busiest part of the store.

Maintaining such a large assortment of produce is tricky, and requires constant attention throughout the day. GroceryCo has installed in every store a custom and proprietary water misting system to keep the produce fresh and looking good. The system runs throughout the day, turning on and off based on sensors monitoring the traffic in the produce area. When there are fewer customers, the system will run, misting cold water in different areas. The system runs much more regularly through the evening. Every misting results in water on the floor, sometimes more than others (particularly in the morning).

GroceryCo places bright colored signs around the produce area. The signs feature their logo and smiling mascot, and read "BE CAREFUL—OUR FLOORS MAY BE A LITTLE WET FROM WATERING YOUR PRODUCE".

GroceryCo has specific training and custom mops and squeegees for the employees. In the morning, the procedure calls for the entire area to be mopped, then squeegeed, then inspected for any moisture on the floor. During misting times during shopping hours, a signal will tell employees that the misting will begin in 5 minutes. During that time, "wet floor" signs are placed prominently around the soon-to-be-wet floor areas. During the misting, an employee is to stand by to prevent customers from entering the area, and to mop/squeegee/inspect the area immediately thereafter before removing the "wet floor" signs.

Paula Plaintiff's first trip was to the produce aisle. Upon entering the area, she parked her shopping cart and began looking at tomatoes. After making her selection, she turned around and took a step back to her cart. Unbeknownst to her, the floor was still wet, and she slipped and fell. As she fell, she hit her head on the display case, resulting in a cracked skull and brain swelling.

As bad luck would have it, the power had surged during the night and the misting system—and its alarms—had reset to initial settings. The backup system had not functioned correctly, and it had been offline for days. Despite having the same routine everyday, the employees who were working didn't notice that the misting system was running when it should not have been, and water was all over the floors. Instead of being on the floor where they were supposed to be, they were huddled up near the front office, looking at one of the employee's phone.

4.3.1   *Essential/Main Fact Witnesses*

Essential (or main fact) witnesses are just that—they supply the ultimate facts that go directly to the elements of the cause of action, crime, or defense. If you have to prove a battery, you will need the person who was touched against his or her will. If you have to prove a negligence case, like the slip and fall, you will need Paula Plaintiff—the person who walked in the store and slipped on a freshly mopped wet floor. You'll need the employees who were working that day, and responsible for store safety. You simply cannot prove the case without these main fact witnesses.

Main fact witnesses prove the ultimate issue. Be very careful to identify your essential main fact witnesses and secure their attendance at trial.

4.3.2   *Support Witnesses*

Support witnesses set the tone of the case, set the scene, and can establish a history of the case. They may not have seen the actual event, but can testify about things that provide *context*. In the slip and fall example above, the clerks who opened the store and cleaned the floors would be support witnesses. They did not see the incident, but they can talk about the condition of the scene prior to the slip. Similarly, a store employee who was not even there the day the accident happened can be a support witness if that person is called to testify about procedures or to authenticate a diagram of the store. The store's custodian of records is a support witness, and may testify as to who was on duty that day or to store's procedure manual.

Together, main fact witnesses and support witnesses combine to paint the full picture for the jury.

4.3.3 Expert Witnesses

Expert witnesses are becoming increasingly important in litigation in America. Due to the complexity of vehicles, medicine, computers/internet/social media, attorneys must rely on experts to explain how things work and how they impact our daily lives.

Rule 702. Testimony by Expert Witnesses

A witness who is qualified as an expert by knowledge, skill, experience, training, or education may testify in the form of an opinion or otherwise if:

  a) the expert's scientific, technical, or other specialized knowledge will help the trier of fact to understand the evidence or to determine a fact in issue;

  b) the testimony is based on sufficient facts or data;

  c) the testimony is the product of reliable principles and methods; and

  d) the expert has reliably applied the principles and methods to the facts of the case.

Someone with the requisite amount of knowledge, skill, experience, training, or education may take the stand and not only discuss the facts, but opine on the ultimate issue. The judge is the gatekeeper of who can testify as an expert. Be sure to find someone who will qualify as the best expert for your issues. Also, be sure that your expert has a good history. You want to avoid using a so-called expert what has been discredited in a trial, or worse—has been prohibited from testifying as an expert by a judge. All of that information is available in the discovery process.

In Paula's case, doctors and workplace safety experts would definitely be needed to discuss injuries and likelihood of recovery, and why GroceryCo's system would have worked "but for" not having the system on a power backup. Experts on damages are also critical to getting Paula the right recovery.

4.3.4   Impeachment Witnesses

In Chapter 1 we identified some witnesses that may serve to impeach or rebut. As with the other witnesses, they should be well prepared and add to your story. They may have little to do with the actual essential (ultimate issue) elements, but can add to the story with 404 testimony, or character/reputation evidence. Be sure the impeachment witness knows the limits of his or her testimony and does not inadvertently say something beyond the scope of their testimony that could be objectionable or cause a mistrial.

4.3.5   Rebuttal Witnesses

Rebuttal witnesses are likely going to be called after and in response to the other side's presentation. A prosecutor or plaintiff's attorney would call them *after* the defense presents its case. The defense would simply present its rebuttal witnesses in its case in chief.

The same considerations apply to rebuttal witnesses as all the others.

4.4 Structure and Organization of Direct Examination

Structure your direct examination into segments—a overall case theory (the overall plot or story arc—the main "why we are here"), themes (sub-plots), and topics (the scenes of the story, play, or movie). All of these end up giving you *target facts*—those precious, undeniable, persuasive morsels of information that tell your story and prove your case.

Remember the difference: the themes and topics stem from and organize the overall case theory, while the target fact is a main thing the examiner has to get out of the witness, or get the witness to admit.

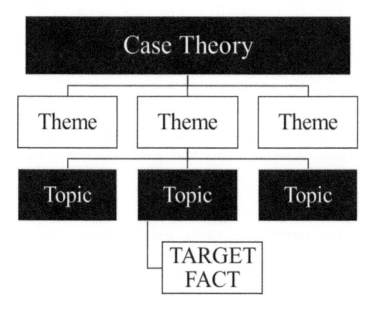

Designing your direct examination is pretty straightforward, but there are some things you should think about when laying it out. What is the best way to present the facts, scene by scene, or person by person? What is the best order of witnesses, and will you have to call some of them to the stand more than once?

4.4.1   *Structural Elements*

Generally, a direct might be arranged something like this:

- Introduction (name, employment, basic relevant biographical information)

- Background information on witness that relates to the case and issues

- Historical info on location, setting, time/date, etc.

- Element facts

- Anticipate impeachment facts and deal with

- Anticipate counterarguments and present facts

- Final facts (strong close, use primacy and recency to reiterate facts/story)

"Storyboard" your direct for a particular witness, see how it plays out. On a piece of paper or posterboard, write each theme and topic, all necessary targe facts, and arrange them in the best order. See below for more.

4.4.1.1   Case Theory

The overall case theory should permeate the direct examination. You can do that by infusing words and phrases that remind the jury of the emotion or feeling of the case from your "rivet phrase". Keep them engaged and interested in resolving the moral, ethical, or legal dilemma that is the theory of the case.

4.4.1.2 Themes

In Chapter 1, we learned about the importance of themes. Laying them out in storyboard fashion will guide your jurors through the direct.

In the *Paula Plaintiff vs. GroceryCo* case example, you could have several themes, such as:

Law created duty of care	GroceryCo knew of duty of care	GroceryCo took steps to comply with duty of care

In this scenario, you are looking at a set of themes that goes to one of the elements of your cause of action: *duty of care*.

4.4.1.3 Topics

Now, within each theme you will have a topics—or, stated another way, within each mini-story you will have important individual scenes. Consider the last theme, above, and lets look at each "scene" that illustrates that theme:

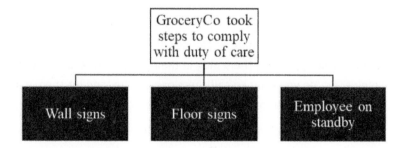

4.4.1.4 Target Facts

It may seem a little "extra" to have a multi-tiered matrix of facts. But going through the process of analyzing the facts accomplishes two main goals: (1) it makes you know your case inside and out, and (2) it lets you think of your facts in "3-D"—thinking of all the ways a particular fact can be used.

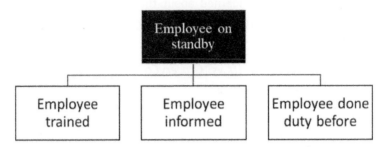

Looking at the "employee on standby" topic (scene), what are the target facts you want to get out to the jury?

In your final closing argument, you have the target facts of a well-trained employee, an employee who was informed of the importance of customers' safety, and that the employee had stood by for the customers on other occasions.

You have solid proof and argument that GroceryCo took steps to fulfill its duties of care.

4.4.2   *Order of the Direct Presentation*

Consider which is better for your case . . . what works best for your story? Are you planning on calling witnesses as they are needed to tell the story, letting them plug in their perspectives as the story unfolds? Or, do you want to call them one by one, and let them get out all of their testimony and move to the next witness?

In cases with complicated facts and issues, the chronological method may work better. Witnesses may testify, leave the courtroom, and come back later to testify some more. This is not odd, as people are used to watching TV shows and movies where scenes go back and forth to different characters.

In cases with narrow issues, or just one or two witnesses, then the witness by witness method works fine. This method could be cumbersome in complex cases—there, the jury is left to hear large blocks of testimony relating lots of facts, then try to shoehorn that into or against the other witnesses' testimony.

4.4.2.1 Scene by Scene (Chronological)

In the slip and fall example, you would have each person called in order of where they appear in the case.

WITNESS	FACTS	WHY CALLING?
Paula Plaintiff (if she is able to testify)	Her morning, slipping and falling	No contributory fault
Patricia Plaintiff	Paula's mother, can talk about the family history with GroceryCo and Paula's regular Saturday morning	No contributory fault
Business records custodian of GroceryCo	To show the Defendant's standard operating procedures	Duty existed, they knew of it
Will Witness	Was there when Paula fell, will testify that he too had slipped in the water (although not as bad) and had gone to find someone to clean it up	Breach of duty; proximate cause
GroceryCo manager	To establish who was on duty that day	Knowledge and breach of duty

GroceryCo records custodian	To show that employees on duty had the safety training, and signed that they knew the SOPs for misting	Knowledge and breach of duty
Wanda Witness	Saw Paula slip and fall, did not see any employees in the area; finally saw them all huddling around one's phone looking at photos and laughing	Causation; breach of duty
Workplace safety expert	Discuss GroceryCo's procedures, and how if they were followed they would be within industry standards to prevent accidents like this one	Duty of care
Edwin Employee	Was on duty, assigned to that section, will say he was distracted by other workers wanting to look at funny videos on social media; was not where he was supposed to be; knew people could slip and fall in the misted water	Breach, causation
Paramedics	Care given on scene	Damages
Doctors	Plaintiff's medical care and future prognosis	Damages

Actuary or financial expert	To discuss defendant's life expectancy and cost of care over her lifetime	Damages
Hospital custodian of records	Medical records and, more importantly, medical bills	Damages
Paula's mother and father	Talk about what it takes to care for Paula on a daily basis	Damages

There may be a good reason to recall a witness or two, here or there, depending on vantage point or intervening acts. Notice, mom is called twice. Will Witness could be called twice—the first time to say what he saw before he, too, slipped and fell. Perhaps the experts in workplace safety could testify about the lack of backup on the misting system. Then Will could get back up on the stand and testify about what happened after his fall, and not being able to find any employees. In calling him twice, you get maximum impact (pun intended). The intervening witness sets the scene for Paula's impending accident. . . the jurors *feel* what is coming. Then a very well-prepared Paula would then take the stand to walk the jurors through her terrible incident. Powerful stuff.

4.4.2.2   Witness by Witness (Point of View)

The *point of view* approach to direct examination has the witness lays out his or her entire testimony in full, from start to finish.

In slip and fall case, you might call Plaintiff's mother and father first, and have them testify about both before the accident and after the accident, all at once. Then you could have the eyewitnesses. Then the paramedics. Then the experts on the industry standard of customer safety and Paula's damages. Finally, you could close with the actuary or financial experts.

Again, note that this approach may work better with short trials and fact patterns.

4.4.3   *Quantity of Details*

Details are important. The more details you have, the more credible your witness will seem. Of course, if your witness remembers A—Y, and cannot comment on Z . . . Z will be the focus of the attack on cross ("If you know all of that, why don't you know this?").

Not every witness needs to give every detail, and not every detail needs ten witnesses. You can avoid bogging the trial down by having witnesses "specialize" in a particular part of the trial. If twenty people see the same thing, do you really need to call all twenty? Sure, the other side can argue that "maybe the eyewitnesses saw something else"—your retort in closing is, "if that is the case, then why didn't opposing counsel call them and let you know that they saw something else?!?" But jurors will zone out if they hear the same thing, over and over. That's *not* maximum impact.

Details will support arguments later. As discussed above, the more details you have, the more facts you can highlight and argue in closing. Jurors are soaking it all in as the trial goes, so you don't have to rehash every direct in your close. Element/ultimate issue facts will be used. Impeachment facts will be used. So, details of *who, what, when, how,* and sometimes *why* have to be included in your direct.

4.4.4 Primacy and Recency

Most Important Questions First and Last. Much like opening statement, a direct can start with a trailer/into—

Q   *Ms. Plaintiff, why are you here today?*

A   *Because I was hurt at GroceryCo.*

Q   *How were you hurt at GroceryCo?*

A   *They left water on the floor, and I did not see it, and I slipped and hit my head. I busted my skull as I fell.*

* * *

Q   *Before we conclude your testimony, Ms. Plaintiff, let me take you back to GroceryCo. Did you anticipate there would be water on the floor?*

A   *No, I have been going there my whole life and I have never seen water on the floors. I never imagined it would be unsafe to walk in there.*

Q   *You said earlier you busted your skull . . . are you still having issues with that?*

A   *Yes. I have constant headaches, my hearing is half of what it was, and I have trouble seeing out of my left eye. I was fine before I slipped in that water.*

4.5 Dealing with Bad Facts

Every case has some bad facts. You cannot ignore them. But you can deal with them. If you have something that will come up on cross, bury it in the middle of your direct. A prior conviction can be slid in the middle of a direct, perhaps with something else not too critical to the case. Use a couple of background facts to bury the bad fact:

Q   *Mr. Witness, where did you first encounter Ms. Plaintiff?*

A   *I was on my way from the loading dock to the front office.*

Q   *Tell us what happened*

[Several questions and answers about the actual incident, which is an allegation that an argument between the two turned into a physical attack on Plaintiff with injuries]

Q   *Let me take you back to something real quick. You said you were on your way through the store. What time did you start work that day?*

A   *I got in at six o'clock in the morning.*

Q   *How long had you worked at GroceryCo at the time?*

A   *I had been there for seven years.*

Q   *By the way, have you ever been convicted of a crime of dishonesty?*

A   *Yes, one, over twenty years ago. It was 1999, I think.*

Q   *Ok. What did you do at GroceryCo?*

A   *I was a shift supervisor.*

And the questioning goes on, into training, duties, obligations to customers, etc. That goes to duty and cause. The conviction is buried in the employment history—strategically. He is honest about the prior. That apparently has not impacted his ability to maintain long-term employment in an important position of trust. The prior conviction has been neutralized.

A prior inconsistent statement can be dealt with the same way. Find an innocuous place in the testimony to talk about it. Get in, have the witness explain the inconsistency, and get out. On cross, the witness has the out of "as I explained on direct, . . .". If opposing counsel insists on asking about it after that, your object to "asked and answered."

Dealing with a bad fact is not so hard after all. But dealing with *why* you didn't address it and were not forthcoming about it is hard and could be fatal to your credibility.

4.6 Anticipating and Dealing with Objections

As will be discussed in Chapters 5 and 7, be ready to defend your witness and evidence. Does the testimony or evidence HOP the BAR? Is it hearsay—and if it is, is there an exception? Is it an estimate based on experience, or an inadmissible lay opinion? And so on. Design good directs and you will largely avoid objections. For those things you have to argue on the fly, have your response and research ready for the judge.

OBJECTION!	WHAT TO DO
Sustained without asking for your response	<ul><li>Ask, "may I respond?"</li><li>If no, ask "may we approach?"</li><li>If no, ask "may I make a proffer outside the presence of the jury?"</li><li>If no, move on; as soon as the jury leaves, ask to make your record as to what your question was and what the witness would have said (in case you need appellate review)</li><li>If the court prevents that, object on the record to being prevented from making a record then file an written proffer after trial (if necessary)</li></ul>

	• If you know you asked a bad question, simply say, "I'll rephrase, Your Honor" and move on
Court asks for your response	• Make a concise statement as to why it is admissible, i.e. "does not go to the truth of the matter asserted" or "effect on the listener" • If you need to elaborate, ask to approach the bench or at sidebar
Court asks you to approach the bench	• Wait for the judge to tell you why he/she wanted you at the bench • Don't argue to loud the jury can hear you • Articulate your argument for admissibility • If sustained, ask if you can approach the question a different way (if you can) to avoid drawing back-to-back objections • Proffer the testimony you want out if you are sustained
Court does not respond, or asks what it was that you just asked	• Judge wasn't listening/paying attention • If no response, simply ask, "Your Honor?" to get his/her attention. You may need to ask to approach • If court asks what the question was, ask, "may I repeat it?" • If you know you asked a bad question, simply say, "I'll rephrase,

	Your Honor"—that should be enough to get things back on track

Sometimes your last question will get an objection that gets sustained. Don't sit down on a sustained objection! That reeks of amateurish concession of defeat. Always have a safe-harbor question you can ask: "one last question—did all of this happen on September 19, 2023?" or "did all of this occur in Stetson County?" Anything to soften the blow of the sustained objection. Of course, if it is important, rephrase and try again.

4.7 Delivery of the Direct Examination

DELIVERY OF AN EFFECTIVE DIRECT EXAMINATION
Must have • Non-leading questions • Logical flow • Hit the elements (the law) • Foundation(s) laid for exhibits, etc.

Many trial lawyers simply muddle through the direct examination, just standing behind the podium and asking, "and . . . what happened next?" So many times the witness is left to struggle to tell the story, not knowing what question is coming next, and sometimes not understanding where the attorney is going with the questions or what is even being asked.

Direct examination must be a carefully coordinated question-and-answer session between you and the witness. Every question, even every word, must be geared to making the witness look and sound great, and in so doing getting the story ingrained in the minds of the jurors.

Jurors can smell a rat a mile away. So, the witness must be credible—in terms of both *substance* and *presentation*.

The *substance* of the witness' story are the words, explanations, responses the jury hears.

The *presentation* by the witness is the body language, neurolinguistic and paralinguistic responses, eye contact, tone of voice, and other commonalities of the witness as perceived by the jurors.

Again, never, ever sacrifice credibility. Remember from previous chapters, deal with bad facts head on. That you have a bad fact is one thing; pretending like you don't, or trying to conceal it, is entirely another. Remember the old cliché that came about from the Watergate scandal: *it's not the crime, it's the coverup*. The act of concealing the bad fact can be more damning than the bad fact itself.

4.7.1   *Non-Leading Questions*

Open-ended questions. You ask the question, the witness supplies the fact—that's direct examination.

Q   *What is your name? Witness supplies the fact, which is his or her name (never mind that everyone had to be told their name, which technically makes it hearsay!)*

Q   *Where do you work?*

Q   *How old are you?*

Q   *Tell us what happened when you opened your front door. (Not technically a question, but statement worded to move the story along.)*

Circling. A tactic that is effective in helping the jury get the message is to circle-back facts back into subsequent questions.

Q   When you opened the front door, what did you see?

A   I saw a man standing in the living room.

Q   What did the man in the living room look like?

A   He was very tall and thin.

Q   Can you describe the tall, thin man's facial features?

A   No, he was wearing a ski mask.

Q   What was the tall, thin man in the ski mask doing?

And so on. This technique is good to emphasize certain facts, the jury hearing them from both the witness and from you. It can become cumbersome and even annoying if over-used, so be judicious in its application.

One fact per question. Direct examination focuses on the witness, so the witness should be the focus. Alternatively stated, get out of the way. The story has to come from the witness stand.

Most lay (civilian) witnesses have not ever testified, so you will need to prepare them for what they have to do on the stand. Remind them of the mantra "I ask you a question, you tell me a fact." Make sure they know it is ONE fact per question. Don't ramble. Be direct and answer only what is asked.

4.7.2   Tone, Tempo

Tone. The *tone* of the direct can be best described as the verbal personality of the witness as observed by the jurors. Different witnesses will have different tones.

WITNESS AND TONE OF VOICE	
Business owner	Calm
Law enforcement officer	Authoritarian

Elderly witness	Kind, gentle
Victim of violent or sexual crime	Caring, being respectful
Expert	Matter-of-fact
Witness with impeachment issues	Contrite, wanting belief

Tempo. Take the time to get the story out there in the most compelling way. Never rush. Don't drag by not being prepared. Conversational tempo is generally fine.

Remember that there will be times you need to stop and drill a while. Be ready to get "off script" and ask a few more questions on whatever topic you are on at the time. Clarifications are an example. Other times you will hear something you were not expecting, and if you can safely drill down, do it. *A lawyer never asks a question for which he or she does not already know the answer.* Be careful.

 Eleazer's Theory of Relativity: talk about important things that happened quickly for a long time at trial; talk about trivial/hurtful things that took a long time to happen for just a short time at trial.

One final note: take time on important topics. Legendary Stetson Law advocacy professor William R. Eleazer taught that important things that took 30 seconds to occur in real time should take 10 minutes to discuss at trial. Conversely, he taught, something unimportant or hurtful that took 10 minutes in real time should only be discussed for 30 seconds in trial. We refer to this as "Eleazer's Theory of Relativity."

4.7.3 Questioning Style

You have to find your own voice as an advocate. You are you and only you! Don't try to be someone you are not. It will be uncomfortable to you and everyone else. Just be yourself. Trial consultant Joshua Carton likes to say *"be yourself—all the other jobs are already taken!"*

What is your style? Are you animated and perhaps a little verbose? Are you reserved, and calculated with every word? Do you have a loud voice, or are you more understated? Some people are large in statute, while others are small-framed. Whatever you have, be professional and tell a good story.

Use the courtroom to your advantage. Here's a diagram of a typical courtroom layout:

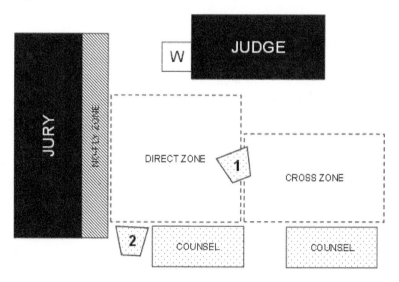

The judge's bench, the jury box, and counsel's tables are immovable. Your position works around those locations.

Podium position 1. This is where the podium or lectern usually sits—in the center of the courtroom. Most judges will require that it remain there. The problem with position 1 on direct is that the witness has to look at you, look at the jury, look at you, look at the jury . . . it can get to look like watching a tennis spectator. Remember to prepare the witness to tell the story to the jury—and watch for cues from you to look at the jurors in case he or she gets stuck looking only at you.

Podium position 2. Many attorneys will ask to move the podium to position 2 for direct examination. From here, the witness does not have to look far from the attorney to the jury. Remember, we want the witness to look at the jury when telling the story. In position 2, even if the witness continues to look at you, at least the jury can see their face and expressions. With the jury in the witness' line of sight, it makes it easier for the witness to engage with them. If that happens, you don't have to constantly cue the witness to look at them.

No-fly zone. The "no-fly zone" is any place immediately around and close to the actual jurors themselves. This is the area that you have to stay out of, save if you are publishing an exhibit and need to get closer to show it—but always ask, "Your Honor, may I approach the jury box to publish the exhibit?"

4.7.3.1　"ABC"—Always Build Credibility

Just a reminder that everything you do reflects on your credibility and liking and the credibility and liking of the witness. Be mindful of your movements, words, and how you respond to the court and opposing counsel. *Always build credibility.*

4.7.3.2　Transitions

EXAMPLES OF TRANSITIONS
Let me turn your attention to . . .
Let's now discuss/talk about . . . .

Do you recall . . .
Now, tell the jury about . . .
Let me show you some exhibits.
Let's move on to . . .
I'd like for you to now tell the jury about . . .

The story cannot just run on and on. Every story has transitions. Think about a movie—there is always some ending to the one scene, and a beginning to the other. Same with chapters in books. This is because the listener or reader needs to compartmentalize and process the story as it is going on. Transitions are mental sign posts on the highway of the trial, letting jurors know where you are going, and giving them a chance to take a mental breather as you go through the story. Transitions also gently guide the witness through his or her testimony.

4.7.4 *Helping the Witness*

Witnesses get nervous. In addition to preparation, there are ways you can help them while they are testifying. First, you can use some of the transition phrases above to refocus them. You can also refocus and redirect them, or simply get them to stop talking for a second and think.

Let me stop you there.

Hold on a moment, let's back up.

Hang on, we'll get to that in a bit. For now, let's get back to . . .

Holding up your hand or hands in the "stop" position can often silence a witness. If you think that the witness is going to say something objectionable, interrupt them. If you think the witness is about to say something so prejudicial that could cause a mistrial, *definitely interrupt them.* You may need to ask for a sidebar conference, and then a brief break so that the witness can be cautioned (or admonished) outside the hearing of the jury.

If they get totally scrambled, use recorded recollections or refresh their recollections.

4.7.4.1   Recorded Recollection

Refreshing recollection. Witnesses get nervous and can forget things, or simply misstate something. You can easily remind them of their testimony by refreshing their recollection. If a witness forgets something, or misstates something, use the following questions to help them—*recorded recollection* and *refreshing recollection.*

If a witness just cannot remember something, Federal Rule of Evidence 803(5) permits you to use a document, etc., to essentially replace their memory with the actual item made at an earlier time.

RECORDED RECOLLECTION
When witness absolutely cannot recall the facts:
Q   Are you unable to remember _____ at this point?
Q   Is there anything that would help refresh your memory on the subject?
=> *Premark; **first show to opposing counsel, ask to/then approach the witness, show to witness** (<u>NOT TO JURY</u>)*
Q   I'm showing you what has previously been marked as [your side]'s Exhibit ___ for identification.
Do you recognize it?
How do you recognize it?
What is it?
Did you create this [report, statement, writing, etc.]?
Did you read it and sign it, or otherwise agree it was accurate?

> Did you do that while the event was fresh in your mind?
>
> Does the writing accurately reflect your knowledge of the event?
>
> => *Have the witness read the relevant portion into evidence*
>
> ---
>
> **NOTE:** *Item is not itself actually admitted/received into evidence unless offered by adverse party. See also FRE 612.*
>
> © *eLEX Legal Publishers LLC (used with permission)*

Sometimes the witness will remember having made some statement, but will not remember exactly what it was. You can assist their memory and recall by showing him or her the document, then asking them to testify from newly-refreshed memory.

4.7.4.2 Refreshing Recollection

When a witness can recall, but is having a momentary lapse, help them by refreshing his or her recollection.

> **REFRESHING RECOLLECTION**
>
> *When witness can recall, but is having a momentary lapse:*
>
> Q Are you unable to remember _____ at this point?
>
> Q Would anything help you remember?
>
> => **[Prompt if necessary]** Would [item, such as deposition or report] help you recall?
>
> => *First show to opposing counsel, ask to/then approach, show to witness* (<u>NOT TO JURY</u>)
>
> Q I am showing you ____.
>
> Please read it to yourself then let us know when you are done.
>
> => *Stop witness if reads aloud*
>
> [Once finished]
>
> Q Does that refresh your recollection?
>
> => *If yes, repeat original question that caused issue*

> **=> *If no, move on***
>
> ***NOTE:** Using Recorded Recollection and Refreshing Recollection are distinctly different, based on total vs. temporary loss of memory of the facts. Also, refreshing recollection and impeachment are distinctly different processes and should not be confused. However, there may be times that you have to refresh the recollection of a witness before or even during an impeachment. You can refresh recollection with virtually anything.*
>
> © *eLEX Legal Publishers LLC (used with permission)*

4.7.4.3   Generally

Witness dossier*.* Always have your witness dossier with you at the podium when you question any witness. Always. You always want to have anything you might need at your fingertips. You never want to have to leave the witness, go back to your desk and start searching for a document or statement. It looks unprofessional. It disrupts the flow of your story. And you leave the poor witness just sitting there uncomfortably.

Keeping the witness on track*.* Again, witnesses get nervous. Some want their day in court and for their story to be heard. Some have agendas and insist on saying things on the stand that may not be relevant or even proper. Never hesitate to corral a witness, with word or gesture.

4.7.5   *Helping the Jury*

Once the direct examinations—*the story*—begins to unfold, the juror will still rely on the virtual video that is developing in their minds, but start to replace and reshape parts of it with more concrete facts. However, they are still comparing the story they heard and made into their own version to the facts that are coming from the stand.

So, help the jurors out. Use photos, diagrams, enlargements, and demonstratives to give them a mental image. More on that below.

4.7.6 *Behavior Sends Signals!*

Your *behavior* plays an important role in the delivery of the direct examination. Be serious, but don't be stoic. Be confident, but don't come across as cocky or arrogant. Walk confidently, don't stumble. Above all else, you have to exude belief in your own story. Same rules apply to the witness (especially experts, who can be a bit too erudite). If you don't believe your witness, how can you expect the jury to believe him or her?

4.7.7 *Defending a Direct*

Be vigilant and ready to respond. You in all likelihood, no matter how much you work on designing objection-free direct questions, you will get objections. First, don't lose your cool. Stay composed. *Listen.* Make sure you understand the basis for the objection. If not, ask the judge to have counsel repeat it ("I'm sorry, Your Honor, what was the basis of the objection?").

Prepare your witness for cross examination. As discussed in Chapter 1.6, mock cross examinations work wonders in preparing witnesses. First, it gets them accustomed to the adversarial nature of the process. Second, it can shake out weaknesses in the witness' testimony. Third, it prepares you for potential issues.

Anticipate cross examination topics and what target facts your opposing counsel will be trying to establish. Again, *listen.* Have your objections ready. Make them timely. In Chapter 7 you will see there are many standard evidentiary objections. Some are for controlling the substance of the witness' testimony, some are for controlling the witness him-/herself, and some are for controlling opposing counsel.

Once your direct is over, your job is not finished. Protect your witness!

4.8 Handling Evidence, Using Demonstratives

Exhibits are not only critical to a case (a contract, a DNA sample, etc.), but they may be excellent tools to assist the trier of fact in understanding details about the case.

4.8.1 *Authentication and Chain of Custody*

It's all about authentication—that the thing "is what it is". Here is the *general procedure* for admitting evidence:

GENERAL FOUNDATION PROCEDURE FOR ALL EXHIBITS
☐ Have **witness review** evidence well before trial (and initial), to later establish he/she reviewed <u>the actual exhibit</u> (esp. w/ recordings)—you can even have him/her initial the item to later prove it is the same
☐ **Pre-mark** exhibits (get with courtroom clerk for labels) and show to opposing counsel before proceeding begins
☐ Have witness again **review** the evidence immediately before trial to confirm it's the same, and have the evidence ready when the witness takes the stand
☐ When ready to admit the evidence, **request permission to approach the witness (DO NOT SHOW TO JURY)**
☐ **Show exhibit to opposing counsel** (can say simply "I'm showing this to opposing counsel" so the record reflects this is being done)
☐ **Show exhibit to witness** and state, "I am showing you what has been pre-marked as [your side]'s Exhibit __ for identification, do you recognize it?"
☐ Ask witness to **identify the item**
☐ Ask witness **how he/she knows what the item is**, and how he/she is familiar with it (WITHOUT yet going into contents)

> ☐ Ask **FOUNDATION QUESTIONS:** "Does this photograph *fairly and accurately depict* the intersection of Tennessee and Meridian streets as it appeared on the morning of June 15, 2023?" or "Is this item in the *same or substantially the same condition* as when you last saw it?"
>
> ☐ **Offer** exhibit into evidence
>
> ☐ Once admitted, **ask to publish** (SHOW TO JURY)
>
> *© eLEX Legal Publishers LLC (used with permission)*

Remember:

- Know the court's preference for numbering exhibits (A, B, C or 1, 2, 3), & how to handle composite exhibits (*ex*: A, 1-3; 1, A-C).

- Know which exhibits require multiple witnesses to establish the chain of custody. Make sure they are in court.

- Provide Exhibit and Witness Lists to the judge, clerk, opposing counsel, and court reporter before trial begins.

- Review all the admitted evidence before closing case and again before it goes back to the jury in deliberation.

- *Publishing* something to the jury means showing it to them. That can be done by holding it up to them, asked the court to hand it to them and let them pass it around, or using electronic presentation equipment

There are two types of physical, tangible evidence: *fungible* and *non-fungible*.

Fungible item. Things that can be mixed in with other similar things and become inseparable are fungible. There is nothing to distinguish them from any other similar thing. Examples are blood, or drugs such as marijuana or cocaine. The witness should have made a unique mark on the item (*see* Chain of Custody, below), such as initialing the item or its packaging.

Non-fungible item. The item itself has unique characteristic that makes it unlike any other similar thing. Examples are currency bills, guns, vehicles, and something with a serial number. Contracts, photos, paintings, diagrams, and the like have no serial numbers but are unique from other things like them, based on content and appearance.

Chain of custody. To authenticate the item as "is what it is", the witness must be able to explain what makes it identifiable. The witness must testify as to how and why that person knows that it is in fact "what it is." Sometimes it takes more than one witness to establish a chain of custody. The chain of custody proves to the jury that the item they are looking at is in fact the one at issue.

CHAIN OF CUSTODY
Each witness in the chain must establish:
☐ The time, place, and circumstances of taking possession of the item of evidence; <u>and</u>
☐ The item was safely kept while in the witness' possession; <u>and</u>
☐ The time, place, and circumstances of how the item was disposed of or placed into safekeeping; <u>and</u>
☐ The item looks to be the same item; <u>and</u>
☐ The item is in the same condition as when the witness had possession (and any differences are explained).
© eLEX Legal Publishers LLC (used with permission)

Be sure to have the proper people subpoenaed and in attendance at trial. Make sure to review the items and these questions with them before trial. Have your witness identify markings used to identify his/her prior contact with the item (initials, dates, packaging, etc.).

4.8.2   Physical Evidence

Guns, knives, contracts, DNA samples, bank records . . . any item of *tangible, physical* evidence. Whatever the object is, there are specific predicate questions (or litany of questions) for establishing the authentication of the item.

You must first establish that the object is unique—that it can be distinguished from similar objects, and it is the one at issue in court. You have to establish that it has not been substantially altered or changed.

TANGIBLE EVIDENCE (OBJECTS), generally
☐   Premark; approach, show to witness (NOT TO JURY)
☐   I'm showing you what has previously been marked as [your side]'s Exhibit ___ for identification. Do you recognize it?
☐   How [do you recognize] [are you familiar with] it?
Establish that the witness has previously observed the object at or near the relevant time, or somehow marked it, and is familiar with its uniqueness or the unique mark.
☐   Is the item in the **same, or substantially the same condition**, as when you last saw it? (may also add, "has it been altered or changed in any way?")
☐   Offer into evidence; ask to publish to jury
© eLEX Legal Publishers LLC (used with permission)

4.8.3   General Evidentiary Foundations

Below you will find the authentication predicate questions for entering into evidence:

- Photos, audios, and videos

- Voice or handwriting identification

- Webpages and social media pages

- Text messages, emails, chats

- Business records

- Summaries

- Copies, reproductions, enlargements

4.8.3.1   Photos, Audios, and Videos

PHOTOS, AUDIOS, AND VIDEOS
☐ Premark; approach, show to witness (NOT TO JURY)
☐ I'm showing you what has previously been marked as [your side]'s Exhibit ___ for identification. Do you recognize it?
☐ How [do you recognize] [are you familiar with] it?
☐ [If audio/video] Have you [heard the recording] [seen the item] marked as Exhibit ___ for identification? When?
☐ Does this photo fairly and accurately depict the [object] [area] [scene] [event] [conversation] [etc.]?
☐ Offer into evidence; ask to publish to jury
© eLEX Legal Publishers LLC (used with permission)

4.8.3.2   Voice and Handwriting Identification

VOICE AND HANDWRITING IDENTIFICATION
☐ Premark; approach, show to witness (NOT TO JURY)
☐ Have you had the opportunity to [hear the voice] [see the handwriting] of [name of person] before? How many times?
☐ How are you familiar with [name of person]'s [voice] [handwriting]?

☐ I'm showing you what has previously been marked as [your side]'s Exhibit ___ for identification. Do you recognize it?

☐ [If audio/video] Have you [heard the recording] [seen the item] marked as Exhibit ___ for identification? When?

☐ Do you recognize the [voice] [handwriting]? Whose is it?

☐ Offer into evidence; ask to publish to jury

© *eLEX Legal Publishers LLC (used with permission)*

4.8.3.3 Webpage and Social Media Pages

WEBPAGE AND SOCIAL MEDIA PAGES

☐ Premark (use actual device if in evidence, otherwise use a printout/screenshot)

☐ Do you have a [name of webpage/ social media] account?

☐ Is it currently active—and if not, why not?

☐ How does the [webpage/social media page] work?

☐ Who has/had access to this page? Is anyone other than you authorized to maintain, update, or edit the page?

☐ Is the page password protected; if so, who has password?

☐ (Approach, show to witness (NOT TO JURY) I'm showing you what has previously been marked as [your side]'s Exhibit ___ for identification. Do you recognize it?

☐ How [do you recognize] [are you familiar with] it?

☐ Is this a fair and accurate depiction of your [webpage/social media] page (can also use "is this a true and correct copy" or "is this a reasonably accurate representation")?

☐ Does it appear to be altered in any manner?

☐ Offer into evidence; ask to publish to jury.

© *eLEX Legal Publishers LLC (used with permission)*

4.8.3.4   Text Messages, Emails, and Chats

TEXT MESSAGES, EMAILS, CHATS
☐   Premark (use actual device if in evidence, otherwise use a printout/screenshot)
☐   Do you and [other party] have email/text accounts?
☐   Have you and [other party] sent messages to each other in the past?
☐   Do you know [other party]'s email address/text number/ messaging name/handle? What is it?
☐   Approach, show to witness (NOT TO JURY)
☐   I'm showing you what has previously been marked as [your side]'s Exhibit ___ for identification. Do you recognize it?
☐   How [do you recognize] [are you familiar with] it?
☐   How was the exhibit created (printed, screenshot and saved, etc.)?
☐   How do you have knowledge of its content?
☐   Is there any reason to believe email/text could have come from someone else, and if not, why not?
☐   If possible, establish how only the other party could have been aware of specific details contained in the exhibit.
☐   Does Exhibit ___ fairly and accurately depict the email/text/etc. exchange between you and [other party]?
☐   Offer into evidence; ask to publish to jury
© eLEX Legal Publishers LLC (used with permission)

4.8.3.5   Business Records

BUSINESS RECORDS
☐   Establish witness' background with business/company
☐   Premark; approach, show to witness (NOT TO JURY)

□ I'm showing you what has previously been marked as [your side]'s Exhibit ___ for identification. Do you recognize it?

□ Can you identify these documents? What are they?

□ Were these documents prepared in the ordinary scope of the business/company?

□ When were these documents made? Who made them?

□ Is it a regular practice of the business to keep and maintain records of this type?

□ Are these documents of the type that would be kept under your custody or control?

□ Do you have knowledge of the acts/events/conditions/ opinions/diagnosis recorded in these documents?

□ Offer into evidence; ask to publish to jury

**NOTES: Trustworthiness of the source and method is key. Be sure to have the proper person subpoenaed and in attendance at trial, and review the documents & these questions with him/her before trial. FRE 901(b)(1); see also 902(11) &(12).

© eLEX Legal Publishers LLC (used with permission)

4.8.3.6 Summaries

SUMMARIES
□ Premark; approach, show to witness (NOT TO JURY)
□ Have you had an opportunity to examine the original documents/volumes that are summarized?
□ Please describe the documents/volumes summarized (number pages, how kept, etc.).
□ Please describe the process used to gather the information to be summarized (how selected, how organized, any highlighting, or other notations, etc.).
□ I'm showing you what has previously been marked as [your side]'s Exhibit ___ for identification. Do you recognize it?
□ How [do you recognize] [are you familiar with] it?

☐ Does the summary fairly and accurately duplicate and summarize the information in the original documents/volumes?

☐ Ask that record reflect that originals volumes were made available to opposing counsel for inspection

☐ Offer into evidence; ask to publish to jury

Consult local rules regarding giving notice of the use of summary witnesses. Plan on offering the original volumes into evidence, generally as a business record.

© *eLEX Legal Publishers LLC (used with permission)*

4.8.3.7   Copies, Reproductions, Enlargements

COPIES, REPRODUCTIONS, ENLARGEMENTS

☐ Premark; approach, show to witness (NOT TO JURY)

☐ I'm showing you what has previously been marked as [your side]'s Exhibit ___ for identification. Do you recognize it?

☐ How [do you recognize] [are you familiar with] it?

☐ Does this copy/reproduction/enlargement fairly and accurately depict the original document, etc. (can also use "is this a true and correct copy" or "is this a reasonably accurate representation")?

☐ Offer into evidence; ask to publish to jury

© *eLEX Legal Publishers LLC (used with permission)*

4.8.4   *Demonstrative Aids (Maps, Diagrams)*

Demonstrative evidence is anything that assists the witness in his/her testimony (diagrams, maps, charts, models, etc.), and can be admitted into evidence. *Demonstrative (visual) aids* (ex: blow-ups of maps/diagrams that witness marks in court and assists lawyers in argument) are generally inadmissible. Problems arise when asking witnesses to mark evidence; generally, *items cannot be marked on/altered once admitted into evidence.* Check local rules or inquire of court before trial as to preferences; there is no universal rule (but see Advisory Notes, FRE 401, 611). May be best to admit an unmarked copy then then have witness mark a second unadmitted copy.

Demonstratives are an excellent advocacy tool, and an important part of good storytelling in direct examination. The witness does not have to have actually made the demonstrative so long as he/she can say it fairly and accurately represents the real place/thing. Admissibility depends on accuracy and relevance (403 balancing test). Be ready to deal with any issues of not being made to *scale* (perhaps ask for a limiting instruction to the jury, telling them it is not to scale and they can give it whatever weight they want). Generally, an item will be admissible unless it is so out of scale or incorrect that it is misleading. If necessary for appeal, move that the visual aid be made part of the trial record by asking that it be a "court's exhibit" (which does not go back with the jury in deliberations).

DEMONSTRATIVE AIDS
☐ Premark; approach, show to witness (NOT TO JURY)
☐ I'm showing you what has previously been marked as [your side]'s Exhibit ___ for identification. Do you recognize it?
☐ How [do you recognize] [are you familiar with] it, and the actual place/thing it represents?
☐ Does this [diagram/map/chart/etc.] fairly and accurately represent the [place/thing described] (can also use "is this a true and correct copy" or "is this a *reasonably* accurate representation")?
☐ [If necessary] Is the [diagram/map/chart/etc.] to scale?
☐ Would this exhibit assist you in explaining your testimony?
☐ Offer into evidence; ask to publish to jury

☐   Ask permission for witness to step down to use the exhibit

☐   Have witness mark/use exhibit as you instruct (ex: "Please point on this map to where you were standing", or "Please write a D where the defendant was standing", etc.), stating after witness points out or marks, Let the record show that the witness has [indicated on] [marked/used the] exhibit as requested.

* FOR EXPERTS: In addition, establish that demonstrative aid (1) was made based on relevant data/facts gathered by the expert, and (2) illustrates expert's opinion of what happened.

© eLEX Legal Publishers LLC (used with permission)

4.8.5   Remember . . .

A few tips to bear in mind during direct examination (and all of the trial):

Understand local rules, preferences, and customs. The best way to avoid any issues is to know the rules. Ask the judicial assistant or clerk of court for help finding them. If not, call the judicial assistant or a local practitioner and ask what the court's preferences are—it will be appreciated.

Never show an exhibit to the jury until it is published. It's not proper—it's essentially giving the jurors evidence that has not become an official part of the trial. And, you'll likely get admonished from the bench.

Do not alter admitted exhibits. Use copies to have witnesses mark up or notate items in evidence, or switch to electronic presentation. Once you have admitted an item of evidence, *it cannot be altered.* Period. You cannot start writing on documents, or opening or manipulating items. The evidentiary foundation for copies and reproductions is above.

Never let your opponent mark or have witness mark your exhibit or demonstrative. Similarly, with your demonstratives, those are *your* demonstrative, and you can ask, "Your Honor, I tender the witness for cross examination but as that counsel not mark or alter the demonstrative [describe or name whatever it is] and that it be preserved in its present condition." They are entitled to make use of it, but they cannot *alter* it.

4.9 Example of a Direct Examination

The following example is from an actual trial of an auto accident case.[1] The plaintiff was suing for injuries sustained based on an accident between his car and a tanker truck. The issue was liability, and the plaintiff was asking the jury to find the driver of the tanker truck negligent by failing to make sure that the lane the plaintiff was in was clear before merging into it.

Note the style of the direct—clear and concise. The plaintiff's story is told beginning with an introduction of who he is and is background. The scene is set for the day and the events leading up to the accident.

Of particular note is how the plaintiff's attorney is able to get the story of the accident oft several times. First, the plaintiff relates it. Then they use a diagram to show the area. Then they use a diagram to illustrate where the vehicles were at all times.

Finally, note how well prepared the plaintiff was for his testimony. Sure, there are a few little hesitations, probably due to nerves. It's obvious, though, that he was well prepared to answer the questions fully and directly. It's also clear that they had rehearsed using the diagram. The attorney's questions were well-designed, as is evidenced by his almost exclusive use of non-leading

---

[1] *Theodore Ervin v. Cindy Young, et al.,* Case Number C-07-1783, Circuit Court for Charles County, Maryland, June 23, 2008. Found at https://www.millerandzois.com/files/trialtranscript.pdf (last accessed May 2023).

open-ended questions. His questions also largely avoided objections.

	MR. BRATT: I'd call the Plaintiff, Mr. Ervin, Your Honor.
	THEODORE ERVIN, a witness, produced on call of the Plaintiff, first having been duly sworn according to law, was examined and testified as follows:
	DIRECT EXAMINATION
	BY MR. BRATT:
In some jurisdictions, the clerk only gives the oath, and the attorney does the intro	THE CLERK: Thank you. Please be seated. Please state your name, address, and occupation for the record.
	A: Theodore Ervin, [ADDRESS REDACTED]. My occupation, Operations Manager, Environmental Services, Fairfax Hospital.
	THE CLERK: Thank you.
Background to establish who witness is, generally	Q: How old are you Mr. Ervin?
	A: I'm [AGE REDACTED].

He's a family man, a generally revered quality in our society	Q: And you're married? A: Yes, I am. Q: Could you tell the jury about our family. A: I have three [REDACTED]. And a wife. Q: And what's your wife's name Mr. Ervin? A: [REDACTED]. Q: And is she here today? A: Yes, she is.
Showing witness is not a "rube", and has credibility as someone who has gone far with his education	Q: Now, could you tell the jury about your educational background? A: Sure. I attended Johnson C. Smith University in Charlotte, North Carolina. Q: And what did you study there? A: Business Management. Q: How long did you go to school there? A: Three years there. Q: Did you graduate? A: No, not from Johnson C. Smith. Q: How far do you—have you done anything else towards your degree besides that education? A: Sure, I've gone—well for—other than military training; yes.

Military service is also an admired quality—builds credibility	Q: In what?
	A: Military training in basic supply.
	Q: Now, how close are you to graduating with your Bachelor's?
	A: I would say about a semester and a half.
Employment	Q: And you testified that you are now employed by Arrowmark as an Environmental Services Manager?
	A: That is correct.
	Q: And is that the same job that you had at the time this accident happened in March of '06?
	A: That is correct.
	Q: Could you explain to the jury what your job entails?
Showing witness' credibility as a manager of lots of employees, i.e. he's responsible	A: As an Operations Manage—Operations Manager at Enova Fairfax Hospital, I—I manage a crew that cleans the hospital. And we're responsible for making sure everything from the front door to the operating rooms to non-clinical and non-clinical areas are—are cleaned and that we prevent any hospital given infections from happening to patients.
	Q: And how many folks do you supervise?

	A: Approximately 50.
	Q: And how do you do your job?
Demonstrates his credibility as a careful observer of his surroundings—which is important later	A: I do a lot of walking on my job. I—I have to be observant of all the surroundings around me.
	Q: Why?
	A: It's very important to keep the hospital clean.
	Q: And so what sorts of things are you typically looking for?
	A: I look—I'm looking in corners and edges for dirt. I'm looking in the ceilings for dust on vents. I make sure that bathrooms are clean. I make sure that the operating rooms are clean so that the next surgery comes in it—that that occurs there's no infections involved in there.
	Q: And do you have any military service, Mr. Ervin?
	A: Yes, I do.
	Q: Could you describe that to the jurors?
	A: I'm a Reservist—part time in the Navy. I also have volunteered to go on Active Duty during the time of the—the last Iraqi war.
This case was in Maryland, where there are many government	Q: And what is your specialty in the military?

employees—establishes familiarity and liking with the jurors	
	A: Supply.
	Q: And specifically what do you do?
Again, his attention to detail	A: I'm in a unit where we have five aircraft that are constantly—hauling anywhere from a Humvee equip—Humvee vehicle to—to—a unit—a—Marine Unit or whatever—wherever they need to go around the world, and those planes have to be on—they—those planes have to be ready to fly whenever they're called upon. My job is to make sure that they have all the supplies and parts that they need. With them constantly flying, a lot of maintenance is required so my job is to make sure that we have the supplies to keep them in the air.
	Q: And in the course of your military duties have you had occasion to serve overseas?
	A: Yes, I have.
	Q: When and where?
	A: I've spent over—
	MR. STEPHENSON: Your Honor, I'd like to note objections to relevance at this point.
	THE COURT: Approach please.

	(Counsel approaches the bench.)
	How is this relevant?
Attorney is telling the judge that credibility is very important and wants some leeway to go be able to establish it	MR. BRATT: Well, Your Honor, this is relevant as to his background and credibility as—
	THE COURT: Well, you—you—he—
	MR. BRATT: His case rests on his credibility.
	THE COURT: He basically covered his—his—well you've covered his pedigree but as far as going into five planes flying around the world and putting parts on them, I don't think that—that's a little bit too far.
	MR. BRATT: But, that was actually the last question I was gonna ask anyway.
	THE COURT: Oh, well. Objection is moot.
Without knowing what the witness was going to say, arguably was irrelevant. Attorney should have proffered for the record what it was the witness was going to say	(Counsel returns to trial tables.)
	Q: Now, Mr. Ervin, where were you living on March 13th, 2006?
	A: 12—12447 Turtle Dove Place in Waldorf.
	Q: And when did you move there?
	A: I moved there approximately—the date was December 28, 2—1999 actually. No, I'm sorry; 2000.

Establishes two things: (1) his stability in life (liking, credibility) and (2) his familiarity with the area	Q: And from December of 2000 until the date of this accident did you live there continuously?
	A: Yes, I did.
	Q: Now, in the course of your military duties where was your job station?
	A: Andrews Air Force Base.
	Q: Okay. And when did you join the Navy Reserves?
	A: I joined the Navy Reserve.
	MR. STEPHENSON: Objection, Your Honor.
	THE COURT: Sustained.
Close call; may not have been relevant, but was not prejudicial (403 balancing)	A: I joined the Navy Reserves in 19—
	THE COURT: Whoa. Whoa. Next question. Sustain the objection.
Again, familiarity with the area	Q: When did you begin—when were you first stationed at Andrews?
Invokes patriotism and makes him likable for responding to his country's needs	A: Right after the 911 incident with the—the bombing of the—the blowing up of the—World Trade Center and the—Pentagon.
	Q: Okay. Now, did you—had you ever had occasion to travel from your home to Andrews Air Force Base and back before March 13th?
	A: Yes.

	Q: How many times?
Familiarity with area	A: Well over 1,500.
	Q: And could you describe to the jury the route that you took on March 13th.
Shows preparation—witness is clear and concise and does not stumble through the description	A: I was just leaving Andrews Air Force Base. I came out the back out which is the Virginia Gate. It comes out onto—Alexander Ferry Road. I made a right turn and I went up two traffic lights to Coventry Way and made a left turn. From Coventry Way I went onto Branch Avenue which is a left lane going Route 5 south. I proceeded into—Charles County and made a left turn onto Mattawoman Beantown Road.
	Q: Okay. Now, on March 13th what was—what caused you to go to Andrews that day?
	A: I wanted to do my required physical training. I usually exercise about two to three times a week. My preferred—the preferred way I like to—work out is by riding my bicycle. So I went to Andrews Air Force Base to ride my bicycle around the base.
	Q: And what time did you leave to go to Andrews that day?
	A: About 10:15, 10:30 that day.

Could you tell the jury what you did from when you left home that morning until you arrived at the scene?

A: I—left my house which is not even a block away from the intersection of Leonardtown Road Leonardtown and Mattawoman Beantown and I went down to Andrews Air Force Base, took my bicycle out the back of my car—out of the trunk of my car. And I rode it around the base, the perimeter of the base. And once I finished I put the bicycle back in the car and left the base. It usually takes me about a [sic] hour to make that ride.

Q: And about what time did you leave the base that day?

A: About 11:30.

Q: And how long of a trip is it to get back home?

A: 20-25 minutes to a half hour.

Q: And you were driving a vehicle?

Q: And what kind of car was that?

A: It's a Honda Accord.

Q: Now, were you involved in an accident on March 13th?

A: I was.

	Q: Can you tell the jury what happened?
FIRST TELLING	A: As I was coming down—Maryland Route 5, 61 Branch Avenue, it'd be right before I turned onto to— Leonard—I mean to Mattawoman Beantown Road. I did observe a Baltimore Tank Line truck and what made it stand out so much was my brother was working for Baltimore Tank Line at the time.
Invokes family and shows why he honed in on the tanker	
	So at the light, the intersection light right there where you make the turn is a three lane turn, I looked up and I just noticed—I didn't see the tractor or anything until I got—until we pulled up next to each other. And I noticed that it was a—a Caucasian man driving the truck and I said definitely not my brother. And I just started to go down—down Leonardtown Road. We were right at the light together next to each other. At some point he turn he went past he drove past me and that is a two lane—that is a two lane highway. I was in the left lane at first. He was in the right lane.
Very prepared, very detailed	
Perhaps a little too narrative; attorney could have interjected questions	And later on he did pass me and get over to the right lane. As we approached Leonardtown Road and the lanes—the lanes start to open up

	and merge I got over immediately. As—the driver kept going straight and I though he was gonna keep going straight where it goes down to Charles—Charles—St. Charles Parkway. And as he kept going straight I pulled up on the side of him about to approach my left lane, my left turn. I was in the far most— the—the—lane number two of the left, of the left turn.
Excellent courtroom procedure and etiquette	Q: May I approach the witness, Your Honor?
	THE COURT: Sure.
	Q: Would you mark this for identification for identification, please?
	(Diagram was marked as Plaintiff's Exhibit Number 1 for identification.)
	Your Honor, may I ask the witness to approach the easel.
	THE COURT: Certainly.
	Q: Thank you. Mr. Ervin, could you come on over here with me?
	A: Sure.

Perfect predicate questions and authentication	Q: The way this courtroom's set up it's a little clunky to do this any other way so I apologize for putting you on display.
	Now, can you take a look at what's been marked for identification as Plaintiff's Exhibit 1? Do you know what this is a diagram of?
	A: This is diagram of—Bean— Mattawoman Beantown Road as it approaches with Leonardtown.
	Q: And does this diagram fairly and accurately represent the way that road was laid out on the day this accident happened?
	A: That is correct.
SECOND TELLING	Q: Can you show me where you were when you first observed that—tractor trailer?
	A: I was back here somewhere. Well, when I first observed it way down— way down on Route 5.
	Q: So you had seen him for the first time sometime before you arrived at the area that's shown on the exhibit?
	A: That is correct.
	Q: Using the exhibit can you show the ladies and gentlemen of the jury how the accident happened.

Very prepared; clear and concise	A: Well, as I say—stated—I was coming down Maryland Route 5, Mattawoman Beantown Road. At about this point right here I know the road—the lane turn—merges for you to get over. I always get over right here. At about right up in this area the Baltimore Tank—Tank Line came over. I was already over in the lane somewhere around here where the second—well, this turn lane here starts.
	So I was about right here. There's a hill right over here. And at that time I saw the tanker coming over and as I—as I saw him coming over I immediately got in this lane. Just as soon as I got in this lane I was rear-ended. The accident happened somewhere around here because the State Trooper came along and when he took my—my bumper off my car he put it over here on the hill. And I asked him was that okay. He said—
Excellent timing of defense objection, as it stopped the witness before the answer	MR. STEPHENSON: Objection.
	A: He said someone—
	THE COURT: Approach please.

Gentle reminder to his probably nervous client about proper decorum	Q: When somebody says objection you gotta stop talking till the Judge decides, okay?
	(Counsel approaches the bench.)
	THE COURT: What's the response gonna be?
	MR. BRATT: I don't really have one, Your Honor. I didn't really need to—for him to tell me what the officer said in the first place.
Seems that the hearsay was unexpected so attorney does not fight for it	MR. STEPHENSON: I—I don't suggest he did. I just wanted to make sure we don't have any inadvertent hearsay.
	THE COURT: I thought he says is it okay to put the bumper over here. I mean is this relevant to anything?
	MR. BRATT: Not really.
	THE COURT: Well, then.
	MR. BRATT: And I wasn't gonna ask him anything else the officer said either.
Good point, Judge: this kindly judge reminds the attorney about making a clear record in case of appeal	THE COURT: Okay. The other thing I've got to warn you about, I don't know if this is gonna be—go up on appeal. It doesn't sound like it's a case you want to. But in any event if he's pointing to this diagram they'll be nothing in the record to show what he's pointing to. So, if you

	want to—you know, draw something on there or so forth but otherwise they won't know what—in Annapolis they won't know what happened, okay?
	MR. BRATT: I—maybe I ought to clean that up with the next exhibit, Your Honor.
	THE COURT: Okay.
	(Counsel returns to trial tables.)
	Q: So, so we're clear for the record, Mr. Ervin, what you're pointing to, the area where the accident took place, is Section c of what's been marked as Exhibit 1, correct?
	A: That is correct.
Proper technique for handling evidence	Q: Okay. Now, I'd like to show you something else. If I can get this marked for ID as well please. Thanks.
	THE CLERK: Um hum.
	(Diagram was marked as Plaintiff's Exhibit Number 2 for identification.)
	Q: Now, Mr. Ervin, I'm gonna show you what's been marked for identification as Plaintiff's— Plaintiff's Exhibit 2. Have you seen this diagram before?
	A: Yes, I have.
	Q: What is it?

A: It's a diagram that actually I created by passing—pasting all the vehicles involved and how the accident actually occurred.

Q: Okay. So, you used the diagram that was produced as part of this litigation by the defense, correct?

A: That is correct.

Q: And you didn't—didn't do it on this size but you used a smaller piece and then I've had it blown up, right?

A: That is correct.

Notice a lot of "okays" preceding the questions; try to avoid the pre-tags in your questioning

Q: Okay. Could you tell the jury what this diagram that you made shows?

A: It shows the location of the—the vehicles and how I perceived them as—as the accidents happened.

Q: And so we're clear, this frame, Exhibit 2, is Part C of the main diagram, correct?

A: That is correct.

THIRD TELLING

Q: Okay. Why don't you tell the jury what you're illustrating here.

Again, very well prepared witness

A: I'm illustrating the three lane—the three vehicles involved; the Dodge Caravan, the Honda Accord and the tractor trailer. As I also stated back here, I merged over into this lane and stayed in this lane. And this is where the next turn lane begins. As

	I'm going up here I see the tractor trailer coming over. He was in this lane at first.
	So, with my vehicle right here I didn't see any any—and I could still see his head come up here. I didn't see any turn signals at all. So when I saw him coming over from the peripheral of my vision, I hurried up—I reacted and got over because I knew he was I—just well I thought he was carrying fuel knowing that Baltimore Tank Line carries fuel. That's from my knowledge of my brother and that's the type of work that he was doing.
	So, I got over in this lane and as I got over in this lane right here I was rear-ended by the Dodge Caravan. And the tractor trailer just kept going straight. He didn't stop or any—
Concedes a *neutral bad* fact on direct that may come up on cross	Q: All right. Now, did you take any measurements or anything like that of the scene?
	A: No, I didn't.
	Q: And so what did you base your placement of these vehicles on?
	A: The hill.

	Q: And that's what you're saying is your knowledge of the hill you testified about earlier?
	A: That is correct.
	Q: And so is—would it be fair to say this is your estimate of where the vehicles were to illustrate how the accident happened?
	A: That is correct.
	Q: Okay. You can take your seat again. Now, Mr. Ervin, you testified that you had initially seen the Baltimore Tank Lines trailer some distance down—Mattawoman Beantown Road, correct?
	A: That's correct.
	Q: Can you describe your observations of that vehicle from there until the accident took place?
What is the basis?	MR. STEPHENSON: Objection.
	THE COURT: Overrule. Continue.
	A: Well, as I stated earlier, we were coming off of 301 and 5; where 301 and 5 merge. We had just crossed— the street where the 7-11 and—and the—the—Wa-Wa Gas Stations are right across from each other. And right—as soon as you pass there there's a—another traffic light. That

	traffic light is Mattawoman Beantown Road and Crain Highway.
	And at that time we pulled up next to each other. I was on the inside lane. He was on the outside line making outside lane making a turn. There's three turns right there. There's three lanes right there. And that's when I looked to the side. Well, I had first noticed him. when I was coming up and I was behind him and I saw the BTL on the back of his truck.
Leading, but seems attorney is trying to move the witness' testimony along	Q: Okay. And you turned onto Mattawoman Beantown Road, correct?
	A: I made a left turn on Mattawoman Beantown Road.
	Q: And after you make that left turn onto Mattawoman Beantown Road, what—what does Mattawoman Beantown Road look like there in terms of the lanes?
	A: Up until you get cross the train tracks right there, there's three lanes.
	Q: And then what happens after you cross the tracks?
	A: They become two lanes.
	Q: And that's two through lanes on Mattawoman Beantown Road?

FOURTH TELLING	A: That is correct.
	Q: And after that turn happened where were you in relation to the tractor trailer?
	A: I was in the left lane. We were at one time side by side but he accelerated past me. The speed limit on that—that route is 45 miles an hour. I was doing 45 miles an hour.
	MR. STEPHENSON: Objection, Your Honor.
	THE COURT: Approach please.
	(Counsel approaches the bench.)
	THE COURT: Okay.
Well-stated 403 objection—relevance vs. prejudice; references clearly established law	MR. STEPHENSON: Your Honor, this is exactly why I objected initially because they're trying to offer testimony of some alleged improper driving by my client prior to the accident which is clearly impermissible under Maryland law. This has no relevance to what happened at the accident. Now he's trying to suggest that my client was speeding prior to the accident so as to prejudice the jury.
	THE COURT: What's the response gonna be?

Attorney properly concedes	MR. BRATT: Your Honor, my response is, is that the objection can be sustained. That's not why I asked him that. All I asked him was—to describe where the truck was and he was in relation to the lanes.
Judge picks up on the cumulative nature of retelling the story	THE COURT: Didn't we cover this once before?
	MR. FORD: Early.
	THE COURT: Earlier.
	MR. BRATT: It's a—it's a long road. It gets a little confusing. Well, I'll make you a bet. Every pet—member of the jury has been on that left turn all the way down to 5 at least a dozen times. I mean, it's a major thoroughfare.
Clear ruling on the relevance objection; does not *specifically* rule on the cumulative testimony or tell the attorney to move on	THE COURT: Well, first of all we'll sustain the objection. But I think you've basically covered this.
	MR. BRATT: Okay.
	THE COURT: Haven't you?
	MR. BRATT: Thank you, Your Honor.
	(Counsel returns to trial tables.)
Leading, but done to refocus and redirect the witness	Q: So, Mr. Ervin, at some point you ended up behind the tractor trailer?
	A: Yes, I did.
	Q: What lane were you in on Mattawoman Beantown Road then?

Notice the tempo slows, and more facts and lots of details are emerging about the critical few seconds before the crash

A: I was in the left lane.

Q: Okay. And what happened next?

A: After we cross—I can't get the names of the streets in my mind right now, but once we crossed that last light before we approached—before we approached Mattawoman— Leonardtown Road, I was behind the B—the BTL truck.

Q: Okay. And at that point were you approaching the area where—where it turns to four lanes?

A: I merged over to that first turn lane.

Q: And when you say the first turn lane, if we're going from left to right, this road has a left turn lane all the way to the left side of the road—a left turn lane to the right of that lane and then there are two through lanes that continue going straight, right?

A: Correct.

Q: Okay. And when you say you were in the—the right lane are you talking about the right sided left turn lane?

A: The right sided left turn lane.

Q: What happened next?

A: I start traveling a few yards and then another turn the next turn lane begins. And that's when the Baltimore Tank Line started to merge over so that he can make that turn as well.

Q: And as you went from the portion of the road that was two lanes to your place in the right sided turn lane, did your speed change?

A: No.

Q: What happened next?

A: At that point I saw, from my peripheral vision I saw the Baltimore Tank Line truck coming over. And that's when I—on sudden reaction I just got out of his way and moved over to the very far left turn lane.

Q: Now, when—right before you saw that tractor trailer start to come over did you see any turn indicators?

A: No, I did not.

Q: Did you see any other signals or brake lights?

A: No, I did not.

Q: How—can you describe how fast it came over?

A: It was—it was sudden.

	Q: And so you immediately went into the—the next sided turn lane to your left, correct?
	A: That is correct.
Good question to keep the witness talking, telling the story and supplying the facts	Q: What happened next?
	A: Suddenly I was rear-ended.
	Q: Okay. What, if anything, did you do before getting over into that lane?
	A: I don't recall.
	Q: And how quickly did you switch lanes into that left turn lane?
	A: Very sudden. It—seconds.
	Q: And what happened immediately next?
	A: I—I was rear-ended.
	Q: Okay. Now, did you—did you see the vehicle that rear-ended you?
	A: No, not at first.
	Q: Okay. Did you subsequently see the vehicle?
	A: After it hit me.
	Q: And what kind of vehicle was it?
	A: It was a green Dodge Caravan.
	Q: Did you have an opportunity to look to your left before changing lanes?
	A: I'm sorry, I didn't hear you.

	Q: Did you have a chance to look to your left before you changed lanes?
Obj: *Asked and answered*	A: No.
	Q: About how long did that lane change take?
	A: Seconds.
Details, details, details! Witness well prepared	Q: And what was the position of your vehicle in the far left lane after you switched over?
	A: After I switched over I was in—in the immediate lane.
	Q: And how was your car oriented within that lane?
	A: It was straight.
	Q: And the vehicle, the Dodge that hit you, what part of that vehicle hit what part of your vehicle?
	A: My left rear corner was hit. And if I'm not mistaken, the—center of the Dodge had hit me.
	Q: What happened after that—strike that. Was there any collision between your car and the tractor trailer?
	A: None.
	Q: And do you know why not?
	A: I had got—I have got out of that lane before it could occur.

	Q: Now, what happened after the Dodge struck the rear of your vehicle?
	A: I suddenly stopped.
	Q: And what happened next?
	A: I just cleared my head for a second and I immediately called my brother.
	Q: Why?
	A: Because I knew that he would give me some information on what—since the Baltimore Tank Line truck didn't stop, I couldn't see the number or anything so I can report it. So I called him for the dispatcher's number to see if they can give me any information of who the driver was or anything.
	Q: And did he—did he give you that information.
	MR. STEPHENSON: Objection.
	THE COURT: Approach please.
	(Counsel approaches the bench.)
Succinct objection	Okay.
	MR. STEPHENSON: First of all, Your Honor, its hearsay. Second of all we have admitted that the driver was the only driver in the vicinity of the accident and the accident location when it occurred. They're now trying

	to imply or inject some sort of cover up or we didn't provide information that was necessary. None of this is relevant to how the accident happened, Your Honor.
Succinct response	MR. BRATT: All I asked him was if his brother gave him the phone number. I'm not taking him through whatever conversations he may have had subsequently to that. We're not trying to interject anything. I'm just trying to show the course of events that happened from collision to the after the collision.
	THE COURT: Well, after the collision basically it's all over, right?
	MR. BRATT: Well there's—there's another conversation that he has with Ms. Young, the other Defendant.
	THE COURT: Oh.
	MR. BRATT: And that's where I'm going.
Is the court's ruling on this issue correct? Why or why not?	THE COURT: Okay. Well, I'll sustain the objection. We don't need to know about the brother.
	MR. BRATT: I'm—I'm not gonna ask him that, Judge.
	(Counsel returns to trial tables.)

	Q: And Mr. Ervin, after you talked to your brother did you talk to anybody else?
Back to giving details	A: Well, I—called the Baltimore Tank Line.
	Q: No, the—let me strike that. Did you speak with Ms. Young?
	A: Yes, we did.
	Q: What, if anything, did you say to Ms. Young.
	A: I think the first thing that I asked her was did you see that truck run me out of my lane.
	Q: And what, if anything, did she say back?
	A: She said she didn't see it.
	Q: Did you have any other conversation with Ms. Young at the scene?
	A: We asked each other where—was everybody—were—were we both okay.
	Q: Okay. And, what happened after that conversation with Ms. Young?
	A: Afterwards we called the police. The police came to the scene. We exchanged information.
	Q: And did you talk to the police officer?

	A: We talked to the police officer.
	Q: What, if anything, did you personally say to the officer?
	A: Well, I told him how I—how the accident happened.
	Q: What did you say to him?
	A: I told him how I was traveling in the direction that I was and how the tractor trailer had run me out of my lane. And—and that was it.
	Q: Okay. And just so we're clear for the record the—what I had shown you is—what was I—identified as Plaintiff's Exhibit Number 2, the diagram you had prepared. Does that fairly and accurately to the best of your recollection represent the area of the collision and what happened?
	A: Yes.
Excellent ending—enter the evidence, thank the witness. Crisp and clean.	Q: Your Honor, I'd ask that what's been ID'd as Plaintiff's 1 and 2 be admitted into evidence.
	MR. STEPHENSON: No objection.
	MR. FORD: No objection.
	THE COURT: It'll be received.
	Q: And I have no further questions for Mr. Ervin.

	THE COURT: Why don't we take our lunch and recess now; it's almost 12:00.

4.10   Checklists

4.10.1 Direct Examination Organization

You may have more or less elements or defenses, and themes/topics/target facts (TF) (this is just a template).

ELEMENTS (PROOF) CHECKLIST	
• List all pleadings (pull from online case docket to be sure you have everything)	
• Include critical pleadings (complaint, answer, indictment, substantive motions) to your case file (*you don't need everything, but be sure to have the important stuff!*)	
• Facts analyzed, categorized, and prepared	
• Witness roles analyzed and categorized	
ELEMENT 1:	ATTACK:
ELEMENT 2:	ATTACK:
ELEMENT 3:	ATTACK:
DEFENSE 1:	PROOF:
DEFENSE 2:	PROOF:

THEME 1
 • TOPIC 1
   ○ TF 1
   ○ TF 2
 • TOPIC 2	

	○ TF 1
	○ TF 2
	<u>THEME 2</u>
	• TOPIC 1
	○ TF 1
	○ TF 2
	• TOPIC 2
	○ TF 1
	○ TF 2

4.10.2 Witness Prep List

	Dossier completed
	Dossier reviewed with witness
	Witness deposed
	Deposition transcript received, reviewed by witness
	Witness meeting
	Witness advised of role(s) on direct
	Questions prepared and reviewed
	Practice direct examination(s) done, result satisfactory

CHAPTER 5

Cross Examination

OBJECTIVES: Cross examination is an excellent tool for uncovering the truth. You can use it to tear down the opponents case, and to use opposing witnesses to bolster your own case. In this chapter, we are going to cover the most important basics of:

- Why cross examination is so important to our legal system

- Preparing for and organizing cross examinations

- How to get those golden "target facts"

- Dealing with objections

- Tools for controlling difficult witnesses

5.1 Purpose of Cross Examination

5.1.1 Importance

 An attorney who can tell his or her story by using the adverse witness is a powerful advocate

Many attorneys consider cross examination to be THE most important part of the trial. The simple reason is *control*. Control of the story, control of the narrative, control of the other side's mouthpiece (witness). An attorney who can tell his or her story by using the adverse witness is a powerful advocate. That attorney gets *two* chances to tell the story—once in his or her own case and again during the opponent's via cross—and bolsters his or her own side in the process. And using the other side's witnesses' own words makes for great material for closing argument.

The importance of cross examination has been discussed and highlighted throughout modern American jurisprudence. Consider these quotes from case law:

> "[W]e must also account for the function of cross-examination in the trial process in construing the Sixth Amendment guarantee of counsel." The age-old tool for ferreting out truth in the trial process is the right to cross-examination. "For two centuries past, the policy of the Anglo-American system of evidence has been to regard the necessity of testing by cross-examination as a vital feature of the law." 5 Wigmore, Evidence § 1367 (Chadbourn rev. 1974). The importance of cross-examination to the English judicial system, and its continuing importance since the inception of our judicial system in testing the facts offered by the defendant on direct, . . . suggests that the right to assistance of counsel did not include the right to have counsel's advice on cross-examination. "The Court has consistently acknowledged the vital role of cross-examination in the search for truth. It has recognized that the defendant's decision to take the stand, and to testify on his own behalf, places into question his credibility as a witness and that the prosecution has the right to test his

*credibility on cross-examination. . . . Once the
defendant places himself at the very heart of the trial
process, it only comports with basic fairness that the
story presented on direct is measured for its accuracy and
completeness by uninfluenced testimony on cross-
examination."*

*United States v. DiLapi, 651 F. 2d, at 149-151 (Mishler,
J., concurring) (emphasis in original) (2nd Cir. 1981)*

*The importance of cross-examination—as the majority
recognizes—is to reveal a witness' state of mind and,
more particularly, the extent of the witness' incentive to
testify to the government's satisfaction.*

*United States v. Larson, 495 F.3d 1094 (9th Cir.) August
2007*

5.1.2   Search for Truth

Courts in America have called cross examination the best tool
for reaching the truth. Here are some quotes from courts around the
country about the overwhelming importance of cross examination in
the search for truth:

*Ours is an adversarial system of justice that relies on the
ability and resources of adversaries to uncover the truth
by testing each other's evidence through a variety of
methods, the most important of which is cross-
examination. Moreover, in an adversarial system, the
defendant has a right to a defense and to cross-
examination. Wolford v. JoEllen Smith Psychiatric Hosp.,
693 So. 2d 1164, 1168 (La. 1997)*

*Cross-examination is the principal means by which the
believability of a witness and truth of his testimony are*

tested. Davis v. Alaska, 415 U.S. 308, 316, 94 S.Ct. 1105, 1110, 39 L.Ed.2d 347 (1974)

[Cross examination is] the greatest legal engine ever invented for the discovery of truth." California v. Green, 399 U.S. 149, 158, 90 S. Ct. 1930, 1935, 26 L.Ed.2d 489 (1970) (quoting 5 J. WIGMORE, EVIDENCE § 1367, at 29 (3d ed. 1940))

An air of unreality pervaded the trial. Obviously, the [expert] witness had an underlying motivation for testifying. Was there a continuing relationship with either the defendant or some members of the defense team? That factor would remain unexplored if a lawyer could not effectively cross-examine the expert without, at the same time, disclosing the client's initial relationship. One may say that it hinders the search for truth not to permit such a witness to testify. One may say, with equal persuasiveness, that it hinders the search for truth to limit the effective cross-examination of such a witness. It is not a matter of letting lawyers shop for a hired gun. It is simply a matter of placing the lawyer who sought the opinion of such an expert in an impossible situation. Countless claims of malpractice would be leveled against attorneys who put unfavorable expert evidence in as part of their clients' case-in-chief. Certainly there are experts who are wrong, and no unfair advantage should be taken of a lawyer's attempt to evaluate a client's case. Our system is committed to a search for truth within the context of the adversary system. Graham v. Gielchinsky, 599 A.2d 149, 155 (N.J. 1991).

The age-old tool for ferreting out truth in the trial process is the right to cross-examination. For two

*centuries past, the policy of the Anglo-American system
of evidence has been to regard the necessity of testing by
cross-examination as a vital feature of the law." Perry v.
Leake, 109 S.Ct. 594, 601 n.7, 488 U.S. 272 (1989).*

5.1.3 Relation to Other Parts of the Trial

5.1.3.1 Cross and Jury Selection

Don't be afraid to ask potential jurors about what you know
will be coming up on cross examination and test people's views on
the matters. It certainly helps you adjust your presentation to your
audience.

Moreover, it gives the jurors a preview of what is coming up
without asking them to pre-try the facts of the case. That, of
course, is not permitted. You cannot pre-try your case. Most judges
will stop you from that, and they should. The *trial* is for trying your
case, not the *voir dire*.

But employing some creative permissible questioning, you can
at a minimum find those that are willing to consider your theories,
themes, and topics. Those that are not are, by definition, biased or
prejudiced.

Consider the following scenarios, and possible *voir dire*
questions:

Cross topic	*Voir dire* question(s)
Witness will be impeached with prior convictions	What would you think of a witness that had previously been convicted of a felony? How would you view the testimony of someone who had been previously convicted of a crime of dishonesty?

Witness will be impeached with prior inconsistent statements	We all value truth, right? Would you agree that truth is of utmost importance in a courtroom? If you were to hear that a witness made inconsistent statements about something, what would you think of that person's credibility? Would you completely discount his/her testimony?
Witness will be shown to have an incomplete memory of what happened	When searching for the truth in a matter, what do you find most important? How important are details? Would someone's lack of details impact how you weigh their believability? Credibility? Would you believe what they can remember, if they should remember other things but don't?
Experts	In most cases, if not all, expert witnesses are hired by the parties to help explain their case. Does the fact that an expert is paid impact how you might view his/her testimony? What about the amount he/she is paid? What things are important to you in weighing if someone is, in fact, an expert in your mind?
Witness will concede many points favorable to your case	Witnesses are usually for one side or the other. If a witness for one side largely agrees with the other side, what does that tell you about the witness? What does that tell you about the side

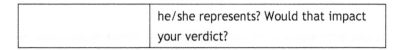

| | he/she represents? Would that impact your verdict? |

As always, follow up with "why?" and "how so?" and "could you tell me more, so I understand more about your opinion." Always follow up—most of the gold is mined in follow up questions, when you get the jurors talking.

The point is to not miss the opportunity to condition the jurors for what lies ahead. As things develop in the trial, it will become clear to the jurors why you asked certain questions in *voir dire*. And it bolsters your case and your credibility that you forewarned them as to the strengths of your case and the weaknesses of the other side.

5.1.3.2 Cross and Opening

In golf, when a player takes a safe shot that has no obvious dangers, it's called "laying up." The idea is to play it safe, maybe take an extra stroke, but not make things worse.

Professionals *go for it*. They know their abilities, they know the course, they know what to do if things go wrong. Most of all, they know that winners take calculated risks. *Go for it* has become a phrase in our lexicon that we use to encourage people to do their best with the chance of an excellent outcome.

In the courtroom, if you have done your preparation and honed your skills, "going for it" can make an incredibly strong statement.

If the advocate has prepared, then there is no reason not to talk about the facts in the opening statement to the jury. Why? Because the advocate knows that the facts will come out.

Many students avoid referencing any potential points from cross examination in their opening statements. The reasoning is, "well, I don't know what the witness will say on cross." That is the mindset of an amateur, not a master. In this example, the attorney is confident she will get certain admissions from the defendant on cross exam. She confidently incorporates those facts into her story in opening.

> *Lots of thought and planning went into this business deal. Many nights laying awake . . . Many days of agonizing hours of design—getting to a plan and ripping it up, only to start over. Lots and lots of drafting and redrafting, writing, and re-writing . . . The countless hours of making sure the deal was "just right" . . . Meeting after meeting with face after face, bad lunches and missing the kids baseball practice to go to a meeting with a stranger over a lousy dinner.*

> *But we're not talking about the business plan. We're talking about the plan Mr. Defendant was developing, the trap he was setting to steal Ms. Plaintiff's business. Mr. Defendant will have to answer today. He will answer to Ms. Plaintiff, he will answer to this jury, and he will answer to me. You will see first hand his responses to my questions as he sits right over here (indicating witness stand). You will observe his mannerisms, see his demeanor. You get to hear him explain—or try to explain—what all of his "planning" entailed.*

> *You will hear him talk about how he carefully worded the documents, why he used certain words and phrases in certain parts of the contract.*

> [Getting into the story you are going to tell on cross . . .]

> *He will admit to you that he had his eyes on this business for a very long time. He will tell you about the trips to visit the shop, the email inquiries, all the online searches about the profitability of this type of business.*

He will tell you that he made over thirty drafts of the sale agreement. He will tell you about the changes he made, changes made after visiting lawyers in other towns and seeking advice on how to write unbreakable contracts. He will admit to you going to the law library downtown and educating himself on legal terms, so that he could make the contract sound more enforceable.

Mr. Defendant will admit to you tricking Ms. Plaintiff into entering this deal. He may not agree to the term "trick", but he will tell you that he was very, very careful to spend lots of time with her, asking about every employee, taking notes about the history of the company . . . basically appearing to care deeply about the future of the company. And he will admit to you that he made elderly Ms. Plaintiff come to think of him as the son she never had. He will tell you about spending Christmas with Ms. Plaintiff right before the contract was presented to her. What a fun day they had . . . just like a family would spend together.

Mr. Defendant will take the stand today and tell you about how all of this was done, over the course of a year and a half. He will walk you through his devious plan, and show you just how badly he pulled the wool over Ms. Plaintiff's eyes.

The jury wants to hear the story. And you want to tell it in a way that gets you their conditional acceptance—they believe your story and want to hear more. If your story pans out, they will render a verdict for you.

Don't be afraid to tell the story as you know it is going to come out on the cross examination of witnesses. If your cross examination is performed correctly, every one of the facts that you mention in that opening will come out. And that cements your credibility, and your case. Plus, as the jurors listen to the directs, they do so knowing that something is coming for the witness on cross . . . it may even put your opponent on edge and force an error in the direct. Alternatively, it may force your opponent to deal with bad facts or impeachment points on direct. That "taking the wind out of the sails" can be flipped on your cross: "remember a while ago when you were speaking with your attorney about having lied? Let's discuss some of those lies." And off you go.

5.1.3.3   Cross and Closing

As mentioned in Chapter 6, it's not always practical or even wise to write your closing argument before the trial. Practically, writing it before the trial helps overall analysis in a general sense. But being married to a canned or scripted is dangerous. Relying on a pre-planned closing breeds inflexibility during trial and inhibits argument. Remember, closing argument is not the time to introduce your case theory; it is the time to tie points up, reinforce the facts with the jury instructions and vice versa.

When planning your closing, have the points available in which to freely use experience and skill to argue. *Argue.* Not rehash what the jury heard, but to *argue* why what they heard means they should find for your client. Above all else, be ready to pivot to things that came out in the trial. Some of those things you may be ready for prior to trial; some may be gifts that pop out in your crosses.

Here is an example of a closing, where the attorney uses real-time cross examination points to hammer the opponent.

Think back to when Mr. Defendant was on the stand. Remember the exchange about the amount of planning that went into this "quote, unquote" [makes quotation marks in the air] deal:

"Mr. Defendant, you had never written a business purchase agreement before meeting Ms. Plaintiff, correct?

Yes.

You had never written any such proposal prior to deciding that you wanted her business?

That's right.

And your computer logs show you revised just this particular paragraph over 30 times before you presented it, right?

Yes.

You knew she was a widow?

Yes.

And you started spending time with her?

I did

More, and more, and more time?

Yes.

Even spent Christmas Eve and Christmas Day with her?

She even started referring to you as the son she never had, didn't she?

Yes.

And all the while you were working hard on your contract?

Yes.

And on December 26, the day she introduced you to her pinochle friends as her son, you presented it to her to sign?

I did.

And she did so without even reading it?

Yes."

Folks, it's obvious why he went to such painstaking effort to get the contract just right—it had to be so wonderfully perfect that poor Ms. Plaintiff would think it just another great thing her "son" [makes quotation marks in the air] had done. And not question . . . just sign. No need for a lawyer when Mr. Defendant had done it better than anyone could.

What level of devious thought compels someone to pay lawyers to advise on how to write iron-clad contracts— especially when those lawyers are out of town, and had no chance of running into Ms. Plaintiff?

What level of treacherous scheming does it take to befriend a lonely widow . . . to prey upon her need for companionship . . . to gain her trust . . . and to use the beauty of Christmas as a part of the plot to rip her off?

All of those horrible things are what Mr. Defendant admitted to me, and to you, during his cross examination. From his own mouth, so you know it's true. He could not hide behind the facts of his own actions and statements.

And his own words paint the picture for you—a man who is absolutely guilty of fraud and theft from Ms. Plaintiff.

This is not a case of an arm's length "get the best deal you can" situation. This is a man without honor, and without any intention of keeping the bargain Ms. Plaintiff thought she was entering.

And so on. The jury selection, the cross examination, and the closing are all telling the same story.

5.2 Preparing for Cross Examination

5.2.1　Identify Objectives of Cross

Each witness is different, but the mantra of cross is always the same: *don't just repeat what was done on direct*. Start with that—it's no objective at all to simply have a conversation with the witness that essentially rehashes the direct.

There are two basic objectives: use the witness to tell your story, or impeach the witness so he or she does not add to the other's side case. Easy. Whatever the objective, that objective comes down to a *target fact*. Getting the witness to admit the target fact, or agree with you on what a particular target fact is—that's the objective of cross.

In Chapter 1, you learned about identifying the different facts and witnesses, and their respective roles. When preparing for cross, think about what target facts you need where. Do you need *concessions* from the other side's witness, to bolster your own claim or defense? Do you need to use the witness to rebut some claim or other witness' testimony? Do you simply need to neutralize the other side's witness by impeaching his or her credibility?

5.2.2　Elements and Defenses

You already know what target facts are—the important facts. On cross, it's a fact that *disproves* an element of the crime. It's a getting a witness to concede an important background fact that could establish a defense. Clearly identify your target facts for cross—these are the "must get" facts for the cross mission.

5.2.3 *Attacking the Witnesses or Using Them as Your Own*

Going after a witness for bias, etc., are based on facts that are pretty readily identifiable, and most come from the rules of evidence.

TYPES OF IMPEACHMENTS AND ASSOCIATED RULES
Contradiction within the testimony at trial: FRE 401, 402, 403
Omission: FRE 401, 402, 403
Lack of personal knowledge, recall, etc.: FRE 602
Bias/prejudice: FRE 607
Prior bad acts/character for untruthfulness: FRE 405, 608
Prior conviction: FRE 609

You may have to use the other side's witnesses to help tell your story—if so, think of what facts those witnesses could give you that help your claim or defense.

5.2.4 *Safe-Harbor Questions*

Some facts can be simple life-lines. For instance, the county in which a crime occurred may not be relevant to anything other than establishing jurisdiction. But if you are in a pickle on cross—the witness has gone wild, opposing counsel is objecting left and right, and the judge is shutting you down . . . think of a fact and ask about it. It can settle you down and give you a moment.

Q   *All of this happened in Stetson County, correct?*

Q   *You're here today in response to a subpoena?*

These safe-harbor questions can stop the insanity, and are also good to use so that you do not sit down on an objection (which is like "striking out looking" in baseball—very embarrassing!).

5.3 Structure: Organization of Cross Examination

Structure your cross examination into segments—a overall case theory (the overall plot or story arc—the main "why we are here"), themes ("mini-stories"), and topics (the scenes of the story, play, or movie). All of these end up giving you *target facts*—those precious, undeniable, persuasive morsels of information that tell your story.

Remember the difference: the themes and topics stem from and organize the overall case theory, while the target fact is a main thing the examiner has to get out of the witness, or get the witness to admit.

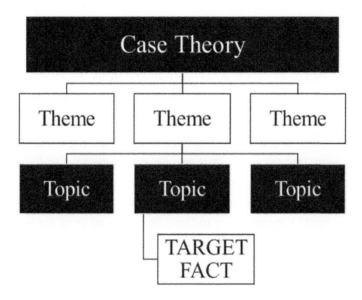

5.3.1 Case Theory

Your overall theory of the case, as discussed above, is generally what happened and what you have to prove. For cross examination, for example, it can be an attack on the credibility of the witnesses to prove that the plaintiff or prosecution's entire case is just a sham. It might be an attack on the quantity and quality of the other side's proof.

5.3.2 Themes

Your themes the mini-stories that support the overall case theory—like sub-plots.

Themes for cross examination might be concepts such as "knowledge" or "intent." Perhaps their opposites, "lack of knowledge" or "lack of intent". Others might be motive, recklessness, malice, lack of mistake. Each of these can play out in one or more topics, evidence specific instances of such theories.

5.3.3 Topics

Recall that topics are the individual scenes that end up on a target fact. Topics are a scene, established by a specific set of questions that support the particular theme and lead to a target. For cross examination, it works differently than topics on direct.

On direct, you are guiding the witness to tell the story, fact by fact until "the thing" is out there. On cross, you have to force the witness, essentially back them in, to the target fact. Adverse witnesses generally do not go along with your desire to tell your own story, right? They are going to fight. So, topics on cross are ways to narrow the questioning and prevent the witness from giving any other logical answer than the one you want.

Think about "2 + 2"—you automatically thought "4". In cross examinations, you don't always have to get the cross witness to say "4". If you can get them to agree to all the elements of the equation, then the jury can conclude the target fact for themselves. THAT is persuasion, and that is a powerful tool.

TOPIC

BROAD QUESTIONS

Narrower questions

Narrower questions

Narrower questions

Narrower questions

TARGET FACT

Take the Star Wars hero Han Solo. His story was *redemption*. There are several scenes that demonstrate how he redeemed himself. First, there was the scene in which he gets the gang safely off of the planet Tatooine. There was the scene where he left the rebellion to go and pay his debt. There was the scene in which he returned to save Luke and help blow up the Death Star. In the new movies, there are the scenes where he tries to, and finally does, save his son Ben from the dark side of The Force.

Your topics do not have to be long series of questions. In fact, they can be short and to the point. But as with the themes, you have to identify the topics and carefully plot them out, so that the jury clearly understands them. When the jury is following your story, you have them on your side.

5.3.4　Target Facts

Not to purposely overstate their importance, but identifying and developing a pathway to get admissions for target facts has to be a main focus of your cross.

5.3.4.1　Witness Target Facts

Do you discredit for bias? How about attacking credibility by showing prior convictions or inconsistencies? Or, do you get the witness to assist you by telling part of your story—there are times when an opposing witness can help you. The witness may concede lack of knowledge or give some bad fact about your opponent. Whatever it is, identify the fact or facts about that witness that are important to you.

5.3.4.2　Ultimate Factual Issue (Element)

Similarly, think of the factual issues that you must establish: the defendant was not present when the crime was committed, or that someone agreed to different terms in an agreement. Whatever it is, identify that target fact and establish it by creating scenes, and topics that clearly emphasize the fact's importance to the verdict.

5.3.4.3   Ultimate Legal Issue (Element)

Issues of consent, waiver, liability, and the like have target facts. Again, identify them and build your topics and themes backward (or upward) from there.

5.3.5   Anticipating and Dealing with Objections

As with direct, *know what is coming*. Look at the target facts you have to get out in testimony. Is the target fact admissible? Will it draw an objection? What will your response be to argue for its admissibility? What about the lead-up questions, that draw down to the target fact? Be ready to either (1) argue for admissibility, or (2) have a "plan B" to get the target fact to the jury.

5.4 Delivery: List of Questions vs. Outline of Topics (Cross Sheets)

5.4.1   List of Questions

Many attorneys diligently write out all of their cross examination questions. Some write nothing, and just "wing it"— which is tantamount to malpractice. Those who write out their questions generally have done their case analysis and have given thought to what their "goals" of the cross. Armed with their list of questions, they rise to engage the opposition witness.

And then everything derails, and the cross is a disaster.

Why? Because as soon as the witness pulls in a different direction, the crossing attorney tied to a list of questions loses control. Most don't know how to regain control. They resort to arguing with the witness, or simply moving on without having fought and ferreted out the required target fact.

USING A LIST OF QUESTIONS FOR CROSS EXAMINATION	
PROS	CONS
• Can be comprehensive • If followed, covers all anticipated themes/topics • Lets you fill in anticipated impeachments • Seems "safe" if you are inexperienced or not confident in your abilities	• Inflexible • No easy way to adapt when the witness goes "off script" • If the cross goes off the list, hard to get back on • No way to plug in testimony from direct that you did not anticipate

5.4.2   *Cross Sheets (Dynamic Outline)*

5.4.2.1   **What Is a Cross Sheet?**

In *Cross Examination in a Nutshell* (West Academic, 2018), I introduced the method of using topical cross sheets. While there is no "official" form, the sheet looks like this:

CROSS EXAMINATION SHEET	
WITNESS:	ARGUMENT FOR CLOSING:
THEME:	
TOPIC:	
TARGET FACT:	
FACTS TO BE ADDRESSED	NOTES FROM DIRECT

PAGE _____ OF _____

Witness. Write the witness' name on every sheet to stay organized. These sheets should not be stapled together, so you have to be able to keep them organized as you re-organize during trial.

Note, some witnesses are repetitive, so you could use the same sheet for them. For instance, at the scene of an accident, there are usually several incidental law enforcement and emergency service personnel on scene. The questions for each of them may all be the same, such as "you did not hear the driver say anything, correct?" or "you had no role in drawing blood from my client". In that case, then you could just write "LEO" or "EMT" as the name and reuse the sheet.

Theme. For organization of your story, put the general theme here—"lying", or "shows intent", for example.

Topic. This is important: each topic has its own sheet or sheets. Why? Because each topic gets to a target fact or facts. For "lying", you may have several instances of lying. Each instance is a scene. You then have multiple situations to go walk the jury through the opportunity to tell the truth that did not result that way.

Target fact. This is even more important: *each target fact has its own sheet*. No exceptions. This is fundamental to this system. By using a single sheet (or two, depending on how many questions it takes to get down to the target fact), you focus on one thing at a time. No matter what happens, you have a pathway and roadmap to that target fact. For the "lying" theme, you have the topic (scene) and the target fact is either (1) the fact that the witness lied, or (2) the lie itself. Or, depending on the case, *both*.

Facts to be addressed. Think OUTLINE of points/facts, not LIST of questions to ask verbatim. An outline has the issues you want to ask leading questions about. A list of actual questions risks you not being flexible or able to pivot to an impeachment, etc., if needed.

Notes from direct. Here, as the direct is proceeding, jot down answers next to your anticipated topics. Be as accurate as possible with what someone said. Instead of having a list of questions and a separate list of what was said—you have it in one place. And you can put the witness' statement right next to what it is you want to discuss, in the topic you have preselected.

Users of this method often use different colors for different things—having designed these sheets, I use these colors:

Witness, Theme,

Topic, Target Fact .... Blue pen

Argument for Closing .... Blue pen, will often add at trial in blue or red

Facts to Be Addressed .... Pencil (*note*: doesn't scan well)

Page numbers............................... Pencil or blue pen

Notes from Direct .... Purple pen

Once direct is complete and it is about my turn, I will ask the judge for a moment, and then organize the attack. I re-order the sheets as to how I want the cross to go, and number the sheets at the bottom with red pen. On each sheet, I will quickly circle the order of attack for each topic. Sometimes things change or something pops up that I want to hit first or save to last. Using the sheets gives me flexibility.

Argument for closing. This section is simply where you write why this target fact (on the particular sheet) is important. Doing this allows two things: (1) analysis and construction of your overall case theory in pre-trial prep, and (2) the ability to change or adjust in real time during trial.

Remember, sometimes you don't have time to prepare for a closing after the case is over. Sometimes you will have overnight, or even over the lunch break. Other times, the evidentiary portion of the trial is over and you move into closing arguments. With your Cross Sheets, you are ready to talk about how *their* witnesses told *your* story, and how you rebutted their case and impeached their witnesses. Everything is right there for you.

5.4.2.2   Why Cross Sheets Are Better than a List of Questions

Why use the Cross Sheets? The best part is the combination of organization and flexibility this system gives you. If you have five target facts ("TF") you need to get to, then you can easily move them around in real time. You may start the trial thinking you will do them in order, but the direct changes that plan. You organize the cross like this:

TF-1

TF-2

TF-2

TF-4

TF-5

On direct, the witness is totally unprepared and makes mistakes relevant to TF-4. The witness also makes important inconsistent statements from depositions as to TF-2. With your Cross Sheets, you can reorganize in seconds to address the cross in a powerful way:

TF-1

TF-3

TF-5

TF-2 (now includes an impeachment)

TF-4 (now includes lack of memory as to ultimate fact)

You can't do that with a list. You can with a physical stack of papers. All of a sudden you have your most powerful points at the end. Or, you could organize like this:

TF-2 (now includes an impeachment)

TF-1

TF-3

TF-5

TF-4 (now includes lack of memory as to ultimate fact)

This is also powerful, as it sets the tone for the cross in light of who the jury now knows to be uncredible, and possibly a liar.

The point is: *flexibility.*

USING CROSS SHEETS	
PROS	CONS
• Easy to reorganize "on the fly" at trial • Detailed as to theme, topic, target • Easy to incorporate into closing • Best place for contemporaneous notes from witness' direct testimony	• Requires preparation • Requires confidence (no list of questions!) • Requires quick analysis of how to reorganize between direct and cross

If you are prepared and confident, there are no cons! Cross Sheets are clearly the better method for preparing and executing cross examinations. NOTE: this method requires you to be able to think on your feet. But, that's the whole art of being a trial lawyer! Practice your crosses to get more confident, creative, and effective.

5.5 Delivery: Leading and Limiting

Almost every teacher of advocacy will agree that there is only one way to deliver questions on cross examination: *lead* and *limit.*

5.5.1 Leading Questions

The most basic and fundamental part of cross examination is to *lead.* Control the witness by asking only leading questions. Do not let the witness run away with an open-ended question. You supply the fact, and do so in such a way that the only answer can be "yes" or "no".

Remember the fundamental flow of questions on cross examination:

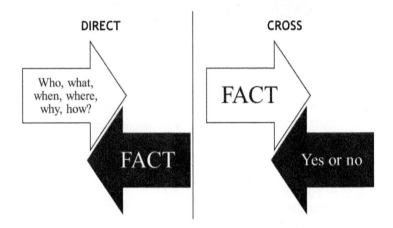

What is a leading question? Certainly not the one posed in the previous sentence—that question is an *open-ended question*. An open-ended question asks the person being questioned to provide the facts that will answer the question. Examples:

Who was your fourth grade math teacher?

What is your dog's name?

When did you first vote in a presidential election?

Where do you get your hair cut?

Why do you want to be a lawyer?

How do you make a peanut butter and jelly sandwich?

Who, what, when, where, why, and how. These are *direct* examination questions. They do not suggest an answer, and allows the questionee to then give the details.

The best way to think of a leading question is to keep in mind that *the fact is in the question itself*. The question supplies the fact, and the answer will either agree with the fact or disagree with the fact. Another rule of thumb is that a well-constructed leading question can only be answered "yes" or "no". Examples:

Your name is Joe Bodiford?

You are a law professor?

You are writing a book on trial advocacy?

You do not like French toast?

You did not swim the English Channel?

A proper leading question contains the fact, right?

Or, in an example from a fact pattern:

Q   *You were standing at the corner of Tennessee Street and Monroe Street?*

A   *Yes.*

Q   *Two particular cars drew your attention.*

A   *Yes.*

Q   *The first car you noticed was green?*

A   *Yes.*

Q   *The second car you noticed was red?*

A   *Yes.*

Q   *The green car was driving west?*

A   *Yes.*

Q   *The red car was driving south?*

A   *Yes.*

Q   *The green car had the green light?*

A   *Yes.*

Q   *The red car did not have a green light?*

A   *No, it did not.*

Q   *The red car had a red light?*

A   *Yes, it did.*

Q   *The red car did not stop at the red light?*

A   *No, it did not stop.*

Q   *The green car was passing through the intersection?*

A   *Yes.*

Q   *The red car hit the green car?* ◀— TARGET FACT

A   *Yes.*

In each of the examples above, the questions contain the facts that the cross examiner wants the jury to hear. Each question is designed for an agreement or an acceptable disagreement with the fact. The questions are all connected and driving toward a target fact.

Further, leading the witness will place you as the provider of facts in the driver seat to control the flow of facts.

5.5.2   *Limiting Question to Only One Fact*

Advocacy teachers will also insist that each cross examination question have a *limit* of one and only one particular fact. No more. When you get your "yes" or "no", there will be no doubt about what fact the witness is affirming or denying.

These canons are the most important things to remember about cross examination—and are the most often violated. Strict adherence to leading and limiting will allow you to control the flow of facts and the witness being cross examined.

In order to maintain control of the questioning and establish the right tempo, you should always be careful to only address one fact per question. It's tough to do, but critical.

Q   Mrs. Witness, you were on the corner of Meridian and Thomasville Roads when the accident occurred?

A   Yes.

Q   The red car was moving?

A   Yes.

Q   The green car was stopped at the light?

A   Yes.

Q   Both were in the northbound lane of Thomasville Road?

A   Yes.

Q   The red car ran into the green car? ◀━ TARGET FACT

Q   Yes.

Simple. One fact at a time. The order is important, and is easy to order and reorder when you are only asking about one fact at a time.

Avoiding compound questions is critical. Consider this mess:

Q   You were at the intersection on Meridian Road when the red car that was going north ran into the green car stopped at the light?

A   Yes.

What is the witness saying "yes" to? That she was there, the ordinal, the colors of the vehicles, the street names, or what?

Limiting *controls*. You control the material being discussed, you control the witness' by narrowing the subject of the inquiry, and you control the jury's focus. Always limit your question to one fact at a time.

5.6 Delivery: Tone and Tempo

Tone. As discussed regarding direct, tone is the approach you take with a witness—a question, or even a word, can be as persuasive as anything else. That is not to say that yelling or being in any way combative or attacking is a good tone. To the contrary, moving away from the bazooka and picking up the scalpel is much more effective.

Think about your normal daily approach to life. Think of how you see others interact. Think about memorable performances on screen or stage. What tone of voice do you associate with certain scenarios or situations?

The tone you establish will set the stage for the exchange with the witness. It will define for the jurors who is in control. Choosing your tone will control the witness, but more importantly, it will control the flow of facts and ultimately the story.

Tempo. Implementing the right tempo for various sections of the cross make it as interesting and captivating as listening to a symphony.

The tempo YOU select will highlight important parts of the cross examination. The right tempo will also control how the witness act and reacts. Setting and controlling the tempo allows you to control the flow of facts, and in turn, the witness.

5.7 Delivery: Transitions/Sign-Posts; Position in the Courtroom

5.7.1 Transitions/Sign-Posts

As with direct examination, it is important to use transitions so jurors know which theme or topic you are on. *See* sections 4.7.3.2 and 4.7.4 for examples.

5.7.2 Position in the Courtroom

Finally, don't forget your position in the courtroom. Remember, you want the witness looking at the jury on direct, you want him or her looking away from the jury on cross. Make the witness look at you by staying the in the "cross zone."

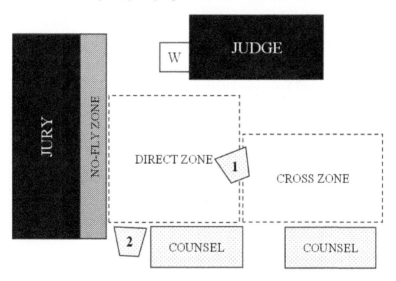

5.8 Impeachments, Refreshing Recollection

5.8.1　Impeaching a Witness

Establishing that a witness was not present for an event, or that he or she may have misheard a statement, or has a bias, are a product of the *theme-topic-target fact* process. There are certain impeachments that must be done a certain way. Those processes must become part of your "advocacy muscle memory" and capable of being performed without the use of a checklist.

5.8.1.1　Prior Inconsistent Statement

PRIOR INCONSISTENT STATEMENT
[After witness testifies differently at trial than from previously]
☐　Your statement today is _____.
☐　You previously gave a statement/deposition in this case?
☐　[If depo] Counsel and a court reporter were present?
☐　[If sworn] You were sworn to tell the truth?
☐　[All impeachments] Everything was clear in your mind? No one forced you to make the statement?
☐　What you said then was accurate and complete?
☐　You've had an opportunity to review that statement/ deposition before testifying here today?
☐　Calling your attention to [page, line], when asked _____, you stated _____.
☐　[If contradiction] You made that statement, didn't you?
☐　[If omission] You never said then what you are saying today?
**NOTE: *This basic framework can be expanded to show the supporting attendant circumstances of the prior statement, such as when made, timing relevant to the issues, to whom made, etc. You do NOT need to show or disclose the statement to the witness, but must to opposing counsel if requested.*
© *eLEX Legal Publishers LLC (used with permission)*

5.8.1.2 Prior Convictions

PRIOR CONVICTIONS
☐   Have you ever been convicted of a felony?
☐   [If so] How many times?
☐   [If non-felony crimes of dishonesty] Other than that, have you ever been convicted of a crime of dishonesty or false statement?
☐   [If so] How many times?
You don't get to double-dip; for example, a felony grand theft conviction is addressed under the first question—you cannot make it seem like the witness has 2 convictions by asking the second question without "other than that".   ****NOTE:** *Most jurisdictions require you to have proof (certified judgments) of the convictions in hand before asking about prior convictions.*   © eLEX Legal Publishers LLC (used with permission)

5.8.2 *Refreshing Recollection*

See Chapter 4.7.4.1 and 4.7.4.2 for the predicates on refreshing a witness' recollection.

Remember, there may be times that the witness does not recall a certain thing, such as making a prior inconsistent statement. In that case, you have to perform the refreshing process, *then* go into the impeachment.

Q   *Mr. Defendant, you recall as a part of your job was to do employee reviews?*

A   *Yes*

Q   *Your 2023 review of Ms. Plaintiff was not good, was it?*

A   *It was not.*

Q   *You said she was too talkative during work hours?*

A   *I don't remember what I wrote.*

Q   *Would anything refresh your recollection?*

A   *I guess if I saw the file I could tell you.*

Then the refreshing recollection happens. After that, back to the question, *you said she was too talkative during work hours?* He answers "yes" and you keep going.

The point is don't let a witness wiggle on cross by pretending not to remember something you know they said or wrote. Confront them with it.

5.9 Controlling the Witness

5.9.1   Tools to Control a Witness

While a great degree of what happens in a courtroom is spontaneous, trial advocates should have solid fundamentals ("advocacy muscle memory"). Having perfect and practiced fundamentals keeps you in control and gives you a move in those cases where you think you are boxed in.

Difficult witnesses present the hardest advocacy situations of all. Wrangling with a difficult witness is unlike anything else in life. Think about it the scene: you alone, in front of a bunch of people, trying to get another person who is clearly against you (and may even dislike you) to agree with you—all for the purpose of your livelihood and career and your client's life. No pressure, right?

Yet this all-too-critical part of the trial is where we see the least amount of skill. Yelling does not work and judges will not permit it—yet we see attorneys simply repeating the question at a higher pitch and louder volume. Just taking the response without trying to get what you want does not work, yet that happens all the time when the lawyer simply moves on.

There are a few solid techniques that the cross examiner can have in the quiver of arrows, or toolbox, that are easy to remember and use, and will produce results.

The following are tools and techniques to have at the ready in order to keep the questioning from derailing.

Composure, listening, navigating the situation. Always listen and think ahead. Where are you going? Where is the witness going? What did he or she just say? The witness is being a jerk—what do I do now? What is the jury thinking about this—and the witness—and *me*?

Asking the witness if he/she understands the question, or needs clarification. While we have some great control techniques listed below, sometimes you might ask a confusing question. That's okay—it happens to all of us. If you see the witness struggling, be the professional and ask the witness if he or she understands. If not, clear it up. Everyone will appreciate it. If the witness is being "that witness" and pretending not to understand, ask a time or two and clear it up a time or two. Then turn it on the witness by asking *"what part of my question did you not understand?"* Usually they cannot explain it, so you return to your original question and continue.

5.9.1.1 That Was Not My Question

After the first nonresponsive answer, pause and then state respectfully, "Perhaps you didn't understand my question. My question to you is . . . (restate the question), listening respectfully and attentively to the answer.

If you get a second nonresponsive answer hold up your hand as they are being nonresponsive. When they stop say, *"Thank you, but that was not my question. Let us try this a third time. My question to you was . . .* (restate the question again)."

Here's a tactic to call attention to the witness' non-responsiveness. If the witness will not stop when you hold up your hand then you should drop your hand, turn away, go to counsel table, and look through your notebook. Once they finish, count to three silently, look up and say, *"Thank you, but that was not my question. Let's try this a third time. My question to you was . . ."* (restate the question yet again)." It highlights the frustration you and the jurors feel at the lack of candor and cooperation.

If you get a third nonresponsive answer then turn and face the judge. State the following, "Your honor move to strike the witness's testimony as nonresponsive"—wait for the ruling.

5.9.1.2　Have You Finished? Let's Get Back to My Question!

Some witnesses will run like a hooked tuna. As much as they can, as fast as they can. These witnesses like to talk, and to oversell to the jury:

Q　*Sir, you were the CEO of ABC Corp at the time the contract was signed?*

A　*I was the CEO at the time when your client breached the contract, swindled me, and cost my company revenue and jobs.*

Ouch. That does not seem good. This witness is either truly aggrieved or looking for an acting award. If he is truly aggrieved, truly injured, and none of it was his fault, then you have to be a little more delicate in correcting his behavior on the stand. If he is overselling and pandering to the jury, then you can snap the collar back much harder.

For the really injured victim:

Q　*Sir, you were the CEO of ABC Corp at the time the contract was signed?*

A   *I was the CEO at the time when your client breached the contract, swindled me, and cost my company revenue and jobs. We had to hire an outside—*

Q   Hold on. Let's get back to my question.

Q   *We're talking about January 2023?*

A   *Yes*

Q   *There was only one CEO of ABC Corp at that time, is that correct?*

A   *Yes, just me.*

Q   *Okay . . . and the contract was signed in January 2023?*

A   *Yes, on January 15.*

Q   *So we are clear, the answer to the original question is "yes", you were the CEO of ABC Corp at the time— January 17—when the contract was signed.*

A   *Yes.*

The idea is to back up a little, add some soft facts using an easier tone and a moderate tempo, and make the questioning less confrontational from your angle. Most witnesses will back down and participate because they either get or merely sense what you are doing. They do not want to look like a jerk, so they tone it down.

Then there is the witness who just cannot resist being either the martyr or the showboat. Witnesses will cry, add irrelevant facts, and do and day other improper things. These witnesses can annoy jurors—watch the jurors, they will let you know.

Here is how the "let's get back to my question" controller would work with a blabbermouth witness:

Q   *Sir, you were the CEO of ABC Corp at the time the contract was signed?*

> A   *I was the CEO at the time when your client breached the contract, swindled me, and cost my company revenue and jobs.*
>
> Q   *Thank you—now, let's return to MY question. You were the CEO, yes?*
>
> A   *Yes.*
>
> Q   *Of ABC Corp, yes?*
>
> A   *Yes.*
>
> Q   *Thank you.*

This type of control can be preceded by a "perhaps you did not understand my question." It is an openly-stated redirection, and a bit condescending. But, there are times that it is needed, and works.

5.9.1.3   The Flip to the Opposite

There are times that the witness will not admit to something blatantly obvious. Sometimes witnesses overtly lie, other times they play games and not admit *exactly* what is asked (even when everyone understands the question).

For example:

> Q   *Officer, you arrived on scene at 7PM, correct?*
>
> A   *I didn't arrive "on" the scene. I arrived at the scene.*
>
> Really? This witness wants to play a game of semantics? Correction must ensue:
>
> Q   *Officer, you arrived on scene at 7PM, correct?*
>
> A   *I didn't arrive "on" the scene. I arrived at the scene.*
>
> Q   *So you did not arrive at 123 Elm Street at 7PM?*
>
> A   *No, I did arrive at that address.*

Q   *You understand what "on scene" means?*

A   *Yes.*

Q   *So, my question again, you arrived on scene at 7PM?*

A   *Yes.*

Is this minor, and perhaps even a bit petty? Yes. But witness control begins early in the process and must be consistently applied. The correction comes in the form of taking the undeniable, finding its opposite, and asking the person if the opposite is true—which it is not, and would be absurd for the witness to admit.

It's not a terribly powerful correction tool, but it trains the witness to stop with the word games, or hiding the answer, and to just come out with it.

5.9.1.4   The Weed-Out Game

Dodgy witnesses do not like to admit the obvious. They like to play semantics games and get cute in front of the jury. Certainly, there are times when the attorney is either the one playing games, or the issue is so narrow that it requires precision. In those cases, the witness is correct to hold the questioning attorney to the specifics. So, be accurate and forthcoming in your questioning.

The elimination game, or weeding out all incorrect possibilities, is a strong way to lock a witness into a specific answer. For example:

Q   *Mr. Witness, when you heard the crash, you looked and saw a dark blue truck, is that correct?*

A   *I don't know if it was blue or not.*

Q   *Truck red wasn't red, was it?*

A   *No.*

Q   *The truck wasn't white?*

A   *No.*

Q   *It wasn't yellow?*

A   *NO.*

Q   *It was blue?*

A   *Yes, yes, it was blue. It was blue.*

You can present enough non-viable alternatives to the witness until the witness has to concede what you want. This technique prevents wiggling and equivocating, and reminds the witness that you are in control. It backs the witness into a corner. One of the best control techniques.

5.9.1.5   Then the Answer Is Yes (or No)

An easy corrective tool is to make the witness say yes or no. That is provided, of course, that you have *asked* a question that calls for a yes or no answer.

This is sometimes a game of repetition, of training of the witness. If you do it enough, the witness may finally resort to simply saying yes or no.

Q   *On December 23 at noon, you were at the intersection of Capital Circle and Apalachee Parkway?*

A   *I was running all my holiday errands that day.*

Q   *Then the answer is "yes", you were at that intersection, yes?*

A   *Yes.*

Q   *And you saw Mr. Defendant's red car?*

A   *I think it's more of a maroon.*

Q   *But the answer is "yes", you saw Mr. Defendant's car approaching?*

A   Yes.

Q   And your light was red?

A   I was stopped, so . . .

Q   So the answer is "yes", your light was red?

A   Yes.

Q   And you turned in front of Mr. Defendant's car, didn't you?

A   Yes.

Consistency is the key to training the witness. It's like correcting a dog—you have to do it at the moment of the bad behavior, otherwise the dog doesn't ever understand the right thing to do. You have to win the battle with the witness, exerting dominance and establishing the understanding that you will never, ever let them get away with not saying yes or no.

Note, there are judges that will permit witnesses to explain their yes or no answers. I submit that there is no room for explaining on cross examination—the flow of facts simply calls for yes or no. Re-direct is a chance to clean up answers and or expound upon facts. The argument is that when a witness is permitted to go beyond yes or no, and get into explaining why he or she answered yes or no, that witness becomes an advocate. By explaining yes or not, the witness gets to choose why and what the explanation is. That requires excellent advocacy, and takes the witness out of the proper role of witness and improperly permits advocacy.

5.9.1.6   You Didn't Understand My Question

As mentioned above, this control technique makes you look like the nicer person. If the witness does not give you a contextually appropriate answer, consider using this technique.

Understand and remember that witnesses will not always give you an answer that you like. There is a difference, however, in the witness answering your question not to your liking, and not answering the question at all. The distinction is important to know and understand, as re-asking the same question when it has in fact been answered will draw a sustainable objection.

5.9.1.7 Re-Ask the Question (With or Without a Control Tag)

This technique is good when you need to get a little more "stern" with the witness. Tags such as "right?" are colloquial, and not necessarily good and proper form. But it's nice. Just asking the question point-blank connotes *I mean business* when it is coupled with a no-nonsense tone.

Q   *After the report was made, you had a chance to review it, right?*

A   *I had a chance, you know, I went in, and I was given a copy of what was filed, and. . .*

Q   *[In a stern tone] You reviewed the report?*

A   *Uh, yes.*

Q   *Thank you. Now, turning your attention to . . .*

5.9.1.8 We'll Get to That in a Second . . . This Question Is About . . .

It can also be used with a slight variation when the witness jumps ahead, and wants to begin a narrative answer. When that happens, cut him or her off after your question is answered:

Q   *A red car was traveling behind the green car?*

A   *It was a red car, yes, and it hit the back of the green car, which was—*

Q   *Excuse me [or, "hang on a second"—its ok to be*
     friendly or familiar], we'll get to that in a second,
     that question was simply about the color. The make
     of the red car was BMW, right?

Be sure to come back to the point the witness was about to
make, or when getting to it, use a short preface phrase such as
"now, about what you saw the red truck do . . ."

5.9.1.9   Interruption

If you have control of the courtroom, interrupting a witness is
not hard. In other words, if you are delivering a well-thought out
objection-free story of a cross, both the judge and opposing counsel
will have little to interrupt or complain about.

Q   *Miss Witness, you did not come in the office on the*
     day of the fire?

A   *Well, no, because I had to—*

Q   *Let me stop you there. You were not there to see*
     who might have been there when the fire started?

A   *No.*

However, if you interrupt a witness, the judge can call you
down with the admonition that the witness should be permitted to
explain his or her answer. If that happens, you should re-evaluate
your questions—most likely you are asking non-leading, open-ended
compound questions that *require* the witness to explain. In the
example above, it is likely completely irrelevant where the witness
was, so she should not be allowed to explain. That's especially true
if she were someplace such as chemotherapy, which would cause
the jury to feel sorry for her. No place for that in a trial, either.

If you sense the witness is about to say something that will
cause a mistrial, stop him or her.

Q   *Mr. Witness, you did not know Mr. Defendant prior to that day?*

A   *I did not.*

Q   *Never seen him before?*

A   *Well, I had seen—*

Q   *Let me stop you there. You had never seen him in person, correct?*

A   *Correct.*

If the answer was "[w]ell, I had seen his fact on the sexual offender list up at the post office", then you would have had a mistrial. Interrupting the witness would be appropriate. Of course, you want to make sure that the witness is instructed not to mention things that may have been prohibited by the court in pretrial motions *in limine.*

5.9.1.10 Simplifying the Question, and "Playing Dumb"

When you get the first nonresponsive answer hold up your hand and apologize: *"I'm sorry, perhaps I wasn't sufficiently clear, let me ask it a different way"* and ask a simpler version of the same question. It works better if you can ask an even more black and white question. This method asserts control as it forces the witness to play along and by "dumbing it down" for you, and so limits the answer.

If you get a second nonresponsive answer you should remain calm, wait the witness out, allowing them to answer completely and then state, *"I appreciate that you said (or felt the need to say) that, but my question to you was (simplest version possible for the question)."*

If you get a third nonresponsive answer you should stay calm but be firm, stating the following:

Q   Sir/Ma'am, we can at least agree that you are the witness?

A   I am the lawyer?

Q   We are in a court of law?

A   Yes.

Q   In a trial?

A   Yes.

Q   And you just testified on direct?

A   Yes.

Q   Now I am asking you questions?

A   Yes.

Q   You are supposed to give answers?

A   Yes.

Q   Thank you. Please answer this question: [re-ask question]

One of the most difficult aspects of cross examination and witness control revolves around balancing the need to be in charge while not appearing unfair, rude, or unethical. Unlike other aspects of trial advocacy, these particular skills are very much dependent upon the situation. Our own sense of self and power in the room are challenged when witnesses refuse to answer. Our need to be "in charge" can keep us from clearly seeing the right question in the right moment. It is important to keep your head about you when this happens. Slowing down, focusing on the moment, and listening critically are all skills that stand each of us in good stead when this happens.

What situations have you experienced and how did you handle (or wish that you had handled) it?

5.9.1.11 Using the Jury to Help Control the Witness (Hammer Phrases)

There is an old maxim, that goes around in various forms, that holds *you should not cut the witness' throat unless the jury hands you the knife*. Great advocates are in tune with the jurors, and know how they are doing against the runaway witness. The jurors' expressions tell it all. When they are looking at you, they are with you. When they look down, perhaps with arms folded, they are tired of the witness and have shut the witness and his/her waning credibility out.

You can take advantage of jurors' moods when controlling a witness.

Tell these folks . . . When you get to a target fact, or to a critical question or two before the target fact (whether the target fact is an actual fact-fact, or a point of impeachment), incorporate your jury into the process by having the witness look at them and give his or her testimony.

Q   *So, please tell these folks [gesturing toward jury, moving closer to the jury box], you knew the gun was loaded, right?.*

Tell these folks again . . . Stepping slightly aside, pausing while looking at the witness, look at the jury. Then look back to the witness and ask him or her to repeat what he or she just said or said on direct. This is an open-ended question, you want them to hear again, so that you can really accentuate the impeachment you are about to do based on that statement.

Q   *Mr. Witness, you recall discussing [issue] on direct examination?*

A   *Yes.*

Q [Pause, look at jury] Please tell these folks again what you said about [issue].

[The idea is to reiterate the questionable testimony, to reinforce that it is in fact not credible. Listen carefully to hear if the witness changes the story in any way. If it does change, confront:]

Q Ok, but on direct examination you told this jury that you were standing behind the car when the shots rang out, didn't you?

One of two beneficial things will happen: (1) the witness will claim not to recall, or (2) the witness will agree to saying the first statement.

You're telling these jurors that . . . To really emphasize a target fact, again, whether an actual fact or a point of impeachment, you can preface your question with "*you're telling these jurors that you did not know the gun was loaded?*"—the implication is that there is no way this witness is really sitting up there lying like that. The witness will likely squirm!

Don't tell me, tell them . . . When a ridiculous explanation is coming out, make the witness try to convince the jury—it forces the witness to confront an already disbelieving jury. Point to the jury, maybe add a "*look at them and tell them* . . ." for effect.

All of these approaches combine well with gestures (see below).

5.9.1.12 I'm the One Asking the Questions

You will at times get witnesses who want you to answer questions they what to ask, in an effort to throw you off.

When a witness answers questions with questions, you have a great phrase to derail that tactic: *I'm sorry, but the rules of court don't let me answer your question. Let me ask mine again.*

It's a great control technique, and effective because the witness now knows that asking questions breaks the rules. The stigma of not playing by the rules is generally enough to prevent further questions back at you from the stand.

5.9.2   *Using Gestures*

There are body movements that you can employ to assist you in controlling the witness. For instance, raising your eyebrows and cocking you head is a sign of disbelief. Holding your hand up in the "stop" position can cut a witness off. Putting your hands up as in disbelief signals just that.

Think about emojis. We communicate on our mobile devices with just an icon. Some people have entire conversations. Not suggesting that you turn into a human emoji, but take a look at some emojis on your phone, and think about what you could do with a simple movement. Sometimes just a stare can say everything. Remember a quote from the late politician Martin Lomasney: *never write if you can speak; never speak if you can nod; never nod if you can wink, never wink if you can do nothing.*

Practice your own individualized gestures on video (remember, the mirror lies to you), and see what you come up with.

5.9.3   *What Does Not Work in Controlling the Witness*

There are some things that simply do not help you in a bad cross examination or with a tough witness. Yet you see them all the time. Avoid:

- Arguing

- Yelling

- Asking the judge for help

- Asking untrue questions or somehow falsifying facts

- Losing your composure and professionalism

- Attacking an honest witness

There are certain objections that the advocate can use to control the speaker on the witness stand. *See* Chapter 7.4 for a discussion of objections you can use to control the subject matter, the witness, and opposing counsel.

No doubt that all advocates, no matter how prepared and polished, will encounter an obstreperous and contumacious witness. It is not unusual for witnesses to want to wiggle, if not outright revolt—most people do not want to be told what to say or to have words put in their mouth.

When the witness becomes uncooperative or combative, use the tools and techniques listed above. One must be (1) skilled and able in the art of witness control, and (2) have enough wits to deal with the situation in real time. Simply becoming argumentative or combative with the witness is ineffective.

5.9.4   *Experts*

The preparation for the cross examination of an expert is really no different than that of any other witness. That being said, there are a few extra issues to consider when cross examining experts.

Target documents will be more extensive. The witness will be very polished. In all probability, the witness will be prepared. Do not shy away from the chance to discredit the expert on cross examination, and make that a part of your story—*the other side is so desperate, they hired a quack!*

Investigate the expert. Be prepared to pick apart the expert's resume or curriculum vitae. The qualifications of an expert to even *be* an expert are a ripe area. Find everything you can—scour the internet, check Lexis and Westlaw, ask other attorneys in the area, ask insurance adjusters. You will be amazed at the amount of information you can amass.

Be prepared to go through every detail of the expert's report or findings. Target facts can be found in the report, such as:

- The absurdity of the opinion

- Lack of or incomplete testing

- Failure to follow standards in the field

- Not taking care to amend if additional work or analysis done

Know and use the standards and opinions of other experts in the area. It is said that lawyers become experts in their own rights in many different areas. This is simply because of having to know so much about an area in order to depose and cross examine the witness. For your cross examination, you have to know whether the witness is really, really good, or simply a "hired gun" willing to say anything for a buck. You have to know the terminology and the procedures. You have to know what prior analyses have revealed, and why those opinions are accepted or not. In other words, you have to be able to know everything the expert knows in order to boil it down for the jury to understand your cross examination.

Acknowledging that your expert is qualified and respected. Perhaps this starts at deposition. Ask the expert if he or she knows your expert. If not, why not—and would the witness be willing to familiarize him- or herself with your expert before the trial. If so, what is his or her opinion of your expert? On cross examination, you have fuel to work with either way.*Preparation for testimony.* Experts are infallible, just like any other expert.

Credibility issue: prior court experience. You must know if the expert witness is a regular in court. Is he or she someone who will say whatever, if the price is right? Has the expert has ever been disqualified, or not permitted to testify—especially if on the specific area you are crossing on. What an amazing point of cross examination!

Q   *Mr. Expert, you were once disqualified as an expert?*

A   *I am not sure what you mean.*

Q   *On this specific issue of _____, a judge in this courthouse refused to let you testify as a witness— don't you recall that?*

A   *What do you mean?*

Q   *Judge Goudie, down the hall—you know who Judge Goudie is?*

A   *Yes.*

Q   *And you remember the Jones case from last month?*

A   *Yes.*

Q   *You were hired by the plaintiff to testify about _____?*

A   *Yes.*

Q   *Exactly like you were hired by the plaintiff in this case to testify about the same topic?*

A   *Yes.*

Q   *And Judge Goudie made a ruling that you were not qualified as an expert in that area, didn't she?*

A   *Yes.*

With a cross examination like this, you have neutralized the expert witness, and have amazing material to support your story!

Credibility issue: dealings with opposing counsel. Lawyers and experts tend to run in packs, especially when both are local. I personally called a particular psychiatrist as an expert in more cases than I can remember—he was local, he was reputable, and he was good. That was mostly at sentencing, so there was no real issue with a trier of fact. The judge understood that the psychiatrist was there to present findings in support of a lesser sentence, and either accepted or rejected the mitigators when deciding the sentence.

But when the expert is called in a trial to assist the trier of fact—*the jury*—in deciding an issue, the close relationship between the expert witness and the lawyer is important. If the expert is making a living testifying for one particular lawyer, his or her credibility becomes an issue. Think about it—in order to keep the cases and cash flowing, the expert witness needs to give the lawyer opinions that the lawyer likes. That sets up some great cross examination:

Q   *Mr. Expert, you are being paid to be here?*

A   *I am.*

Q   *You make your living testifying at trials like this one, right?*

A   *Partially.*

Q   *You're not saying you have income other than being a witness, are you?*

A   *Well, no, but it involves more than just testifying.*

Q   *You only do expert work, don't you?*

A   *Yes.*

Q   *And being an expert means you have to do an analysis, right?*

A   *Yes.*

Q   Form on opinion?

A   Yes.

Q   Possibly give a deposition?

A   If asked, yes.

Q   And testify at trial, right?

A   If asked, yes.

Q   All of that is what you do as an [makes quotation fingers in the air] expert witness?

A   Yes.

Q   And you get paid to do that.

A   I do.

Q   You get paid hourly, right?

A   Yes.

Q   For reading, reviewing, analysis, and that, you get paid?

A   Yes

Q   For that you get more than one hundred dollars per hour, right?

A   Yes

Q   More than two hundred dollars per hour, right?

A   Yes.

Q   You get paid even more than three hundred dollars per hour, don't you?

A   Yes.

Q   And that's not in-court work, right?

A   Correct.

Q   *For non-court work, you get three hundred and fifty dollars every hour?*

A   *Yes.*

Q   *Now, once you get to court, that rate goes up, right?*

A   *Yes.*

Q   *That rate goes to five hundred dollars per hour.*

A   *Yes.*

Q   *You have been on the stand for two hours so far today, right?*

A   *Yes, I believe so.*

Q   *[Turning to jury] That means you have earned one . . . thousand . . . dollars . . . while these people have been sitting here?*

A   *Yes.*

Q   *And that amount is paid by that man over there, right? [pointing]*

A   *Yes.*

Q   *And his attorney, Mr. Lawyer, hired you, right?*

A   *Yes.*

Q   *This is not the first time you have testified for Mr. Lawyer?*

A   *No, it is not.*

Q   *He hires you quite regularly, doesn't he?*

A   *Yes,*

Q   *He hires you for five cases or so a year, right?*

A   *Yes.*

Q   And your average billing to his clients is about ten thousand dollars, right?

A   Yes, as an average.

Q   So Mr. Lawyer give you fifty . . . thousand . . . dollars per year of work?

A   Something like that.

Q   Your relationship with Mr. Lawyer is important, isn't it?

A   As it is with all my lawyer clients.

Q   And that is because without a good relationship, you do not get hired?

A   I would assume not.

Q   Without Mr. Lawyer hiring you, you would lose fifty thousand dollars a year from his cases?

A   Yes.

You do not have to go any farther—the target fact (that he is all about the money) is clear to the jury.

Credibility issue: _extent of witness willingness to testify for anyone who pays_. Much like the above, get out of the witness how many times he or she testifies for pay. If you can adduce instances where he or she has testified for the same side as yours, even better.

Credibility issue: _opinion contradicts prior opinions in similar cases_. Finding out about other opinions is not too hard if you just look. Ask other attorneys about the witness, pull transcripts, look for publications. Jurors are very keenly interested to know if witness is a hired gun or a real analyst. The difference in credibility assigned by the jury between the two can make or break your case.

Credibility issue: objectivity. Playing off of the "keep the hiring lawyer happy" theme, bring out any evidence that the analysis or opinion is not based on any objectivity. Compare to your own expert, especially if they are far apart in their opinions, to show the opposing expert's opinion is simply not reasonable—and therefore should be rejected as it is not objective but subjective based on the paying side's position.

Another important issue is knowing where you are—and knowing who the jurors are that are listening to the expert. Regionalism is a real thing in trial work. Big city, fancy suit wearing lawyers are not welcomed with open arms in rural communities. We would be kidding ourselves to think that race and gender do not continue to play a role in how people are accepted in some parts of this country. All that to say that there are reasonable "persona" issues that can be exploited before the jury. Imagine an expert from a large city, with a big practice in an urban area. How he or she conducted his or her review, and how he or she testifies in a small Southern town could be an issue. Urbanites tend to be busy folks, accustomed to the fast pace of city life. They do not get offended by short, direct, even curt responses. Southerners might revile such a presentation, and not trust the expert—that is wholly within their purview.

If the witness is an older, established, kindly person with a good reputation, don't attack him or her. If he or she is of another national origin, be careful that the jury doesn't think you believe the expert to be a lesser person because of that—never be thought of as racist, sexist, or otherwise.

However, if the witness is talking down to you and the jury, exploit that:

Q   *The initials DNA stand for deoxyribonucleic acid, right?*

A   [Sighs] I'd assumed you wouldn't know that, but yes.

Q   Really. You also assume that these folks in the jury box don't know it?

A   No.

Q   You assume they we are not smart enough to know what DNA stand for?

A   No.

Q   Do you think you are smarter than the folks here?

A   No, that's . . . that's certainly not it.

Q   You don't know who in this room knows what, do you?

A   No.

Q   So you should not assume anything, should you, doctor?

A   No, I'm sorry. DNA stands for deoxyribonucleic acid.

Q   Thank you.

Perhaps a far-fetched example, and maybe a little argumentative, but know that experts will test you, and will try to exert superior knowledge on you. You have to control them.

If the witness is unprepared and uncredible, but has that "aw-shucks" likability, be super nice and just as endearing—all while getting the witness to agree that he or she did not analyze or consider certain things, did not fully prepare—and generally cannot be believed.

Q   Hey, I was looking at your report, and looks like you didn't take any measurements of the other's car's tire skid marks?

A   Where you looking at?

Q   *Page three—under the third paragraph.*

A   *Well, let me look.*

Q   *Sure, take your time.*

A   *You know, I thought I took those measurements, and put it in there.*

Q   *You probably had a lot going on at the time, right?*

A   *Oh, sure, I have quite a few clients.*

Q   *And you do your best for them, of course?*

A   *Absolutely.*

Q   *But sometimes we all miss something, right?*

A   *I suppose we do, because that other car's skid mark measurement sure isn't in this here report!*

You don't pile-drive the affable witness. Your point is made and preserved. You have established a key deficiency in the expert's work, but done so with a nice tone. The jury will respect that you were nice to the nice, and take the witness' concession of error as honest. You didn't have to beat it out of him, which makes it genuine. What great material for closing argument!

5.10   Example of Actual Cross Using Cross Sheets

My client was arrested for a driving under the influence. A seemingly run-of-the-mill DUI—she had one of the best videos I have ever seen, but blew *twice the legal limit* in Florida (.08, pursuant to Florida Statute section 316.193). Certainly, there was some really great things to work with, but also a really bad fact that had to be overcome—specifically, the really high breath test result.

This was the narrative portion police report:

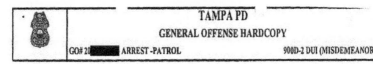

Related Text Page(s)

Document: INITIAL REPORT
Author: 49005 - ████████████
Related date/time: May-████13 ████ 146

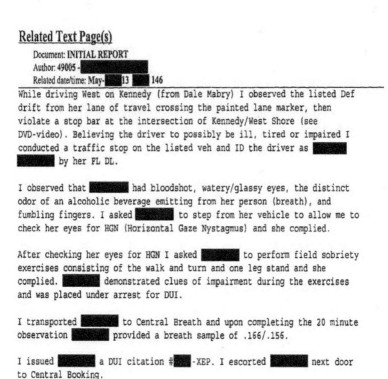

While driving West on Kennedy (from Dale Mabry) I observed the listed Def
drift from her lane of travel crossing the painted lane marker, then
violate a stop bar at the intersection of Kennedy/West Shore (see
DVD-video). Believing the driver to possibly be ill, tired or impaired I
conducted a traffic stop on the listed veh and ID the driver as ████████
████████ by her FL DL.

I observed that ████████ had bloodshot, watery/glassy eyes, the distinct
odor of an alcoholic beverage emitting from her person (breath), and
fumbling fingers. I asked ████████ to step from her vehicle to allow me to
check her eyes for HGN (Horizontal Gaze Nystagmus) and she complied.

After checking her eyes for HGN I asked ████████ to perform field sobriety
exercises consisting of the walk and turn and one leg stand and she
complied. ████████ demonstrated clues of impairment during the exercises
and was placed under arrest for DUI.

I transported ████████ to Central Breath and upon completing the 20 minute
observation ████████ provided a breath sample of .166/.156.

I issued ████████ a DUI citation #████-XEP. I escorted ████████ next door
to Central Booking.

The officer's dashcam video was available, and showed the
traffic stop and the interactions with my client. She looked very,
very good on the video—which was completely contrary to what was
in the report.

I set my case up my case theory to be "rush to judgement."
Because the video showed my client driving without any issues, and
performing the roadside tests almost flawlessly, the case theory was
"believe your eyes, not what you are told." Boiled down to a word,
it was a case of *believability*—everyone has seen someone who had

too much to drink. People form their own opinions based on prior life experience.

Themes: This was a bad arrest based on a rush to judgment by the cop. After he smelled alcohol on her breath, he was going to arrest her no matter what.

Topics: No bad driving, no indicators of impaired driving, cop predisposed to arrest, other innocent reasons for her appearance, excellent performance of physical tests.

The Cross Sheets looked like this:

CROSS EXAMINATION SHEET	
WITNESS: Arresting officer	ARGUMENT FOR CLOSING:
THEME: BAD ARREST!	Believe your eyes - NOT
TOPIC: "STANDARDS" of driving	what you hear! Her
TARGET FACT: DRIVING WAS JUST FINE!	driving was JUST FINE
	per "the standards"

FACTS TO BE ADDRESSED	NOTES FROM DIRECT
"NHTSA" - 3 "phases" ① -weaving (across lanes); straddling; swerving; turning w/ wide radius; drifting; alm. striking obj/veh - stopping problems; vary. speed (↑↓) too slow; speeding - wrong way, wrong lane; slow to react/resp. to signs/signals; stop for no reason; no lights on; improp/unsafe turn; drv. off road; inapprop. resp. to ofc; "unusual beh." - "appearing impaired" - STOP: troub. control, exiting; fumb. w/ docs; d/n understand; → slurred speech, leaning on veh; repeats Qs, wrong ans.; "ODOR OF Alc" ⇒ INNOCENT REASONS FOR HER DRIVING! - "DRIVING" is a "normal faculty" - ONLY 1 NHTSA "cue" (stop bcz viol ≠ NHTSA!) - You changed lane in intersection!! ≡	✱ 1:30-145 AM; business area He says: - drifting to Ⓛ, "almost striking median" [NOT IN RPT! NOT ON VIDEO] ≡ - pulled Ⓛ ?? "EASY, SAFE" She's a young female !! - siren to get throug traffic ??

PAGE 1 OF 4

CROSS EXAMINATION SHEET	
WITNESS: Arresting officer	ARGUMENT FOR CLOSING:
THEME: BAD ARREST!	Beleive your eyes -
TOPIC: "Standards" for driver	She appeared/acted A-OK
TARGET FACT: She looked fine / YOU WERE GOING TO ARREST ANYWAY	per "the standards"
FACTS TO BE ADDRESSED	NOTES FROM DIRECT

Facts to be addressed:

Ⅱ "PERSONAL CONTACT"
- know her EVERYDAY APPEARANCE?
  (so... no baseline?)

- EYES: smoke? contact lenses?
  time of day? crying?

- COOPERATIVE:
  ✱ TOLD YOU SHE HAD A
     BAD EVENING!
     - crying ... alone ...
- Fumbling? normal - everyone
- Alc. containers?
- Slurred speech? Abusive?
➡ QUESTIONING TECHNIQUES
   - divide attention
   - purposely confuse
   - no unusual reactions
   - followed instructions
   - got out OK (veh in gear,
      closed door, d/n lean -)
➡ INNOCENT REASONS FOR HER
   APPEARANCE!

Notes from direct:

〉 DISTINCT
   ODOR ????

1:20

} She was trying to
  tell you What
  was wrong - you
  just wanted to put
  her through phys. tests!
- you d/n care why she
  was upset!

PAGE 2 OF 4

CROSS EXAMINATION SHEET

WITNESS: *Arresting officer*	**ARGUMENT FOR CLOSING:**
THEME: *BAD ARREST!*	*Believe your eyes —*
TOPIC: *"standards" for physical abilities*	*She 100% passed all of*
TARGET FACT: *She could do everything 100%*	*his "rigged" tests!*

FACTS TO BE ADDRESSED	NOTES FROM DIRECT
③ "PRE-ARREST" screening	"standardized" ≠ validated
So... GOING TO arrest !?!	
✗ COMPLEX INSTRUCTIONS IN SHORT TIME {	takes just seconds on video
W.A.T. — go through Rpt. factors	— mental/phys @ same X
vs.	
VIDEO	distracted ≠ impaired !
NHTSA- reg's "designated straight line"	COPS FINGER SIGNALS ??
(Imaginary line - yours or hers?	Telling jury he sees
size? color? length?)	something they can't ?? }
- "IMAGINE" } "AS STRAIGHT As you can"	
SLOPE DOWN ↓	4 "clues" - swaying - "dropped foot"
O.L.S. — PERFECT	
	NOT ON VIDEO
✗ INNOCENT REASONS FOR HER PERFORMANCE	— — —
- fatigue	You [DEMONSTRATED??
- stress	—More like ½ demo!!
- nerves	
- rough pavement on feet	
- lights in eyes	
20 min —	→ You weren't watching her— You WERE DOING PAPERWORK

PAGE **3** OF **4**

CROSS EXAMINATION SHEET	
WITNESS: *Arresting officer*	**ARGUMENT FOR CLOSING:**
THEME: *BAD ARREST!*	*SHE WAS NOT*
TOPIC: *By law, she was not impaired*	*IMPAIRED BY ALC-*
TARGET FACT: *NOT LEGALLY IMPAIRED!*	*by cop's own standards*
	or by the jury's ★

FACTS TO BE ADDRESSED	NOTES FROM DIRECT
(Legal definition of "normal faculties")	"I DONT
Ability to	LOOK FOR
- SEE	NORMAL
- HEAR	FACULTIES"
- WALK	_____ .
- TALK	
- JUDGE DISTANCES	
- DRIVE	
RESP TO EMERGENCIES: pulled over properly	
DRIVE AUTO: she drove w/o issue	
DAILY MENTAL/PHYS TASKS: took off shoes - high heels - no problems - d/n even sit down! (knew sandals were in her car)	

PAGE 4 OF 4

I have noted in the transcript below where the Cross Sheets change as I change themes and topics. You should be able to discern as you read the transcript where I was on the sheets. Remember, *I do not use a list of questions*. I think in 3D as I go, using the sheets as a guideline for my questions. My questions are born of telling the story from the skeleton of the sheets.

Here is the transcript of the cross examination—it has been edited for brevity, but is available in full at www.bodifordlaw.com/cross-examination.

	Q. Good morning.
	A. Good morning, sir.
I start with **Cross Sheet 1**, and set it up by using the witness to give some background of his training and techniques.	Q. All right. Let's go through these— this investigation and all this. Now, you start with—there's three phases to a DUI investigation per NHTSA, right?
	A. Yes, sir.
	Q. And then—and NHTSA is N-H-T-S-A, right?
Cross Sheet 1 of 4: NORMAL FACULTIES: SEE, HEAR, WALK, TALK, DRIVE	A. Correct.
	Q. National Highway Traffic Safety Administration.
	A. Yes, sir.
	Q. And they're the ones that have somehow standardized this process that you go through when you're doing a DUI investigation.
	A. Correct.

	Q. And standardization means all of you supposedly do it the same way—
	A. Yes.
	Q. —or supposed to do it the same way, right?
	A. Yes, sir.
	Q. There's a difference between standardization and validation, correct?
Now I proceed into the facts of the case, starting with Cross Sheet 1 of 4.	A. Yes, sir.
	Q. Okay. The first phase is vehicle in motion, correct?
	A. Yes, sir.
	Q. Okay. And then your Phase I observations, there's any number of things that you can look for according to NHTSA, right?
	A. Yes, sir.
	Q. And you're familiar with those, right?
	A. Yes, sir.
	Q. So things you could look for according to NHTSA are weaving, both within the lane, and across the lane lines, correct?
	A. Yes, sir.
	Q. Straddling the lanes as you drive down the street?
	A. Yes, sir.

Q. Swerving?

A. Yes.

Q. Turning with a wide radius?

A. Uh-hum. Yes.

Q. Drifting?

A. Yes.

Q. And drifting is when they're kind of just going one direction, and they correct it, right?   And they drift over, and they come back, correct?

A. Yes, sir.

Q. Okay. And almost striking a vehicle or object, that's a sign that you could look for as far as Phase I, correct?

A. Yes, sir.

Q. Other things that NHTSA puts out are stopping problems; do you agree?

A. Yes, sir.

Q. Varying speeds, meaning somebody'll go fast for a while, and then they'll go really slow for a while, that's a—that's a cue, right?

A. Correct.

Q. Or rapid acceleration, burning out at a stop sign, or slamming on brakes, deceleration, those could be clues, correct?

A. Yes, sir.

Q. People that just get over there and go too slow, they're going like 25 in a 55, that could be a clue of impairment, right?

A. Correct.

Q. And to the contrary, speeding could be a clue.

A. Correct.

Q. Could be a clue. Okay. How about going the wrong way down a one-way street? NHTSA says that's a clue, correct?

A. Yes, sir.

Q. And there's others, driving in the wrong lane; do you agree?

A. Yes, sir.

Q. Being slow to respond to traffic signals or an officer's direction, that's a clue, right?

A. Yes, sir.

Q. You know, when an officer's directing traffic, and the person just goes right by them, you know? Is that right?

A. Yes, sir.

Q. People that stop for no reason, that—that could be a clue of impairment per NHTSA, correct?

A. Yes.

Q. That would fall in the category of those folks that you see that are sleeping through a cycling green light, you know, they're just there for apparently no reason, that's a clue that somebody could be under the influence, right?

A. Yes, it is.

Q. Clearly. Somebody driving with no headlights at night, right, that's a clue?

A. Yes, sir.

Q. NHTSA also says that making an improper or unsafe turn is a clue of impairment, right?

A. Yes, sir.

Q. And also driving on somewhere other than the roadway, you know, like driving on the sidewalk, so to speak. That could be a clue of impairment, correct?

A. Yes, sir.

Q. Inappropriate response to an officer's signals, or other unusual behavior, those are all clues, correct?

A. They can be, yes, sir.

Q. They can be. And those are ones that are—that NHTSA has come out and said, officers, look for these things, right?

A. Yes, sir.

Q. Okay. Now, do you have your NHTSA manual with you today by chance?

A. No, I don't.

Q. You didn't bring it? Okay. NHTSA also says that looking at the actual stop itself once you've activated the lights to conduct the stop, that there's continued clues that you can continue to see, right? Such as trouble with the controls on their car, you know, they put the left blinker on; and then the right blinker; and then the left, that could be a clue, correct?

A. Yes, sir.

Q. Trouble exiting the car. You know, when people get out and they fall over, that's a clue, right?

A. Yes, sir.

Q. Now, fumbling with documents, you've told us about that, and certainly you think that's a clue, correct, that's a NHTSA clue?

A. Yes, sir.

Q. Not understanding what you as the officer are telling them, right?

Over 40 questions in a row with only a "yes" or "no" response—the questions, tone, and pace were designed and delivered to assure those responses from the witness.

Open-ended question, but no harm done. If he said yes, he has to give me the answer I wanted. If he said no, shows he comes to trial court unprepared.

A. Correct.

Q. So these are all things that you can look for as far as drivers and to determine whether they are impaired.

A. Yes, sir.

Q. Now, in this situation, you're telling us that you saw on her vehicle in motion, Phase I detection, before any contact with her, you've essentially seen her drifting to the left almost striking a median; is that what you said?

A. Yes, sir.

Q. Okay. Now you remember reporting this case; did you not?

A. I did.

Q. Do you have your report with you today?

A. I have a couple of the pages, just my narrative—

Q. Okay.

A. —that I brought with me, yes, sir.

Q. Right. And in that narrative you mention drifting, but nowhere in your report do you say anything about almost striking a median, did you?

Negative impeachment—highlighting what should be there by showing it is not.	A. Just that she crossed over the line. Q. Right. Now, that report was made that night, correct? A. Yes, sir. Q. And it was made based on your observations while they were still fresh in your mind, right? A. Yes, sir. Q. And the reason that you make the reports is so that you can have a fresh memory when you come in five, six months later at a trial, right? A. Yes, sir. Q. Okay. And it's important that you make those reports accurate? Yes? A. Yes
By going through the timing of writing the report, and why it was important to write it, I was able to highlight its importance, and credit its contents.	Q. And it's important that they be all-inclusive— A. Yes Q. —correct? Good, bad, and the ugly? A. Correct. Q. Right. So almost striking a median is a fairly significant driving indicator, isn't it? A. Yes, sir.

An admission that a fact was made up at trial. I used "in front of these jurors" to imply he was lying to *them*, not to me.

**NOTE: In the notes section on the right of Cross Sheet 1 of 4, you see my notes from direct examination about his "drifting" comments.

Add to the fact that it's not in the report, and he's just now making it up, the jury is reminded that the video is the true measure of

Q. And that's—but that's— conspicuously you've left that out of your written narrative at two different places in your report, you would agree?

A. The actual wording of that, yes, sir, but—

Q. Right.

A. —which there is a line right next to the median.

Q. But striking the median—striking a median, the first time we've heard of that is today in front of these jurors.

A. Yeah. That she almost struck the median, yes, sir.

Q. Okay. And that's also not on the video.

A. Correct, yeah.

Q. Today you said that she drifted several times, right?

A. Several times to the left, yes, sir.

Q. Okay. And again, looking at your report, you say that she drifted from her lane of travel, then violated a stop bar. You say in your report she drifted once, correct? Are you— you've read your report in preparation for today, right?

NOTE: Terrible question— compound—more than one fact.

whether he's telling the truth or not.	A. Yes, sir, I did.
	Q. Okay. And so you make it seem in your report is that there's one incident of drifting.
	A. Well, prior to the other one— there was the one that's—that I put in the report, but then the one that was not captured on video, which— she went towards me—
	Q. So you're only—
	A. —and put that on—
	Q. —putting on—in the report what's on the video?
	A. I—I don't know. Could I—if—if I could look at my report again.
At this point, I knew that I had him on the ropes. What's better, I knew that he knew it, too. He was about to make up another fact, and I was going to let him and punish him for it.	Q. Sure.
	MR. BODIFORD: Judge, may I approach?
	THE COURT: Yes, you may.
	THE WITNESS: Just to verify exactly what I said.
	MR. BODIFORD: Mine—yeah, mine is the—your narrative's going to be on these two pages, and I've got some notes which I don't mind you—
	THE WITNESS: Okay.
	MR. BODIFORD: —seeing or anything like that.
	THE WITNESS: All right, sir.

MR. BODIFORD: So that's—let's go (unintelligible) to your recollection is refreshed, and we shall proceed.

THE WITNESS: (Witness reviewed documents). I stated that she was observed drifting from her lane of travel crossing the painted lane marker. Yeah, that's what I stated (unintelligible)—

MR. BODIFORD: Okay.

THE WITNESS: —drifting, that she drifted from her lane of travel, crossing the painted lane marker.

Now that his recollection is refreshed . . . I would have given him the facts for him to agree to, but he just repeated what he'd read in his report, so there was no need.

BY MR. BODIFORD (CONTINUING):

Q. All right. So in your report, you make it sound as if that's one incident (unintelligible), correct?

A. Yes, sir. But it was actually several.

Q. So now that we're in trial, now you're telling us there's more than just one.

A. There was at least two, yes, sir.

I knew what was on the video from my pretrial preparation, and the jury had just seen it on direct. I knew it was not there, and it was going

Q. Okay. And none of them are depicted on this video.

A. I believe they are.

Q. Can you—can you point out where she's drifting over a—on—over a lane marker—

to be interesting to see him try to point it out.	A. Yes, sir.
	Q. —in this video?
He receded from the crossing the lane marker because it was not on the video, and he realized it. He was now trying to claim going back and forth (essentially weaving) in the lane had resulted in her tires going over the line and consequently that she had left the lane of travel. I knew how to clear that up.	A. Drifting over to the left. I—I don't know if her tires actually crossed the lane marker, but she drifted over to the left several times.
	Q. And—and so we're clear, when you're driving a car in the state of Florida, you're allowed to use the entire lane, right?
	A. Yes, sir.
	Q. If you want to drive on this side of the lane, as long as you stay in that lane, that's cool, right? Yes?
	A. Sure.
	Q. And if you want to drive over on— move over to the left or right, and drive on that side of the line, as long as you don't go over, it's cool, right?
	A. Yes, sir.
	Q. All right. And that's what's depicted on this video, correct?
	A. Yes, sir.
	Q. There's no—there's no swerving, there's no—let me ask it to you this way: Do you agree that all—all the other NHTSA indicators that we've

We went through this at the beginning, and the jury heard all the things that are indicators. Now he's trying to add something in—I had to highlight that.

He was trying to gain some ground back by saying that stopping over the big white stop bar at the intersection is an infraction, and essentially any and all infractions are indicators of alcohol impairment. That opened a huge door for me . . . again, I knew the video incredibly well from watching it over

talked about here this morning, other than this drifting issue, none of those are on the video.

A. She violated the stop bar, sir.

Q. But that's not a NHTSA indicator now, is it?

A. It's a traffic infraction, it is a—

Q. Do you—

A. —NHTSA indicator.

Q. In all the things that NHTSA has said, is failing to stop at a stop bar, or failing to obey a traffic light, or a stop signal, is it an indicator?

A. Failing to stop at a stop bar is a traffic violation.

Q. Okay. So a traffic violation would be an indicator of impairment, right?

A. Yes, sir.

Q. Okay. Is failing to—or is changing lane at an intersection, is that a traffic violation? If you change lanes while you're in an intersection under a light, that's—

A. I believe it's within 50 feet, yes, sir.

Q. Okay. So you—you can't—so we're clear, if you're going under the light and you're in the four-way, and over in pretrial preparation . . . and I knew HE had committed a traffic violation! Time to use it against him.

Point made—the video clearly shows him committing an infraction, and certainly he had not been drinking, so his traffic infraction was not an indicator of his impairment. But he sensed it coming.

you can't be changing lanes, right? That's a—

A. You're not—

Q. —traffic violation.

A. —supposed to, yes, sir.

Q. Okay. You do that on this video, don't you?

A. I don't know if I was within 50 feet.

Q. Okay. But you weren't impaired that night.

A. No, sir.

Q. Okay. So by you committing a—a violation as you go through the intersection, that's not an indicator in any way of you being impaired, correct?

A. I'm not sure where exactly you're talking about. I'm—I'm sorry.

Q. When—when you—when—

MR. BODIFORD: Let's see if I can make this thing work.

A. Okay.

(Whereupon, the video recording was published to the jury).

Q. Technology sometimes fails us, doesn't it, Officer?

Seemed to me he was trying to make it look as if I were trying to confuse him. Back it up, go forward again, and make it clear it's not me who's being duplicitous, it's him.

A. I'm just not sure exactly at what—what intersection you're referring to, sir.

Q. Well, how many intersections did you go through with her? Do you recall?

A. Well, there was the one at Westshore, and then—I'm not sure if there was one prior—

Q. All right.

A. —to that.

Q. I can't tell where on the video we are, but you are traveling, would you agree, looks like through—is that Lois? And you're in the—

A. Yeah—

Q. —middle lane.

He was trying to justify what he did and avoid my point—I was in control, and I did not let him wiggle out of it . . .

A. —that—that's—

Q. There you go.

Finally—he admits it. But not after I had to hold his feet to the fire. Time to move on . . .

A. —approximately Lois.

Q. You just changed lanes in the intersection; did you not?

A. Yeah, that's—that's right after I observed the vehicle, so I wanted to get—get up to the vehicle. Yes, sir.

Edited for brevity. . .

Moving on to Cross **Sheet 2 of 4	Q. All right. Now, we go to phase— the next phase of the three phases, and this next phase is known as personal contact. Right?
	A. Yes.
	MR. BODIFORD: Hold on.
	Q. And the personal conduct—I'm sorry, personal contact phase of the investigation is—is strange because you don't have a baseline to start with with these people. Do you understand what I mean by a "baseline"?
	A. If you could explain just what you're—
	Q. You've never met [CLIENT] (phonetics)—
	A. —referring to.
	Q. —[CLIENT] before that night in your entire life, had you?
	A. Correct.
	Q. Okay. So not having any knowledge of her, you don't know what she's like under regular circumstances, do you?
	A. That's correct.
	Q. Okay. You have to take her as you find her.

A. Yes.

Q. Now, with you—you said that when you first got up to her, you noticed several—several things that added into these clues or cues of—of impairment, what you call the totality of the circumstances? One of which was that her eyes were red, right?

A. Yes, sir.

Q. 1:30 in the morning, certainly an innocent explanation for having red eyes is that somebody's just been up for a long time, and they're tired, correct?

A. Correct. It could be.

Q. And somebody that may have been in a place where somebody was smoking, smoke can cause eyes to turn red; do you agree?

A. Yes, sir.

Q. She told you she was wearing contact lenses, didn't she?

A. Yes, sir.

Q. And certainly contact lenses can make somebody's eyes red, right?

A. Possible, yes, sir.

He knows that the video shows my client crying and upset at the time of the very first contact, and her explanation of why. He knows I am going to make him out to be a bad guy for arresting her after she fought with her boyfriend.

**NOTE: this was on the note section of Cross Sheet 2 of 4, from my notes of his direct testimony.

Q. Is there anything else about Ms. [CLIENT] that night that you observed that would have led you to believe why her eyes were red—or understand why her eyes were red, other than alcohol?

A. She said she had a rough night. I don't know if it was pertaining to a boyfriend or some situation. But—

Q. And she was—

A. —she did state that. At one point she started crying, yes.

Q. She was crying. She was crying when you got up to her. And crying will make your eyes red, won't it?

A. It can, yes, sir.

Q. It can. And that's—crying is not an indicator of being under the influence of alcohol, is it?

A. She wasn't crying when I first walked up to her.

Q. Well, it's interesting you talk about that. First of all, she was fully cooperative with you, you agree with that.

A. Oh, yes.

Q. Okay. Now, as far as this having a bad evening, she—she stops and tells you initially, I'm having a bad night. And there's a long pause in the video, and you begin to talk to her again, and she says, I'm having a bad evening. She starts to try to tell you, she—she pauses—do you remember that, she pauses, and you're listening, right?

A. Okay.

Q. You've got to—do you remember that on the video?

A. Yes.

Q. Okay. You've got a young female who's alone in a car at 1:30 in the morning who's crying. That you knew at that point in time, correct?

A. Yes, sir.

Q. And when she pauses saying she's had a bad evening, you didn't say why; you said, let's get out and do field sobriety exercises, didn't you?

Edited for brevity. . .

Took a chance here, asking for an open-ended narrative. I am comfortable using this, but do not recommend to everyone. I knew he'd just spit out all his "totality of the circumstances" points and I would address them one by one. I was

Q. All right. So finally, if you will, please explain why that when given the opportunity to find out what had been going on with her that evening, you chose instead to do the physical sobriety exercises.

A. Well, based on my observations up to that point; and the distinct odor of an alcoholic beverage coming from her breath; the fact that she was fumbling around with

ready for it on Cross Sheet 2 of 4.	her paperwork, at that point I was ready to conduct a DUI investigation, ask her to step out of the vehicle. If I would start diving into a conversation as far as what's going on with her that evening, I would have gotten off track as far as my investigation. And as a police officer, every time I stop somebody for whatever reason, everybody always has a story or a personal situation that they're going through. And if I took the time to listen to everybody's situation every time I made a traffic stop, I'd never get my job done.
He we go . . .	Q. Distinct odor of an alcoholic beverage. So from this distinct odor, can you tell us, was it strong, was it moderate, was it weak, or was it just distinct?
	A. Enough to smell it coming off of her breath, yes, sir.
	Q. Okay. And just smelling something on somebody's breath does not give you an indication of how much they have had to drink, right?
	A. Correct.
	Q. Or what it was they had to drink, right?

	A. Only that it was an alcoholic beverage, yes, sir.
	Q. But you can't distinguish beer, wine, liquor, any of that. Just that it's there.
	A. Correct.
	Q. Okay. Or when, you can't tell from that odor when they had it, right?
	A. Correct.
	Q. And this—this issue of fumbling, now, are you telling us that she's in there just—you know, there's papers flying everywhere; or was it that you're telling us that she was looking for these things?
	A. She was looking for the items and passed over them several times when they were right in front of her.
	Q. You have in your report noted that she had fumbling fingers, right?
	A. Yes, sir.
Negative impeachment	Q. Nowhere in there do you say, and she passed over the documents that I had asked of her—
	A. No.
	Q. —did you?

	A. That's—that's inclusive in the fumbling of—the fumbling of fingers.
	Q. Okay. So the first time you've articulated that she passed over documents is here before this jury today, right?
Not on my sheet, just happened in real time	A. That's my explanation as far as fumbling fingers, yes, sir.

Edited for brevity. . .**

Back to the Cross Sheet, "Questioning Techniques". . .	A. Yes, sir.
	Q. Uh-hum. All right. Now, your questioning techniques. NHTSA talks about how to do these questioning techniques to, if you will, simulate this driving divided attention skills thing, right? You're trained how to do that.
	A. Yes, sir.
	Q. So when you're up—up at the car, and you're asking for this, and you're talking about that, that whole interaction is designed to divide the driver's attention, isn't it?
	A. When you ask for, like, several different documents, yes, sir.
	Q. Right. So you're coming out of the gate trying to trip somebody up.
	A. I wouldn't say I'm trying to trip them up, I'm just trying to introduce

	a question that would cause them to have to use divided attention. Q. Uh-hum. And she—at your Phase 2 personal contact with her at the car, she did those things correctly, didn't she? A. Yeah. She—I asked her for the documents, and like I said, she had difficulty locating them, but eventually did. Q. Uh-hum. And no unusual reactions other than her crying, right? A. Correct. Q. She followed your instructions while at the car; did she not? A. Yes, sir. Q. And when she got out of the car, NHTSA says if somebody gets out and they're leaning and, you know, not being able to balance, that's a clue. She didn't exhibit those clues, did she?
Free-styling off the Cross Sheet, I incorporate the video that the jury has just seen.	A. Correct. Q. She was able to get out, close the door, and go directly to where you wanted her to stand, right? A. Yes, sir, she did. Q. And she stood there like a statute; did she not?

	A. She stood there, yes, sir.
Not letting him wiggle or equivocate	Q. What—when you—when she first goes and stands behind the car while you're moving hers, are you telling us that there's something wrong with the way she's standing there that gave you any clues at—at that point in time—
	A. No, sir.
	Q. —she was under the influence?
	A. Not at—no, she stood fine.
	Q. Okay. Now—and again, back to these—this totality of the circumstances, you're adding these clues into your overall investigation as you're going, right?
	A. That's correct.
	Q. Okay. So—but by the same token, all of these things that we've just talked about when we first get to the car are all also very indicative of innocent behavior, too. Right? Like a distinct odor of alcohol on her breath, of—of—of alcohol on the breath, it's not illegal to drink and drive, right?
	A. Correct.
This was addressed in jury selection, so now I have the arresting	Q. It's illegal to drink too much and drive.

officer admitting what the jury knows to be the law. They can now hold him to that standard.

A. That's correct.

Q. So that odor in and of itself is consistent with innocent behavior; is it not?

A. It can be, yes, sir.

Q. Right. And—and the fumbling and trying to get the documents, you've probably stopped thousands of people in your time, and that's something you see all the time, isn't it?

A. Sometimes it happens, yes, sir.

Q. Even with people who are stone cold sober.

A. Sometimes.

NOTE: now I move on to **Cross Sheet 3 of 4, "FSE's [field sobriety exercises] were great"; you will note there are more notes from direct on my sheet than with the other sheets. You will see below how I incorporated them into my cross.

Q. Right. Okay. Now, the next phase, Phase 3, what is Phase 3 called? It's called pre-arrest screening.

A. Yeah. Pre—yes, pre-arrest.

Q. NHSTA calls it pre-arrest screening. You're familiar with that, right?

The jury thought this was funny, which signaled to me that they were with me and understanding the story I was telling about this cop being prone to arrests.

A. Yes, sir.

Q. And you're trained on that, right?

A. Yes, sir.

Q. And pre-arrest screening begs the question that this is going to lead to an arrest, doesn't it?

A. Possible.

Q. Well, they don't call it "pre-let-them-go" screening, do they?

A. Well, if someone does the exercises and fails to demonstrate clues of impairment, then they would not be placed under arrest.

Q. And—and so we're clear on how this works, your—your pre-arrest screening captured on the video so that once you—you've arrested them, you've got a record to show the jury. Very simple how—why this video is taken, correct?

A. Yes, sir, that's—that's a part of the reason, yes, sir.

Q. All right. Now—and we've talked a little bit about this before, but you described for Ms. Muller (phonetics) the fact that the—these instructions are designed to be both mentally—give a mental and a physical thing at the same time to simulate this divided attention. In other words, you want to distract

	them while you're giving these instructions, correct?
	A. That's correct.
	Q. Yeah. But distraction isn't the same as impairment. You can be a distracted driver and not be impaired, right?
	A. Could—could be, yes, sir.
The following came from my notes on the Cross Sheet from the direct examination, regarding there being "complex instructions in short time".	Q. Okay. So the idea behind these are to give these things—but these are—you know, give these divided attention instructions. But don't you agree, there are a lot of instructions in a very short period of time. Right? Stand like this, I'm going to tell you to do this, put your hands down, you walk here, you turn this way, you walk back, you got it? Go. That's how it works in a short period of time. Right?
	A. I understand what you're saying, yes.
	Q. So it is—you—do you agree—
	A. I don't think it's a lot—
	Q. —that the idea—
	A. —of instruction. But—
	Q. Hmm?
	A. I don't think it's a lot of instructions. But—

Q. But the—

A. It's enough to cause divided attention.

Q. Okay. Right. There you go. And—and—and so you—you demonstrate that here, now, you've done these exercises countless times—

A. Yes, sir.

Q. —agreed? Okay. The walk and turn. Now, the factors—well, stop here real quick. These things are pass/fail, right? You either pass them, you go home; you fail and you go to jail. That's how it works, right?

A. It's not a pass/fail, it's whether they demonstrate any of the clues of impairment.

Q. Okay. So you don't look at it and say, boy, they really failed that exam. You're just trying to build whatever clues you can find to make an arrest.

A. I look for clues of impairment, yes, sir.

Q. All right. Now, the walk and turn. You said that NHTSA gives us eight actual clues to look for. And those are the ones that you're looking for, no more, no less—

A. Correct.

Q. —right? Uh-hum. And on this one, she, in your estimation, exhibited four, or—

A. Right.

Q. —50 percent of the—of the—of the ones that are out there.

A. That's correct.

Edited for brevity. . .

Q. All right. Let's stop here real quick. One of the things that NHTSA tells you in their manual is if somebody's wearing high heels, they can take them off, correct?

A. That's correct.

Q. She did that, right?

A. Yes, sir.

Q. She stood on those, what, 3- or 4-inch high heels, bent down, unbuckled them, took them off, and never even teetered, did she?

A. I—I think she did a little.

Q. Well, you've done the—you've done these—

A. Right.

Q. —field sobriety tests a billion times. You ever stood in high heels and tried to bend down and take them—

A. Never wore—

That was the kill shot in the trial—and he knew it. There was no way he could overcome by his testimony the images on the video. My client in no way appeared to be under the influence of alcohol or drugs.

Q. —off?

A. —high heels in my life.

Q. Okay. So we know that you're not trying to take them off either. That's a pretty impressive feat that she just does there, isn't it?

A. Yeah, I would have to say yes. I don't know how anybody walks in them.

Edited for brevity. . .

(Whereupon, the video recording was published to the jury).

Q. Okay. The first thing you said was imagine a straight line between her—where you're at and the car.

A. Correct.

Q. Now, NHTSA says—NHTSA says that in order to do the walk and turn, it requires a, quote, designated straight line, right?

A. If possible. If it's available.

Q. You're in a mall parking lot, aren't you?

A. Uh-hum.

Q. There's about 5,000 straight white lines within 20 feet of you, aren't there?

A. It was a very lit area, and I decided to do it just right there because I don't like taking people away from the scene.

Edited for brevity. . .

A. I chose to do the exercises right there, yes, sir.

Q. Okay. So you're telling her, imagine this line. This imaginary line, how long was this imaginary line?

A. I just told her to imagine it from where she was standing, towards my vehicle.

Q. Well, did you tell her how wide to imagine it?

A. No. I just—

Q. Are you talking about a—

A. —I just told here I just wanted her to walk as straight as possible.

Q. Okay. Well, were you—or were you wanting her to imagine a pin-stripe, or say, like maybe a football, or likely be a stop bar? Did you tell her?

A. No, I didn't specify, sir.

Q. Okay. And you didn't tell her what color this imaginary line was or how long this imaginary line was, or anything, did you?

A. No, sir.

Q. Okay. And that's not what NHTSA standardizes, is it?

A. NHTSA said to use a line if it's available—

Q. Okay.

A. —in—the best location.

Q. All right. So—by the way, while we're standing here, so that we're all clear, she's not leaning like this to her left, is she?

A. Could be the camera—

Edited for brevity. . .

(Whereupon, the video recording was published to the jury).

Q. —what you said this morning, she steps off the line. Now you tell us when she steps off the line.

A. When she fails to maintain, you mean?

Q. Okay. Now, she's in position.

A. Yes, sir. Watch her. Just watch her feet. While I'm demonstrating.

Q. Uh-hum. Is that it?

A. There's one more after that.

Q. Now, it—

A. Right there.

Q. —part of the—Okay.

A. Right there.

Q. So when you're walking in front of her, then she—she—

A. Moves her—

Q. —moves her—

A. —foot to the side.

Q. —she moves her right foot—Okay. At this point in time, she's been standing one foot and the other for almost 30 seconds, correct?

A. I didn't time it. I don't know, sir.

Q. But that's part of the test. That's part of what the test is, is just saying, okay, sit here and listen to me, you put them in this position—

A. Correct.

Q. —because you know that it—at some point in time, the likelihood of them falling out of that position is going to be very real. Right?

A. Just following what I'm trained to do, sir.

Q. Okay. So then we go through— does not touch heel to toe.

(Whereupon, the video recording was published to the jury).

Q. Now, your explanation of that was that you're giving a signal on a video to—

A. Correct.

Q. —to what, to them, to the jurors?

A. Just indicated on my video that when she missed this heel-to-toe.

Q. Okay. So what would—what would be the downside of shooting this from the side so we could actually see whether they're touching the heel to toe?

A. Sometimes I do. It all depends on where my vehicle is and where I line up the camera.

Q. Okay. Well, you could have—you know, you had any number of options, but you told her very specifically, you took her to that spot, and you told her, walk towards the camera.

A. Correct.

Q. And you know that that's not going to show whether she's heel-to-toe. You've done this 1,000 times. You—

A. Well, if—

Q. —know whether or not it shows—

A. —if it clearly doesn't show, that's why I always point my finger out.

Q. So basically you're—you're trying to tell the jurors something they can't see.

	A. I—I'm not sure what you're implying, sir.
	Q. Well—
	A. Are you saying I'm lying or—
	Q. No. I'm saying that—that the way this video was set up, we cannot see whether she's heel-to-toe, so you're on the—you have the good vantage point, and you're signaling when she misses to us.
	A. That's why I'm—
	Q. If that signal—
	A. —signaling.
	Q. Hmm?
	A. That's why I'm signaling.
Another kill shot. . .*and goes to the theme of the opening* (see section 3.3)	Q. Okay. So the signal is so you can tell them what they might not be able to see with their own eyes.
	A. I guess so, yes, sir.
	Q. Okay.
	(Whereupon, the video recording was published to the jury).
Edited for brevity. . .	
	Q. And again, there are innocent reasons for why she may have done what she did: Fatigue, stress, nerves, all of those things could factor in, right?

A. That's possible, yes.

Q. Okay. And by the way, you're counting—you're having her count to see whether or not she's—you're looking at your watch while she's counting to see if, again, mentally she's able to keep—and she kept pretty dang close, didn't she, doing her, one, Mississippi; two, Mississippi.

A. Yes, sir.

Q. I mean, she maybe got off a second or two, right?

A. Yes. She did—

Q. And that—you agree—

A. Very well counting, yes, sir.

Q. She did well counting, correct?

A. Yes, sir.

Q. Okay. All right. So you go out to the—you go out to the—oh, before you leave there—so you arrest her, she doesn't flip out on you, correct?

A. Correct.

Q. She understands and is still cooperative with you, correct?

A. Yes, sir.

Q. And, in fact, she has presence of mind enough to tell you about the flat shoes in the car. You were nice

	enough to say, hey, do you want to— what do you want to do with your shoes; and she remembered that there were those shoes in her car, and you got them for her, right?
	A. Correct.
	Q. So it's a combination of you, you know, being nice to her; but also her having the presence of mind to be able to respond and to remember that that was there. And that's certainly not an indicator of somebody who is under the influence, right?
	A. I—I don't know, sir. But it—
	Q. What, the ability to—
	A. —that is (unintelligible).
Here, I get into the final Cross Sheet, **Cross Sheet 4 of 4**, regarding the normal faculties.	Q. —well, do you—do you understand what—you know what the normal faculties are, correct?
	A. It all depends on someone's level of impairment.
Setting him up for final destruction. . .	Q. So, Officer, what are the normal faculties that we are looking to see if they are impaired, what are they?
	A. A normal faculty would be someone who's able to listen, comprehend, and perform normal

	functions would be normal faculties, if I understand what you're asking—
	Q. Uh-hum. Yeah.
	A. —and saying.
	Q. No—I mean, you—but I mean, you're vested with enforcing the DUI laws, correct?
	A. Correct.
	Q. And—and so the definition of normal faculties, do you not have a succinct legal definition for what normal faculties are?
	A. I'm just not sure what you're asking for. I mean, I—I would—
	Q. Please define—
	A. —give you my personal opinion what normal faculties are. I mean, normal faculties are basically a person who's able to perform the normal day-to-day activities and—and—is that what—is that what you're asking?
Not letting him get out of it, or throw it back on me. He arrested my client and he must be accountable to explain why.	Q. Well, no. Because—I'm actually asking you if you know what the legal definition is because you're the one that says that she broke that law. So for you to be able to know what law she broke—to be able to say whether she broke a law by driving with normal faculties

	impaired, it would seem that you would know what the normal faculties are. So please tell the jury what the legal definition of normal faculties is.
	A. I base—if I can elaborate a little bit—
	Q. Sure.
	A. —I based my conclusion on making a DUI arrest based on whether or not they demonstrate clues of impairment. I don't particularly look for normal faculties because I've seen, and then certain— in all the DUI arrests and investigations I've done, there are some people who can look perfectly normal and act perfectly normal, but they are impaired.
The jury has heard all of this, and they already know that each of these things my client did correctly. Short, succinct validation of her defense.	Q. How about the ability to see, is that a normal faculty?
	A. Sure.
	Q. Hear?
	A. Correct.
	Q. Walk?
	A. Yes, sir.
	Q. Talk?
	A. Correct.
	Q. Judge distances?

A. Yes, sir.

Q. Respond to emergencies?

A. Sure.

Q. Drive an automobile?

A. Sure.

Q. And as you've said, do all the daily mental and physical tasks that we have in our normal lives, those are normal faculties, right?

A. Yes, sir.

Q. Okay. And—but you put those aside, and all you do is just plug the person—or run the person through the NHTSA standards and see whether or not they're yes or no.

A. Yeah, I would have to agree with that. I mean, we—we look for the abnormal faculties, the—you know, for a person doing out of the norm is what stands out as far as possible clues of impairment.

Q. So what do you give greater weight to, what you know to be normal faculties, like you've described somebody's ability to do daily functions; or the NHTSA standards? What do you give greater weight to when formulating probable cause to arrest her?

	A. I would have to lean towards the NHTSA standards and look for the clues of impairment that people demonstrate, because that's—that's what we're looking for.
Doesn't matter what he says, as the jury already knows the answer!	Q. So in other—
	A. (Unintelligible)—
	Q. —words, you just disregard your own common sense.
	A. I wouldn't say that, no, sir.
	MR. BODIFORD: Judge, I have nothing further.

The jury returned a *not guilty* verdict.

5.11   Checklists

5.11.1 Cross Examination Organization Checklist

You may have more or less elements or defenses, and themes/topics/target facts (TF) (this is just a template).

ELEMENTS (PROOF) CHECKLIST	
• List all pleadings (pull from online case docket to be sure you have everything) • Include critical pleadings (complaint, answer, indictment, substantive motions) to your case file (*you don't need everything, but be sure to have the important stuff!*)	
ELEMENT 1:	PROOF:
ELEMENT 2:	PROOF:
ELEMENT 3:	PROOF:

	DEFENSE 1:	ATTACK:
	DEFENSE 2:	ATTACK:

	THEME 1
	• TOPIC 1
	○ TF 1
	○ TF 2
	• TOPIC 2
	○ TF 1
	○ TF 2
	THEME 2
	• TOPIC 1
	○ TF 1
	○ TF 2
	• TOPIC 2
	○ TF 1
	○ TF 2

5.11.2 Cross Sheet Prep

Use the Cross Sheet found earlier in this chapter.

	Witness dossier completed
	Cross sheets prepared
	Depo sheets prepared
	Impeachments ready

5.11.3 Witness Control Tools "at a Glance"

- That was not my question

- Have you finished? Let's get back to my question!

- The flip to the opposite

- The weed-out game

- Then the answer is yes (or no)

- You didn't understand my question

- Re-ask the question (with or without a control tag)

- We'll get to that in a second . . . this question is about ___

- Interruption

- Simplifying the question, and "playing dumb"

- Using the jury to help control the witness (hammer phrases)

- I'm the one asking the questions

CHAPTER 6

Closing Argument

> **OBJECTIVES:** In this chapter, we will discuss argument as opposed to discussion, and how to wrap all of the story into the facts to lead to asking the jury for a verdict that they probably are already willing to give you. We will cover:
>
> - Preparing for closing argument
>
> - Ideas for structuring a closing argument
>
> - The importance of using the law (jury instructions)
>
> - The importance of "The Ask"
>
> - Techniques for delivering a persuasive closing argument

While it is probably true that if you wait until closing to present your theory of the case, it is too late to even try, an effective closing argument is the capstone all of the proceedings. It is a time to really cement commitment, to reconcile any seemingly unanswered questions, to rebut the opposition, and to ask the jury once again to "do the right thing" (i.e. find for your side!).

6.1 Purpose of Closing Argument

WHAT THE JURY IS DOING DURING CLOSING
• Corroborating
• Corresponding
• Concluding

There is a trial advocacy theory out there that posits that by the time the trial gets to closing arguments (also called "summation", which undermines its importance), most jurors have already made up their minds. Jurors *create* their own metal version of your client's story based on their own life experiences. That begins in opening statements, and they adjust their version as the case progresses, looking for *corroborating* evidence to support what they think happened. Then they will look for the verdict that *corresponds* with their version, to resolve the case and harmonize their decision with the facts and law. Their service and search for justice *concludes* with their verdict.

Assuming that process to be true and applicable one hundred percent of the time (which is may or may not be, depending on based on the evidence, law, the witnesses' performance), closing arguments are key to assist jurors in making the correct choice based on where your trial story/strategy has already taken them. Closings are showing them the off-ramp—it is the time to explain all the turns and twists along the way. It's not the time to begin telling them why they are on the trip to begin with!

Thus, closing arguments are a critical time, and a last change to either change a mind or cement a commitment. Jurors on the fence about their decision can be swayed with a powerful closing argument. Jurors who are already committed—to a decision or even an indecision—can get assurance in their decision while listening to a persuasive closing. The jurors can be your allies and surrogates in the deliberation room. But, again, closing argument is not the time to reveal your story for the first time.

The two main things to focus on in closings are *organization* and *presentation*.

6.2 Argument vs. Discussion

Remember, *there is a difference between arguing and discussing*.

A discussion is merely kicking something around, "spitballing", exchanging ideas, and the like. "Maybe", "perhaps", and "it's possible" are discussion feeders. They have no place in your closing argument.

An argument is an engagement wherein opposing parties want the other to bend to their belief—while refusing to bend to the other. Arguing is an art by which you use terminology that analyzes and evaluates facts to draw conclusions.

Why did Mr. Defendant pull the trigger? Because he had five hundred thousand reasons to . . . all in the form of the insurance policy on his wife.

or

What does [fact] mean to this case? Think about it . . . its because [argument].

or

The defense wants you to believe that Ms. Witness is not credible, not believable. The defense wants you to completely disregard her testimony because she worked for Defendant Company, and has long-term relationships with the management. But she of all people should be believed. She should be believed because [argument].

Simply discussing the evidence is insufficient. It's not persuasive. It's boring. Use phrases that drive home the point as irrefutable.

Drawing a conclusion
In conclusion, . . .
One can easily conclude that . . .
Therefore, . . .
In summary, the evidence establishes that . . .
It seems clear that . . .
[Fact] tells us that . . .
[Fact] lets us know (or believe) that . . .
Connecting the element(s) to the conclusions shown by the facts/evidence
[Element] is shown by . . .
[Element] is indicated by . . .
[Element] is proven by . . .
[Element] is established by . . .
Terms driving to the conclusion
So . . .
Thus . . .
Therefore . . .
It can be concluded that . . .
Consequently . . .
Showing how evidence leads to a conclusion
[Fact] shows that . . .
[Fact] indicates that . . .

[Fact] proves that . . .
[Fact] entails . . .
[Fact] implies that . . .
[Fact] establishes that . . .

Use inductive and deductive reasoning to flesh out easy to follow arguments. Logic is your ally—especially in circumstantial evidence cases. Jurors will reject arguments that require too great a leap in logic.

Take a look at the following types of arguments. There are many ways to achieve maximum impact with your arguments. Different cases, different fact patterns, and your personal style will dictate which tool to use.

WAYS TO ARGUE	
Analyze	Break down the facts and explain how they relate to one another
Assess	Explain the importance or value of a fact or witness
Compare	Demonstrate the similarities or differences in facts
Contrast	Focus on the differences
Criticize	Point out the faults and limitations of the other side's argument(s)
Define	Explain the precise meaning of a fact or testimony (especially experts)
Describe	Give a review of a theme or topic from direct or cross

Evaluate	Explain the importance or value (or lack of) of a particular fact or facts
Examine	Explore and question the relevance of facts or opposing arguments
Explain	Show reasons for why or how something is as it is
Illustrate	Use examples from the facts and testimony to demonstrate why an element is proved (use items of evidence and demonstratives)
Justify or prove	Argue for a verdict by using supporting facts and logical reasoning
Review	Examine how facts relate to the overall story/case theory
Summarize	Outline the main points of testimony or an argument

6.3 Preparing for Closing Argument

Everyone prepares differently. Some say "write your closing first". That seems to tie one down and make it harder to incorporate what is actually said at trial. Trials are dynamic; trials have a basic process, but the myriad of facts and personalities of all involved can turn things on their head.

A better approach would be to have an outline of where you are going, and fill it in as the trial progresses.

A shell outline can be started almost as soon as you take the case and start discovery. You'll want to include:

- **Rivet phrase**

You want to lead off with this in closing, to cement what the jurors heard at the beginning of your opening.

Reiterate from opening the 2-3 sentence statement of the case, fine tuning with specific issues that case out at trial. Can preface with phrase like "as you all now know" or "as you all have now seen".

- **"Mini-stories"**

  - Chronology or witness-by-witness list

Whatever the best method for your story, tell "the big story" by arguing what the evidence means vis-a-vis the law.

- **Argument about how the law and facts merge to prove your case**

Know what the elements are, and have them listed and ready. You will gear all of your closing arguments to proving the elements.

- **Rebuttal of the other side's case**

Clearly set out your counterarguments and argue why the other side's case theory fails.

  - Counterarguments/defenses

A key part of arguing is rebutting and refuting the other side. You should know from your experience as well as the pleadings and cross examination exactly what the other side is going to argue. Be ready to deal with it before trial, and list as you go specifically how it was rebutted.

- **"The Ask"**

You know what you want the jury to do . . . why you want them to do it, and why they should do it is the focus of closing arguments. When you get to "the ask", have everything proved to justify it.

Saving important stuff from trial. As you go, keep a list of things you want to talk about in closing argument. Use your Center Sheet (Chapter 1.8) and your Cross Sheets (Chapter 5.4.2). Anything that is said, interesting "a-ha" moments, misspeaks that go uncorrected . . . anything of note. Write it down, who said it, where if occurred in the trial, and what was going on (i.e. during the defense case, during the testimony of the medical examiner, X happened).

Quotes, quotes, quotes. Take careful notes in the trial, and use as many direct quotes of witnesses to prove your points.

> You heard Ms. Defense Witness tell you, "Mr. Plaintiff did not start the fight." Those are her words . . . not mine, not Ms. Defense Attorney's words. Her own words. It's very important, members of the jury, for that fact to come from that side of the courtroom. The defendant's own witness' words convict him.

Evidence, demonstratives. Hold up your evidence. Touch it, make it real. Show it to the jury and argue why it is important. Remember, usually the jurors will have only seen the evidence for a fleeting moment at the time it was entered into evidence and published. You can use it very effectively to make the items of evidence additional uncontroverted witnesses.

Demonstrative can help you explain. Draw a map, make a list on a whiteboard. Visual learners in the jury will appreciate it.

6.4 Structure of Closing Statement

On a basic level, there are three main ways to organize the facts in a closing argument: by element, or (as we discussed about openings) chronological, or witness by witness.

Closing Organization Options
• Elemental
• Chronological
• Witness by witness

6.4.1   *Telling the Story Element by Element*

This is not the most desired way to tell a story, but it can work. With this method, you simply work your way through the jury instructions, arguing what evidence proves each of them. In a limited fact pattern and a short jury instruction, this may be a way to streamline your closing argument. But, it may not be the most compelling for a longer, more complicated case.

6.4.2   *Telling the Story Chronologically*

Certain cases have more complicated elements that have to be proved. Others have several elements, but only one is in dispute. In these situations, it may be advisable and best to simply set out what is agreed upon, mention it briefly, then focus on the only source of dispute.

As with witness-by-witness recounting (below), a chronological recitation of the entire case can be boring, uninspiring, and totally unhelpful. It is up to you to use active and engaging terms and phrases to tell their stories. *Make it compelling!*

6.4.3   *Telling the Story Witness by Witness (Perspective)*

Going witness by witness and simply recapping their testimony is boring and usually does nothing to help the jury. But, in situations where there are huge discrepancies between the witnesses' testimony, then the witness-by-witness approach may work best.

Even then, it may be best to be nested within the topical/elemental or chronological structure.

6.4.4   Get the Facts Right

No matter the organizational system you use, *get the facts right*. "Facts are stubborn things". First, you don't want to create cognitive dissonance between something you are saying (and perhaps relying on) and what the jurors remember. If you get the fact wrong, then you lose critical credibility. If the jurors have gotten the fact wrong, you did a poor job presenting it during the trial. *Be accurate.*

6.4.5   Admitting Bad Facts, Dealing with the Impact

In previous chapters we looked at the ever-present issue of bad facts. Running away from bad facts can be seen as admitting them. In law, just as in life, *flight is evidence of guilt*. With bad facts, you can ignore them or you can deal with them. If you ignore them, your opponent and the jurors have the opportunity to point out just how bad the facts are for you, as you didn't want to even talk about them. If you address them, you at least have the opportunity to put your interpretation on them and perhaps plant some seed of doubt about the bad facts.

- Compare them to the favorable facts you have (tip the scale)

- Point out how the source of the bad fact is not credible or has some bias

6.4.6 Rebutting the Other Side's Arguments

Always find a place in your closing to rebut the other side. Usually you can do it after your discussion of the law. Be direct and argue why the other side is wrong.

> Now, the defense has spent a great deal of time in this case attacking the credibility of the arresting officer's investigation. You've heard it over and over in this trial: "Officer, you jumped the gun arresting Ms. Defendant?", and "Officer, you didn't follow up on this lead" or "Officer, you didn't follow up on that lead?" and the officer's explanations.
>
> How many leads does the officer need, when he has a video of the defendant breaking into the jewelry store after hours? None, really. Remember, a picture is worth a thousand words.
>
> So the idea that somehow you, the jury, cannot render a verdict until the earth has been scoured for every possible clue and every conceivable scrap of evidence is simply unreasonable.

6.5 Using Jury Instructions, Verdict Forms

Perhaps the most important thing for closing, other than accuracy in the facts, is accurately using the law to your benefit. Wielding the law effectively makes for a powerful and persuasive closing argument.

6.5.1 Elements

Repeatedly in this book, we have discussed elements. You know where to find them. *Use them* when arguing to the jury. There is no other way—a closing without discussing the law is per se ineffective.

> *Members of the jury, in order to prove negligence, we have to prove four elements to you. Elements, as you know, are the individual specific facts that the law requires to be proved. Let me show you this chart, which has the elements. First, as you can see, we have to prove that a duty of care existed. Second. . .*

6.5.2   Defenses

The elements of defenses are in the jury instructions. Use them just as you would elements of the cause of action or crime charged.

6.5.3   Instructions on Witnesses

Standard instruction will contain instructions that provide guidance to jurors when sizing up the witnesses. Example:

> *Members of the jury, the law gives you some instructions on evaluating witnesses. Let's look at one—I have it enlarged for you here. It says, "[i]f you find that any witness has intentionally testified falsely as to any material fact, you may disregard that witness's entire testimony. Or you may disregard so much of it as you find was untruthful, and accept so much of it as you find to have been truthful and accurate. Think about Mr. Plaintiff's testimony and what the law tells you about such testimony. It means . . .*

Each jurisdiction has these instructions. They are a valuable way to encourage jurors to believe or disbelieve a witness, when coupled with the facts that show the witness to be uncredible.

6.5.4 *Instructions About Experts*

Instructions on experts are largely the same as for lay witnesses, but contain admonitions that the jury can believe or disbelieve whatever parts of the testimony it wants, and usually points the jurors to consider the expert's training, education, and experience. Be sure to review them and use expert jury instructions in your closing.

6.5.5 *Constitutional Issues*

There are constitutional rights that attend criminal trials. Jurors have to be reminded of them. For example, one is the very high burden of proof "beyond a reasonable doubt." Another is the right to remain silent and not testify and not have that silence held against the defendant. For example:

> *Members of the jury, there is a specific instruction I would like to point out to you. It is number 3.3., entitled "Defendant's Decision Not to Testify." It's in your instructions, and have a copy of it here. It says, "[a] defendant in a criminal case has a constitutional right not to testify. In arriving at your verdict, the law prohibits you from considering in any manner that the defendant did not testify." That means the government has the entire burden, and the law places no duty on a defendant to explain anything. That is a right every citizen of this country has. . .*

This instruction was taken from the Ninth Circuit's standard jury instructions, found at https://www.ce9.uscourts.gov/jury-instructions/node/336.

6.5.6   What Jurors Are NOT to Consider

Be sure to stay away from pleas that go into inflaming the jury (section 6.8.3) or asking them to ignore the law (section 6.8.4).

6.6 "The Ask": Plea for the Verdict

Your final words to the jury are critical. They cannot be a wimpy "thank you for your time, we hope you do the right thing" sort of thing. Your final words to the jury must stir them to action, and move them to do the thing you are asking for.

6.6.1   Challenge to Your Opponent

When making arguments and counterarguments, a tactic is to throw your opponent's case back in their face. Challenge you opponent to "get up and explain to you, member of the jury" whatever fact or defense they have been hanging on during the trial.

> *My time is almost up, member of the jury. Mr. Defense Attorney will have a chance to speak with you. Throughout the case, the defense has spent a great deal of time in this case attacking the credibility of the arresting officer's investigation. We have seen the video of the jewelry store break-in. Now, we concede that we do not have everything we could, like DNA or fingerprints. Perhaps the defense will explain how those shortfalls overcome the most powerful item of evidence there is: video of the defendant committing the crime. Perhaps Mr. Defense Attorney will talk about that video.*

6.6.2   Challenge to the Jury

Along those lines, challenge the jury (and indirectly challenge your opposing counsel.

Members of the jury, the defense spent a great deal of time in this case attacking the law enforcement officers and the "lack of evidence" in this case. When he gets up here, ask Mr. Defense Attorney to explain to you why you should ignore the video of his client. Ask him to explain how a lack of fingerprints should make you just ignore his client's face on that video. Ask him to explain how not having her DNA somewhere in the store overcomes a video where we—all of us, Mr. Defense Attorney included—can clearly see his client breaking into the store.

6.6.3   *Empowering the Jury*

This part is very simple and very important. Remind the jurors of their great power and their great responsibility.

Members of the jury, you have the power to right this wrong. You have the power to render a verdict that will find Mr. Defendant liable for the injuries to Ms. Plaintiff. And you have the power to make him pay, and ensure that she will receive the care she needs.

Members of the jury, you have the power to tell the government NO. You and only you can stop the government from obtaining a false conviction. Your verdict of not guilty will prevent a great injustice. We ask that you exercise that great power, tell the government no, and find Mr. Defendant not guilty.

This is different than inflaming the jury or asking for nullification. You are simply reminding the jurors that they have both an important duty to perform, and great power with which to do it.

6.6.4   *Examples of Closing Lines*

Here are some ways to close your summation:

With that, members of the jury, we leave the case in your hands. We know that you will make a wise and legal decision. We are confident that you will find in favor of my client, Mr. Plaintiff. Find Mr. Defendant liable.

Your attention to this case is very much appreciated. The work you have done has one part left—that is, to confirm with each other and render a verdict. Your last duty is the most important of this whole trial. Find Mr. Defendant not guilty.

Members of the jury, as I conclude my argument, I am reminded of one thing. I'd like to share that with you. Before me is an incredibly powerful group of people. They have the power to right a wrong. They have the power to make Ms. Plaintiff whole again. We know that you will use your power as the facts of this case suggest— that Mr. Defendant is liable.

Develop a strong parting statement that lets the jury know that they can changes lives, that empowers them to act, and gives them a call to action.

6.7 Delivering the Closing Argument

6.7.1   *Style and Storytelling (the "Arc")*

Trial lawyers are story tellers. Our whole existence in the courtroom is to tell our clients' story.

When using the chronological method of telling the story, think about the overall story—the story arc. A classic story arc is (1) we meet the hero, (2) something bad happens to the hero, (3) the hero goes on a journey to solve his or her dilemma, (4) there are bad guys along the way, and usually a guide that helps the hero, and (5) the dilemma is resolved and the hero is redeemed.

In trials, you can use that same story arc to tell you client's story. In the slip and fall example from Chapter 4, you (1) meet Paula Plaintiff and talk about her life-long love of shopping at GroceryCo, (2) Paula slip and falls and is severely injured, (3) you work though GroceryCo's safety protocols and discuss its misting system and how/why it failed, (4) you attribute fault to the "bad guys" (i.e. the employees who were not doing their job and could have prevented her accident and injury) and hail the "good guys" (the doctors that patched her up and the experts who can explain why this could have been prevented), and (5) "The Ask" is the redemption for Paula. The best part about this is that the jurors become the "guide" (like Gandolf or Obi-Wan Kenobi) who can assist in the final scene—the rendering of a verdict in Paula's favor!

6.7.2 *Linking to Common Emotions, Feelings, Etc.*

Remember, no one wants to listen to a boring presentation. I am never madder at myself in court than when I am presenting, and a judge or juror yawns—or worse, starts to nod off. I don't blame them, I blame myself. It is my job to keep them spellbound and on the edge of their seat, and I fail when they are lulled into boredom.

There are many things you can do to avoid jurors' daydreaming, and have them laser in on you and your client's story.

Using moralities, emotions, etc. As with the rest of the trial, tapping into common morals, emotions, mores, and the like is key to connecting the jury to your cause in a deep way.

- It's not OK to steal
- Lying in court is never acceptable

- Our system of justice depends on . . .

- Honoring one's commitments

In our slip and fall case, one very common theme is looking out for our brothers and sisters. Another is accountability.

Members of the jury, we all have duties every day. At home, washing the dishes or taking out the trash. We have duties at work, like completing TPS reports everyday. But we have duties one to another. Not only does common decency require that, but so does the law.

or

Everyone makes mistakes. They happen. Some are unavoidable. Others are completely avoidable with just a little care taken. Either way, with a mistake comes accountability. Everyone must account for their mistakes. GroceryCo is no different. It must account for what it let happen to Paula Plaintiff.

Likability. Be direct, be open, be clear and concise. Don't waste people's time. Make every effort to be heard and say things plainly. Don't come across as too "lawyerly."

You hear these things in trial advocacy classes and CLEs all over the county. Every trial attorney and advocacy professor has their own advice to impart on how to behave in front of a jury. All of it can be taken for something, whether as a "to" or as a "not to."

It all comes down to this—does the jury like you? They don't have to love you to death, and to want to strike up a friendship after the trial and get together for monthly dinners. But, they also can't not want you to shut up and sit down. Somewhere in the middle is *likability*.

Liking removes the static and noise that prevents consideration of the matter. If you don't like someone, it is going to be difficult to listen objectively to that person. If you like someone, you can listen to what they are saying and decide on the content whether you agree with the premise. But "shooting the messenger" in trials is fatal, as you never even get the chance to have the jurors consider your arguments.

What makes someone likable? What makes *you* likable? What do you like to hear when listening to someone? What turns you off to a speaker? Identify that and work it in to your presentation.

Word selection. Words matter, and how you say things matters. It is said that you should always gear public comments to a third-grade level, so everyone can understand you. How sad, that we are told to "dumb down" our words and phrases.

Use the thesaurus to come up with different words for certain actions or concepts. "Duty" can also be described as responsibility, obligation, or burden. "Breach" can also be described as a break or violation.

6.7.3   *Above All Else, Persuade*

Persuasion is *convincing.* It bears stating again, if you have waited until closing arguments to set forth your case theory, then you have waited too long and there may not even being a point in standing to address the jurors.

But if you have been clear all along, with your case theory and telling the story with themes and topics, and your target facts are obvious, you have already won some of the jurors—maybe all of them. Convincing them to do the right thing will be easy.

In close cases, carefully linking up your facts to the law, and showing the jurors that there is no other way to conclude, will get those who may be on the fence to find in your favor.

Be sincere, be accurate, be complete. Use the law. Show them the way.

6.7.4 *Practicing, Rehearsing*

Cicero said (and Aristotle agreed) that delivery was the most important part of the art of persuasion. As with the performing arts and sports, "practice makes perfect."

 Don't practice in front of the mirror. The mirror will lie to you.

Video, not mirror. The mirror will lie to you. The mirror will not do you any favors, and will lie in your face. The video is like your mother and will tell you the truth whether you want to hear it or not.

Using any number of readily-available video recording devices, record you performance. Then wait a day. Watch it. How bad is it? Are you asking yourself, "Do I really sound like that? What am I doing with my hands? *Why can't I stay still?*"

Take notes, and think about why you do not like what you see and hear. Re-record . . . repeat the evaluation. . . re-record . . . repeat the evaluation. Then show it to your friends or family all three, and which works best. Ask them why, and what about your delivery do they like or don't like. Adjust accordingly. Some things will be universally loved . . . some of what you do no one will like. Get rid of it before the jury sees it!

 Memorize the facts. Don't rely on your notes as a crutch.

Memorizing. Jurors are probably largely unimpressed with attorneys that are able to memorize quickly their names and call them by name in *voir dire*. It almost comes off as a parlor trick,

There are several things that you should not do, and some that you absolutely should not do in a closing argument. Committing these "fouls" and result in an irreparable loss of credibility. And, if we know anything from this book, when you lose your credibility, you will likely lose your case.

6.8.1   *Misstating the Facts (Facts Not in Evidence)*

Be careful to get the facts correct. Make sure if you are going to attribute an exact quote to a witness, that you quote it *exactly*. Your credibility can crash and burn if you try to tell the jurors they saw or heard something that they clearly did not.

6.8.2   *Misstating the Law*

Be absolutely sure you cover the elements by accurately explaining them to the jury. Be sure to argue the correct burden of proof. Not only is this objectionable, but you will lose serious credibility with the jurors if your opponents objects and the judge corrects you.

6.8.3   *Inflaming the Jury*

It is improper to improperly use passion and prejudice to sway a jury to do something it would not otherwise do. You cannot inflame the juror to try to get him or her to ignore the facts or the law, or any reasonable arguments, and simply decide out of blind emotion. Avoid references to current events, such as highly-publicized school or officer-related shootings. Avoid references to the Bible, as to not have religious beliefs trump the duty to follow the law. Avoid asking the jury to "send a message" to the community—that is not their job.

Avoid infusing racial, gender, or cultural references, stereotypes, or prejudices into your arguments. Cases are decided on facts and law, and not on a party's race or other group membership.

All of this is unethical, as to do so is to ask the jury to ignore the law.

6.8.4   *Suggesting Jury Nullification*

Jury nullification is the idea that a jury, as representatives of the community, can convict or acquit as they see fit. Jury nullification, or a "jury pardon", actually happens when a jury, based on its own concept and feelings about what is justice, ignores the law and facts and acquits a criminal defendant. This is when the evidence clearly points to conviction, and yet they acquit anyway. The idea is that a jury is empowered to not follow the law if they see fit to do so.

You must understand that American jurisprudence recognizes the jury's power to engage in jury nullification. However, jurisdictions and jurisprudence is divided on whether *you* can ask them to ignore the law. For example, the Florida Supreme Court recognized that a jury pardon is in fact a jury's right, and may be motivated by lenience or mercy. *Sanders v. Florida*, 946 So. 2d 953 (Fla. 2006). However, the court went on to hold that such right is one without legal foundation and requires the jurors to ignore its oath and the court's instructions to follow the law. Attorneys cannot ethically ask jurors to ignore the law or their oaths to do their duty under the law. It is best to avoid overtly asking for a jury nullification. If you think of attempting it, make sure your research is perfect or your malpractice insurance premium paid up.

6.8.5   *Personal Attacks on Witnesses or Counsel*

Avoid disparaging the witnesses or opposing counsel. Facts about witnesses are just facts—you can argue what those facts should tell the jury. What you cannot do is call the witness some disparaging name. A liar is a liar, and if the facts show that he or she lied, then you are safe to point that out. But if the facts are at issue, be careful about going too far in name-calling.

The same goes for opposing counsel. It is one thing to say, "Mr. Plaintiff's Attorney argues that X. Members of the jury, consider Y. Which is the more logical conclusion?" It is entirely another to say, "Mr. Plaintiff's Attorney is trying to trick you, and confuse you." Not appropriate. Stick to the facts and make counter-arguments based on logic and reasoning.

6.8.6 *Personal Opinions*

Some trial attorneys get emotional and very involved in their cases. Sometimes passions run high and attorneys get carried away. What you think of the case personally is of no import to the jury or its decision. You can argue, you cannot give your personal opinions. Framing an argument should be based solely on the facts and the law.

Avoid trying to bolster your case by referring to irrelevant matters. Don't vouch for a witness by giving your own opinion as to credibility—simply stick to pointing out the important facts about the witness, and ask the jury to draw their own logical conclusion.

6.8.7 *Conceding Something Your Client Has Not Agreed Upon*

There will be times that you have to concede certain things. Sometimes for credibility's sake, sometimes because the facts simply do not conclude anything differently. Your client is ultimately the final decision maker in most things. Anything that may come back later on a claim on ineffective counsel or malpractice must be discussed fully with the client in advance. Be sure to note your file. For example, when conceding guilt to a lesser charge, and asking the jury to convict not "as charged" but to a lesser included offense, get the client's consent beforehand (preferably in writing). Similarly, when conceding any amount of liability requires the client's consent (again, preferable in writing).

6.9 Example of Closing Argument

Below is a mock closing argument for the plaintiff's side in the case of *Paula Plaintiff v. GroceryCo*, from the fact pattern in section 4.3.

The comments on the left point out aspects of the closing that have been emphasized in this chapter. This is a basic, straightforward closing argument that powerfully presents Ms. Plaintiff's story.

Remember, everyone's style is different . . . *find your own voice as an advocate.*

RIVET PHRASE OPENING	Safety doesn't happen by accident.
2-3 sentences that summarize the case	GroceryCo failed Ms. Plaintiff. GroceryCo and its employees knew that safety doesn't happen by accident. They researched it . . . they planned for it . . . they all knew what they had to do to make the store safe. Yet when Ms. Plaintiff needed them most, they failed in their duty.
	That failure is negligence. And negligence is why we are here.
MINI-STORIES	June 15 of last year changed Paula Plaintiff's life. She didn't ask for the change. She didn't anticipate

In this case, to highlight the employees' negligence, the mini-stories will be chronologically. This not only helps the jury recall the order of events, but it builds tension as the story progresses to the incident. And because GroceryCo planned to avoid this accident, I can extend the timeline back for maximum impact.

the change. She didn't even see the catastrophe coming.

But GroceryCo did. They saw it coming. In fact, this story began long, long ago.

You all know that they saw it coming. GroceryCo's manager testified about their foresight when he told you about GroceryCo's safety goals. You have copies of their store operating manual and employee training manual in evidence. That they knew what could happen to Ms. Plaintiff is in writing. Let's look at parts of those manuals, on the screens in front of you. Here are Plaintiff's Exhibits 1 and 2:

[READS PERTINENT PARTS OF MANUAL, PERTAINING TO OPERATION OF THE MISTERS]

Since 1930 when it was founded, GroceryCo has proclaimed to both its customers and its staff that it's "safety first" in their stores. The manager received safety training, and each of the employees on duty received safety training. Again, looking at the monitors, here are Plaintiff's Exhibit 15 and Composite Exhibit 16 A-C. They are the manager's safety training

Using exhibits from trial for emphasis

	certificate, dated [YEAR−2], Employee 1's safety training certificate, dated [YEAR−1], Employee 2's safety training certificate, dated [YEAR−1], and Employee 3's safety training certificate, dated [MONTHS−9]. And remember what the manager
Using a direct quote from a witness	told you: "we preach safety to our employees every day."
	GroceryCo knows the public will be coming in for its self-proclaimed "world's greatest produce section." Each of the employees testified that the produce section is to be treated like gold, like the
Biblical allusion	promised land. And GroceryCo goes to great lengths to ensure that its vegetables and fruits are not only fresh but beautifully displayed.
Personifying the machine, to make it sinister to create tension	That's where the culprit-the misting system-comes in.
	Days before Ms. Plaintiff's June 15 trip, or should I say "slip", danger was already lurking. The backup for the misting system was offline. Remember Plaintiff's Exhibit 9?
Use of undisputable evidence from an exhibit	Here it is on the overhead: this is the computer printout of the misting system and its backup,
Rivet phrase again	showing that it was off since June 12. Safety doesn't happen by

	accident, yet GroceryCo did not follow its own safety guidelines in conducting a daily check of system functionality. Had the employees simply done their jobs, they would have caught this problem. Recall the technician from the company that designed and installed the system. Remember her testimony that simply looking at the display on the unit would have instantly brought the problem to one's attention: "a child could have seen that it was off."
Use of a direct quote from a witness	
Using witnesses' equivocating to show their consciousness of guilt	On Ms. Plaintiff's fateful day, June 15, Employees 1, 2, and 3 were at work. It was over the previous night that the produce misting system had reset itself to initial settings. All three employees told you from that witness stand right there that they believed, or thought, or "kinda remembered" looking at the system. But not one of them could be sure; they were all evasive. But you all know that they did not look at it; had they done their jobs on even a basic level, the misting system's malfunction would have been noticed. Safety doesn't happen by accident.

Using the machine "doing its job" to highlight that (1) it only does what it is told to by humans, and (2) the danger was imminent (creating tension and suspense)	So, in the hours before Ms. Plaintiff's morning visit, the misting system waited to turn on, not registering that it was about to do the wrong thing at the wrong time. The system was counting down to do its job, to spray water at the time its mechanical brain told it to, at 7:55am. Problem is, as we know from the procedure manual, it was supposed to be 4:55am. Minutes before Ms. Plaintiff arrived, the misting system did what its programming told it to do, and blasted out water that coated the floor. The floor where Ms. Plaintiff would shortly walk, blissfully and unwittingly looking at the beautiful fruit, not contemplating what awaited her.
Using the ultimate evidence—the accident itself, which creates sympathy with the jurors	Plaintiff's Exhibit 3, folks. The system report showing that the mister operated at 7:55am, spraying the tomato section. And then [video clip played], Plaintiff's Exhibit 1 . . . Paula Plaintiff slipping, her arms flailing, her head slamming into the tomato display case, and her lying unconscious.
Rivet phrase again	Safety doesn't happen by accident. Where were the employees? We know they did not hear the usual

Again, using the machine to show that it needed the employees to function correctly	"hey, I see there is nobody here, so I am going to water the fruits and veggies" signal from the system. We know why: it had reset and none of them bothered to notice. But the store was open. Open for business. Open for customers. Where were Employees 1, 2, and 3 when Mr. Witness fell just a minute before Ms. Plaintiff [plays video clip]. This is Plaintiff's Exhibit 4, showing Mr. Witness falling and, fortunately, getting up to go find an employee. Where were they? Where were they ultimately found?
Using the metaphor "AWOL" which has a terrible connotation	Away from their posts. AWOL, absent without leave, as the military calls it. In a totally different section of the store looking at some video they all thought was so funny [plays video clip]. Here they are, in Plaintiff's Exhibit 12, yukking it up while
A little vernacular to paint the employees as stooges	customers walk by, and Ms. Plaintiff was lying unconscious under the apples.
	That's the story. A story of negligence of the highest order. A story of how simple safety precautions could have prevented this terrible injury to Ms. Plaintiff.
Rivet phrase, with a twist	Safety doesn't happen by accident,

	and accidents don't happen with safety.
THE LAW	Let us now turn to the law. The law that controls this case. The law that you all must now apply in order to be able to hold GroceryCo liable for Ms. Plaintiff's injuries and suffering. As Judge Sestak mentioned to you all at the beginning of the trial, there are instructions on the law that will aid you. Let's look at those now, if you all will, on the monitors before you.
Critical to the jurors' deliberations is the law—what must be proved. Using the actual JIs on the courtroom projector so jurors can easily follow	
Here, we make it easy for them by first listing, then arguing, then summarizing in a paragraph.	For GroceryCo to be liable for Ms. Plaintiff's injuries, the following elements must be proved to you:
	First, that a duty of care existed.
	Second, a breach of that duty of care.
	Third, proximate damages caused by that breach.
	Fourth, damages caused by the breach of the duty of care.

	Let's take those one by one, and look at the facts that support each of those elements.
No need to rehash all the testimony; rather, a succinct argument as what facts prove each element	First and foremost. A duty of care existed. GroceryCo is open to the public. It exists for the sole purpose of people coming in their stores. It seeks them out by advertising on TV, the internet, social media, and sending flyers and coupons to people's homes.
Moral connections of duty, community, neighbors, etc.	Our system of law, and our obligations one to another, create a duty to be sure that those who come to our businesses can do so safely. It doesn't take a whole lot of legal knowledge to understand why that is . . . what society would we be in, if it were that to step into a store was to do so at your own risk? No, to the contrary. The law protects citizen shoppers by requiring stores such as GroceryCo to keep their establishments reasonably safe.
Clear, concise argument	So, it should go without saying that a duty of care existed each and every day that GroceryCo invited shoppers onto its floors. A duty that they would be safe. A duty that its employees would do their safety-related jobs. A duty that

Reminder that defendant knew of the duty	employees would be vigilant over the shoppers. So, yes, a duty of care existed—and GroceryCo acknowledged and embraced that duty by having internal policies and procedures to execute that duty and for its customers to be safe. GroceryCo knows that safety does
Rivet phrase again	not happen by accident.
Linking up the mindless machine to the duties of the humans to operate it	Second. Did GroceryCo breach that duty of care? Yes, without question. The mister should not have been running. That's not the mister's fault-it's just a machine. It was the humans, the employees, who didn't do their duty and check it out. The employees should have seen that the mister ran, and that the floor was wet. Had they been where they were supposed to be, in the produce section, they would have. They are trained as a part of their duty to constantly be checking for water on the floor. They failed in that duty, by being
Alluding to what some consider stealing (moral link to jurors)	AWOL and nowhere to be found . . . goofing off on company time.
Explaining in an easy-to-understand alternate way	The third element is that of "proximate cause", in other words, that the damages Ms. Plaintiff incurred were directly caused by GroceryCo's lack of care. To put it

Direct argument, using "we" to create an unspoken link/bond between Ms. Plaintiff and the jurors	another way, her damages had to have been linked to the breach of duty. For example, that she wasn't hurt by being pushed down by another shopper. We are assured that Ms. Plaintiff's injuries were caused by GroceryCo. She was a healthy person and had no trouble walking. We know her injuries happened while she was in a GroceryCo store, in their "world-famous" produce section. We know that Mr. Witness, another perfectly healthy person, slipped and fell just minutes before Ms. Plaintiff did. We know that the misting system timers were off, and that they were running when they should not have been, and that the floors were wet. We saw with our own eyes the GroceryCo surveillance videos, showing Ms. Plaintiff minding her business, then slipping and bashing her head. We know that the doctors and experts can directly attribute her injury and life-long disabilities to that fall. There is no question about element three.
"Bashing" is stronger than "hitting"	
No sugar-coating: this is about money, and this	Finally, damages. Why Ms. Plaintiff had to file this lawsuit against GroceryCo. You all heard testimony from several experts who tell you

sets up the argument below	that it will take a lot of money to care for Ms. Plaintiff for the rest of her life. Recall the actuary, who told you about Ms. Plaintiff's life expectancy, and that she could easily live another 50 years. Remember the economist, who calculated the cost of living over 50 years, and probably scared everyone in this courtroom with her predictions about inflation. Remember the medical financial expert, who told you about the costs associated with long-term care for people like Ms. Plaintiff, people who require constant care and have no chance of real employment. It will cost millions of
Teasing the amount so there is no sticker-shock later in "The Ask"	dollars for Ms. Plaintiff to have basic everyday daily-life care. That doesn't even get into her quality of living. But I will come back to damages in just a bit.
Recap of the law	That, members of the jury, is the law and elements. GroceryCo owed Ms. Plaintiff a duty that she could safely shop in their store. GroceryCo's and its employees breached that duty when they let its water misting system spray water everywhere at the worst possible time. They breached their duty when no one was in place to

	clean it up and warn customers to be careful. Ms. Plaintiff was the victim of the negligence, and nothing other than GroceryCo's negligence caused her to be hurt. The damages she received, still has, and forever will have, are the product GroceryCo's gave her.
A little play on words	
REBUTTAL	GroceryCo has made some curious points throughout the trial. During cross examinations, there were lots of questions about fault. Questions
Reminding jurors of the "bad act" of victim blaming	about looking out for one's self. Questions about what customers should be expected to do in a store. It seems as if GroceryCo is trying to blame this on Ms. Plaintiff, so that they can argue
Verbiage to say, "I can't believe this is their argument!"	that there is no proof of elements two and three. Is GroceryCo trying to claim there was no breach of their duty, and that the cause of Ms. Plaintiff's damages was, well, Ms. Plaintiff herself?
	Think carefully about those arguments. Look at the surveillance video and recall the testimony of the witnesses. Apply
Invoking common sense, which they all have	your common sense, your experience, and your intelligence. When Mr. Opposing Counsel comes up to address you with his closing

Challenging opposing counsel, which forces him to answer (which he cannot)	argument, ask him to explain why no one had seen that the backup system was offline. Ask him to explain to give you a good, and I mean a really good, reason that no one had noticed that mister ran at the worst possible time and that the floors were wet. Ask him to justify why Employees 1, 2, and 3 were goofing off when they should have been in the produce section. Make him explain to you why any of this is the fault of Paula Plaintiff.
"THE ASK" Now about the money. . .	As I conclude my time with you, I want to return to the issue of damages. Money. Funds owed to Ms. Plaintiff to make her whole. She'll never be physically whole, but GroceryCo can certainly provide enough to make her life livable.
Rivet phrase again, moving into a moral/ethical argument all the jurors will understand	Safety does not happen by accident. Safety is a duty we all owe one to another. Accidents happen, yes, but accidents are preventable by doing one's duty. Members of the jury, we all have duties every day. At home, washing the dishes or taking out the trash. We have duties at work, like completing TPS reports every day. But we also have duties one to

	another. Not only does common decency require that, but so does the law.
Reminding the jurors that this was an egregious breach of duty	GroceryCo knew that. They knew it, they planned for it, and when it came to Ms. Plaintiff, they failed. Despite all the time and effort to write their manuals and train their employees, and "preach safety", they failed in the worst way. GroceryCo is a billion-dollar company. They will go on, keep selling their produce, keep opening more and more stores, and keep raking in the money and piling up the profit.
Invoking sympathy for Ms. Plaintiff without overdoing it and for good purpose	But Ms. Plaintiff's life is permanently marred. She will have a life, yes. But her life will be far from normal, far from happy, and she will struggle greatly.
Using a demonstrative (summary of expenses, etc.)	Numbers don't lie. Let's look at this summary on the video monitors. You can see the medical bills from the time of the accident until now. You can see what the experts say the medical bills will continue to be through her life. Ms. Plaintiff will require at least $10 million dollars for basic care the rest of her life. Her mother and father, who care for her now, will

Reminding jurors of how hard her life is going to be	not be here forever. One day, Ms. Plaintiff will rely on a trust fund and a trustee to see that she has her basic needs met. She might be able to work, but we know that her injuries will only let her do the most menial of jobs. The most menial of jobs come with the most menial of pay. Whatever she earns will not even begin to support her.
The actual figure	An award of $10 million dollars from the billion-dollar company that hurt her will support her. Please, hold GroceryCo responsible and award her that amount. It may seem like a lot, but remember we are talking about a life forever altered.
Punitive damage argument (perhaps this is not a punitive damages case, but the argument is here for example purposes)	Safety does not happen by accident. GroceryCo ignored that and two people succumbed to their negligence that day. One was fortunate enough to be fine. The other [gesturing to Ms. Plaintiff] was not. GroceryCo must never, ever forget the lesson that Ms. Plaintiff's plight teaches. Safety does not happen by accident. They must pay a civil price for ignoring that, even once, and so callously allowing a quote-unquote valued customer to be severely injured. This just has the power to punish

	their cavalier and lackadaisical attitude about the public's safety. Punitive damages in an equal amount of $10 million is more than appropriate in this case.
The final push . . .	Members of the jury, as I conclude my argument, I am reminded of one thing. I'd like to share that with you.
. . . empowering the jury to do the right thing	Before me is an incredibly powerful group of people. They have the power to right a wrong. They have the power to make Ms. Plaintiff whole again. They have the power to ensure that she does not suffer and struggle for the rest of her life because GroceryCo cast aside its duty of care. We know that you will use your power as the facts of this case suggest-that GroceryCo is liable, and Ms. Plaintiff should be awarded $20 million for what
Rivet phrase one last time, for consistency	GroceryCo let happen to her. Safety doesn't happen by accident. Thank you.

6.10   Checklists

6.10.1 Closing Checklist (Elements, Witnesses, Etc.)

	"Rivet statement" incorporated into beginning
	Jury instructions ready to show and argue to jury (enlargements, overheads)
	Demonstratives ready to show and argue to jury
	Presentation tools ready (easels, pointers, markers, or electronic equipment) and working
	Practiced and prepared in order to meet any court-imposed time limit
	Story ready (chrono or by witness)
	Cross Sheets ready to argue counterpoints or impeachments
	"The Ask" clear, concise, and supported by arguments

6.10.2 Basic Structure: Chrono

Use as many mini-stories as you need to tell the story (you are not limited to three, this is just an checklist template).

	"Rivet statement" incorporated into beginning
	2-3 sentence re-introduction of the case (with added specifics from trial)
	Mini-story 1:
	Mini-story 2:
	Mini-story 3:
	Argue the law (how elements proved, by what witness or item of evidence

Rebut the other side's case with arguments as to why their case theory is wrong, or their witnesses/evidence should not be believed
"The Ask"

6.10.3 Basic Structure: By Witness

Use as many witnesses as you need to tell the story (you are not limited to three, this is just a checklist template).

"Rivet statement" incorporated into beginning
2-3 sentence re-introduction of the case (with added specifics from trial)
Witness 1:
Witness 2:
Witness 3:
Argue the law (how elements proved, by what witness or item of evidence
Rebut the other side's case with arguments as to why their case theory is wrong, or their witnesses/evidence should not be believed
"The Ask"

6.10.4 Ethical Rules for Closings

Don't misstate the facts.

Don't misstate the law.

Don't inflame the jury.

Don't ask for a jury pardon unless the law permits it.

Don't personally attack a witness or opponent.

Don't give personal opinions.

Don't concede something unless your client consents.

6.10.5 *"Important Stuff" Working Checklist*

	Center sheet updated through trial
	Pre- and in-trial rulings clearly noted (so you know what you can and cannot talk about)
	List of specific quotes attributed to witnesses (name, day/part) of trial, subject/context, EXACT words)
	Notes on witness behavior (name, day/part of trial, subject, what observed)
	"Ah-ha" or "gotcha" moments (when, who said it, what happened)
	Important impeachments noted
	Any diagrams that you had a witness mark are preserved and ready for closing
	Notes on anything important that popped up in trial

CHAPTER 7

Evidence and Objections

OBJECTIVES: Knowing "the code" cannot be more important. Understanding evidence is critical to success in the courtroom. In this chapter, we are going to cover the most important basics of:

- Authentication of evidence

- Evidentiary objections to control the substance, the witness, and opposing counsel

- When to make objections

- The proper technique for making objections

- Preserving the record if overruled

7.1 Importance of Knowing "the Code"

Every trial attorney with any modicum of skill knows to anticipate objections. Anticipating and preparing for objections is a simple matter of knowing the facts and knowing the Evidence Code.

Numerous sources for evidentiary objections are readily available, so not knowing the code and the many objections is inexcusable. That, and the fact that any trial lawyer has by definition taken evidence in the accredited law school that led to his or her admission to the state bar. Simply stated, ignorance is not an excuse. It is malpractice.

In preparing for trial, if you have done your factual analysis and prepared your direct examination questions or Cross Sheets, it is not hard to anticipate the objections you will draw and the ones you will make. Hearsay is obvious and usually has a corresponding rule for or against. Relevance can be a tougher sell—be ready with argument and case law. And so on.

If you know you will draw an objection, you must first ask yourself if you can ethically ask the question in good faith. Is there a hearsay exception? Is the evidence self-authenticating? Then have the rule number noted and argument ready for the bench conference.

If you know you can make an objection, weigh whether to even make it, and if you have to, have the rule and case law ready to back your argument.

Motions *in limine* are an excellent way to control the admission of evidence (see Chapter 1). The good part of motions *in limine* are that they are outside the fast pace of the trial, and can get more time and attention from the judge. The con of motions *in limine* is that (1) you tip your hand to objections that may otherwise catch your opponent unawares, and (2) the judge may not have enough context in the pretrial setting to be able to render a ruling—any may defer until the actual testimony is happening. Even then, you have cued the court in on a potential problem he or she will have to address later.

"Bench briefs" are short memos on the topic. They are usually limited to a page or page and a half, and has the case law attached. In the case law copies, highlight the pertinent text in both the court's and opposing counsel's copies. The bench brief is very handy for arguing complicated or very important issues. Some judges will even take a short break to go in chambers and read the bench briefs—or give them to a clerk to quickly confirm the research. Some even consult other judges. Not only that, but having taken the time to not only identify the issue, but also to brief it, looks polished and professional.

Remember, too, that a *contemporaneous objection* is required to preserve any appellate review—even if a pretrial motion is filed and denied, an objection has to be made in real time when the objectionable evidence or testimony is presented.

Follow this checklist when analyzing your facts for admissibility:

	Is this piece of evidence or testimony objectionable?	*Spoken words always get a hearsay analysis. . . everything has to pass 403 muster. . . analyze everything, ESPECIALLY your target facts*
	If so, what is the objection?	*Hearsay? Best evidence? Privilege? Identify the objections to the testimony/item of evidence.*
	Is this piece of evidence or testimony critical and material?	*Ultimate issue fact? Impeachment fact? Why do you need this evidence before the jury?*

	Is the issue clear on its fact, such that can be argued on the face of the rule?	*If it is obviously inadmissible, consider a motion in limine*
	If the issue so complicated that it requires case law authority in order to properly argue it?	*Complicated issues need argument time, so consider a motion in limine well before trial; also prepare a "Bench Brief" on the issue*
	Should a motion *in limine* be filed?	*Think strategically—can you easily win the issue in trial? Do you think your opponent will miss the objection? Think it through.*
	Should a bench brief be prepared?	*Know your issue . . . know your judge!*
	What is the proper legal objection to be contemporaneously made in trial?	*Have the proper objection ready and TIMELY make it in the proper manner*

7.1.1   *Designing Non-Objectionable Questions*

As we know, one of the best ways to make a smooth, zen-like examination is to design (and deliver) questions and question sets that are not objectionable.

Analyze the facts. Then ask yourself, "if I were my opponent, what would I argue is objectionable about this fact?" Think about whether it is relevant, whether it is hearsay, is there a better source of "best evidence" . . . is it cumulative, or does any other evidentiary rule apply that could impact the admissibility of this fact? Is it an opinion, or call for an opinion?

The best practice is for evidentiary issues to be dealt with and resolved before trial starts—long before the propounding of questions to the witness. It is generally not wise having the issues identified and researched prior to trial. In the event it has to wait for trial, be ready with arguments to the evidence code citation and have supporting case law.

Apply the law (the evidence code). When looking at themes and topics, think "BARHOP". You may deduce that this is a version of the old law school mnemonic "BARPH" (<u>B</u>est evidence, <u>A</u>uthentic, <u>R</u>elevant, <u>P</u>rivilege, <u>H</u>earsay), which has been modernized here and modified to reflect the most often lodged objections over evidence to the least. However you look at it, this is the only way to prepare questions—while keeping in mind the rest of the evidence code, as well as any statutory provisions that may apply.

7.1.2 "HOP the BAR"

Or, "BARHOP" (depending on if you're more likely to remember Thumper or a favorite watering hole). Use the following process chart to plot out each fact. In doing so, if you can answer "yes" to each question, then the fact is admissible. This process can be used to deal with themes (broad), topics (narrower), and target facts.

Evidentiary concern	Pass?	Why?	Admissible under code provision?
<u>B</u>est evidence	Y/N	Argument:	
<u>A</u>uthentic	Y/N	Argument:	
<u>R</u>elevant	Y/N	Argument:	
Not <u>h</u>earsay (or exception applies)	Y/N	Argument:	
Not <u>o</u>pinion	Y/N	Argument:	

Not privileged	Y/N	Argument:	
ADMISSIBLE			✔

It is important to note that this analysis can be applied by any advocate during any part of the trial—if in trouble, use your "advocacy muscle memory" and stick to the basics.

Again, that there is always an opportunity to test the admissibility of your questions (at least your topics and themes) thought motions *in limine*.

7.2 Whether and When to Object

7.2.1   *Should I Object?*

To object or not to object? That is the question! It's accurate to say some things are just too trivial to matter. For instance, does that hearsay statement really hurt your case? Do you want it to come into evidence because it helps your case? Does it matter?

If you hear something that is objectionable, think about whether to object or to let it in—but have a valid reason for not fighting the objectionable testimony or tangible evidence. Perhaps you want to set up an impeachment on cross, or perhaps the objectionable evidence *helps* your case. But whatever it is, do not simply miss your opportunity to object. Remember, you know your themes, topics, and target facts long before trial starts. You have plenty of time to anticipate the direct questions and what the other side may try to get before the jury. So, be wise and be vigilant.

Some attorneys think that objecting will aggravate the jury, and make the attorney look bad. Courts around the country regularly instruct the jury that it is the job of the attorneys to make objections, and to not hold that against the attorneys. For instance:

(1)   There is one more general subject that I want to talk to you about before I begin explaining the elements of the crime charged.

(2)   The lawyers for both sides objected to some of the things that were said or done during the trial. Do not hold that against either side. The lawyers have a duty to object whenever they think that something is not permitted by the rules of evidence. Those rules are designed to make sure that both sides receive a fair trial.

(3)   And do not interpret my rulings on their objections as any indication of how I think the case should be decided. My rulings were based on the rules of evidence, not on how I feel about the case. Remember that your decision must be based only on the evidence that you saw and heard here in court.

United Stated District Court for the Sixth Circuit Pattern Criminal Jury Instructions 1.09 (Lawyers' Objections).

There are rules that control what can be received into evidence. When a lawyer asks a question or offers an exhibit into evidence, and a lawyer on the other side thinks that it is not permitted by the rules of evidence, that lawyer may object. This simply means that the lawyer is requesting that I make a decision on a particular rule of evidence. You should not be influenced by the fact that an objection is made. Objections to questions are not evidence. Lawyers have an obligation to their clients to make objections when they believe that evidence being offered is improper under the rules of evidence.

United States District Court for the District of Rhode Island, Model Civil Jury Instructions for the District Courts of the Third Circuit 1.5 (Preliminary Instructions—Evidence).

Sometimes the attorneys will disagree about the rules for trial procedure when a question is asked of a witness. When that happens, one of the lawyers may make what is called an "objection." The rules for a trial can be complicated, and there are many reasons for attorneys to object. You should simply wait for me to decide how to proceed. If I say that an objection is "sustained," that means the witness may not answer the question. If I say that the objection is "overruled," that means the witness may answer the question.

When there is an objection and I make a decision, you must not assume from that decision that I have any particular opinion other than that the rules for conducting a trial are being correctly followed. If I say a question may not be asked or answered, you must not try to guess what the answer would have been. That is against the rules, too.

Florida Standard Jury Instructions in Civil Cases 202.2 (Explanation of the Trial Procedure).

Florida is serious about making sure lawyers are not themselves put on trial:

Remember, the lawyers are not on trial. Your feelings about them should not influence your decision in this case.

Florida Standard Jury Instructions in Criminal Cases 3.10 (Rules for Deliberation).

So do not be afraid to protect and control. If done appropriately and professionally, the jury will respect you—and in turn, perhaps give you and your story the benefit of the doubt or a second consideration.

TO OBJECT OR NOT TO OBJECT, THAT IS THE QUESTION	
Testimony is clearly objectionable but does not matter or is not hurtful	If no reason to object, let it go; but see below about bumbling opposing counsel
Testimony is clearly objectionable and is damaging to your case	Object to make and preserve a record in case of appeal
Witness is being objectionable (giving opinions, narratives, going into irrelevant areas) but does not hurt your case	IF the witness is sensitive (ex: elderly, a child, or sex abuse victim), consider letting it go If the witness needs "training" or corralling, object as a control technique
Witness his hostile and purposely trying to hurt you	Object; consider asking for a sidebar to have the court admonish the witness for bad behavior
Opposing counsel is bumbling around and asking inappropriate questions	Object without a harsh tone; jury will know other attorney is not skilled or bumbling around
Opposing counsel is purposely eliciting inadmissible testimony, offering evidence that is inadmissible, or generally being inappropriate with questions or actions	Object—you need to control the courtroom and the jury expects someone to call down bad behavior

7.2.2 When to Object

If you decide to object, be sure to do it *timely*—object before the question ends or as the witness is giving the hearsay statement: "Objection, Your Honor, hearsay." Have the rule ready, and if it is complicated, case law and maybe even a bench brief. This is a *contemporaneous objection*, and is almost always required by appellate courts in preserving issues for appellate review.

Again, if the issue is complicated and obvious (meaning not something you think your opponent has missed), consider a motion *in limine* to have a meaningful motion, hearing, and argument.

A final reminder. *Listen*. You must listen to the direct examination and react. You cannot be caught up in your notes, or looking through transcripts, or daydreaming. If you hear anything that sounds like an attempt to elicit hearsay, or a witness about to make a hearsay statement, be on your feet and object. It's better to object, and withdraw it, than to miss it altogether.

7.3 Making the Legal Objection and Response

NOTE: the objections are universal, and can be used on direct and cross examinations.

The proper way to make an objection is to stand and state "Objection, Your Honor, _____" (wherein you *state the legal objection*). "Speaking objections" are generally improper and against local rules and judges' individual preferences. If further argument is needed, ask to approach the bench or for a sidebar.

OBJECTION TECHNIQUE	
Proper technique	**Improper** ("speaking objection")
"Objection." (use this when its super obvious)	"Objection, he can't be bringing all that irrelevant stuff up here!"
—or—	*—or—*
"Objection, Your Honor, relevance."	"Objection, the witness doesn't have personal knowledge of something he didn't see."
—or—	*—or—*
"Objection, Your Honor, privilege. May we approach? (or "may we be heard at sidebar?")	[Silence—missed the objection completely!]

Also improper: "Objection! Sidebar!" You can *ask* to be heard at sidebar, but not make the declaration that everyone should convene for you. Try, "may we be heard at sidebar?" That is much more professional.

If you are unable to get a sidebar conference, out of the hearing of the jury, at least object. Then you can ask to put something on the record after the jury leaves, when you have a little more leeway in professionally insisting that you be allowed to make a record. If that also fails, you can file a written motion to reconsider with your reasons. Your record will be complete.

Just remember, the key is to *contemporaneously* (i.e. AT THE TIME, not later) object and state your legal objection, as described above.

Responding to the objection will depend largely on the judge. If the judge is clear on the testimony or evidence and understands the legal objection, he or she can rule with a simply "sustained" or "overruled." Sometimes the judge will ask counsel to approach the bench for a sidebar conference out of the hearing of the jury, so that further argument can be made and instructions given on the ruling (i.e., you can ask this, but not that).

Some judges will simply say, "ask another question" or "move on", which is not a ruling and is not capable of appellate review. All parties to the litigation are entitled to a clean record, and it is not at all rude or unprofessional to ask the judge if the objection was sustained or overruled. Sometimes you have to ask to approach to get that ruling. And, sadly, some judges will not allow that—and you have to explore other ways to make your record, as discussed above and in section 7.8.

7.4 Controlling the Substance

Remember—whoever tells the better story, *wins*. To have the better story, not only do you have to be the better storyteller, you have to have better *substance*. The substance comes from the facts or tangible evidence. The jury will hear both stories, and human nature will cause the jurors to gravitate to the version that has the more believable, more persuasive, more easily understood facts. Substance matters to jurors. Jurors matter to your success.

So, *control the substance!*

When you can control the substance, the better chance you have of controlling the outcome. Plus, if you anticipate a certain cross examination, you do not want the other side to impede your cross by adding in superfluous and irrelevant testimony, or improperly propping up and bolstering the witness' credibility. Controlling that is the essential to your success on cross.

Controlling the substance is done through imposing the right evidentiary objections at the right time. The code mandates that evidence (either testimonial or tangible evidence) has to pass muster (i.e. "BARHOP")—be relevant, not be hearsay (an out of court statement) or be admissible hearsay with a valid exception, be capable of authentication, be the best evidence of the statement or item, and that it be complete. All counsel have an ethical duty to adhere to court rules (including and especially the rules of evidence). When that doesn't happen, you have the opportunity to shut it down.

Here are the most common objections to use to control the substance of an examination:

7.4.1 *Hearsay*

Hearsay	
Also: hearsay within hearsay	
Problem testimony	**What to argue**
Counsel asks for, or the witness states, something that was SAID out of court. Requires knowledge of the exceptions	Counsel is asking for, or the witness is testifying to, an inadmissible out of court statement

7.4.2 Relevance

Relevance	
Also: irrelevant	
Problem testimony	**What to argue**
The testimony or item of evidence has nothing to do with a material issue	The testimony does not have a tendency to make a fact more or less probable; the testimony has no consequence in determining this action

7.4.3 Authentication

Authentication	
Also: lack of authentication; lack of foundation	
Problem testimony	**What to argue**
Counsel is trying to put in evidence without passing the most basic test of whether the evidence is what it purports to be	Counsel has not laid the proper foundation (or predicate) for the admissibility of this testimony/evidence

7.4.4 Best Evidence Rule

Best Evidence Rule	
Problem testimony	**What to argue**
The witness is testifying about a writing, recording, or document without the item (or a permissible copy) being	The best evidence of the thing the witness is trying to testify about is the thing itself

at the trial and available for the jury	

7.4.5 Rule of Completeness

Rule of Completeness	
Problem testimony	**What to argue**
The evidence is only a part of a writing or recorded statement	Fundamental fairness requires that the entire writing/recording be presented to this jury for consideration

7.4.6 Privilege

Privilege	
Problem testimony	**What to argue**
The substance is about communications that are privileged under the Construction, a statute, or rule	This testimony/evidence violates the attorney-client (or other) privilege

7.5 Controlling the Witness

You can't just sit there while the witness takes over the show and starts being the main storyteller. Jurors expect lawyers to defend their clients and not sit like a bump on a log.

Here are the most common objections to use to control a witness during an examination:

7.5.1 *Hearsay*

Hearsay	
Problem testimony	What to argue
Counsel asks for, or the witness states, something that was SAID out of court; requires knowledge of the exceptions	Counsel is asking for, or the witness is testifying to, an inadmissible out of court statement

7.5.2 *Opinion*

Opinion	
Improper opinion	
Problem testimony	What to argue
Counsel asks for, or the witness states, an opinion beyond relating a fact or observation	The witness is offering a improper opinion

7.5.3 *Narrative*

Narrative	
Problem testimony	What to argue
Witness is going on and on, beyond the subject of the question asked, and/or adding irrelevant facts or opinions	The witness is simply going on and on, not in response to a proper and specific question
TYPE 1: Counsel asked question so broad that it will let the witness go on and on	TYPE 1: Counsel is asking the witness to control the flow of information, which is improper.

(objection would be *"calls for a narrative"*)	Counsel should be instructed to ask a series of questions so that the witness does not go on aimlessly, and potentially into inadmissible and perhaps mistrial areas
TYPE 2: The question was OK but the witness is rambling on and on	**TYPE 2:** The witness is not responding to questions, but is simply talking on and on

7.5.4 Speculation

Speculation	
Also: lacks personal knowledge; improper opinion; call for a conclusion	
Problem testimony	**What to argue**
Witness does not know the answer or fact asked for, but is clearly just guessing or opining	The witness is not providing a fact in response to a proper question, but it guessing/opining

7.5.5 Nonresponsive

Nonresponsive	
Problem testimony	**What to argue**
Question is on point, but answer is on a different point (or no point at all)	The witness is not directly answering, or has nor directly answered, the properly asked question

Controlling the witness takes on two dimensions. First, you have to try to control the substance of what the witness is saying.

Second, you have to control *how* the witness presents the story. Controlling the "how" comes in the form of fighting a witness' attempts to talk about what someone else said, speculating about things the witness did not witness, and just sitting there and rambling away.

You will find two types of witnesses: those that innocently violate the rules, and those that intentionally violate them. Lay witnesses are not skilled in the rules of trial combat, so they tend to run afoul of them and immediately back off. There are those that are of the personality that they will just run wild in any setting. Those witnesses are easier to snap back into place.

The intentional violators are the seasoned witnesses—law enforcement and experts. They know when to take the direct question and run with it, and they know how to sneak in an inadmissible statement here and there. And they do it. You have to be prepared to fight that witness and corral him or her back into submission. Specific control techniques are found in section 5.9.

7.6 Controlling Opposing Counsel

Controlling the substance of what comes out in court is critical, and a great part of accomplishing that control is making sure opposing counsel sticks to the rules in questioning on direct.

Here are the most common objections to use to control opposing counsel:

7.6.1 *Leading*

Leading	
Problem testimony	**What to argue**
Question calls for a yes or no as the answer	Counsel is suggesting the answer in his/her question,

	which calls for a yes or no instead of being open-ended and asking the witness to provide the facts

7.6.2 Counsel Testifying

Counsel testifying
Also: facts not in evidence

Problem testimony	What to argue
Opposing counsel is bringing up specific facts in the question, instead of asking "who, what, when, where, why, how" open-ended questions that ask the witness to provide the facts; counsel is the one putting the fact into evidence, not a witness or item of evidence	Counsel is injecting facts into this trial as if he/she were a witness. Counsel should be admonished to simply ask and open-ended question without suggesting facts, so that the witness may do his/her job and provide the facts

7.6.3 Arguing with the Witness

Arguing with the witness
Also: "badgering the witness", improper, inflammatory

Problem testimony	What to argue
TYPE 1: Anything that attacks the witness, or comes across overly confrontational; listen for tone of voice and common argumentative statements	**TYPE 1**: Counsel has resorted to arguing with this witness, which is not proper or permissible cross examination

TYPE 2: Making an argument to the jury guised as a question to the witness	**TYPE 2:** Counsel is arguing the ultimate facts to the jury in the form of a question, by asking for a conclusion or opinion that invades the fact-finding province of the jury

7.6.4   Calls for . . . (Conclusion, Opinion, Etc.)

Calls for . . .
•   *Conclusion*
•   *Opinion*
•   *Hearsay*
•   *Speculation/opinion*
•   *Narrative*

Problem testimony	What to argue
Opposing counsel's question asks the witness to do something other than provide an admissible fact	Counsel is asking this witness to do something other than provide an admissible fact, in the form of [conclusion, opinion, etc.] Counsel should be instructed to ask a series of questions so that the witness does not go on aimlessly

7.6.5   Improper (Various)

Improper
•   *Ambiguous*

- *Asking witness to comment on another witness' testimony*
- *Improper character evidence*
- *Bolstering*
- *Violation of a pretrial order*
- *Improper impeachment (prior statement, prior record, etc.)*
- *Antics (sighing, eye-rolling, etc.)*
- *Injecting personal beliefs*
- *"Golden Rule" violation*

Problem testimony	What to argue
There are several things opposing counsel can do that are improper; listen for anything that is not asking for a relevant, admissible fact; for this objection, it is advisable to add "may we approach?" or "may I be heard at sidebar" to your contemporaneous legal objection, so you make a proper record Watch for opposing counsel making facial expressions, or getting to close to the witness in an intimidating manner Asking the witness to put him-/herself in the place of another witness, victim, the defendant, etc. (the "Golden Rule") clarification; counsel is	Counsel is attempting to: • ask a question that can be interpreted different ways, counsel should be more specific • have this witness comment on another witness • place improper and inadmissible character evidence before this jury • bolstering this witness which invades the province of the jury • violating your pretrial order regarding ____ • conduct an improper impeachment

putting his/her own "spin" on the facts	• acting inappropriately and pandering to the jurors
	• improperly stating his/her own person beliefs, which are irrelevant
	• violate the Golden Rule by asking this witness to put him-/herself in the place of the victim, etc.

7.6.6 Misstating the Evidence (Mischaracterization, Misleading, Confusing)

Misstating the evidence	
Also: mischaracterization, misleading, confusing	
Problem testimony	**What to argue**
A poorly worded question that can lead to the witness misunderstanding the question and potentially giving an innocent, well-intentioned answer that could lead to an impeachment; the witness does not understand the question but doesn't ask for clarification; counsel is putting his/her own "spin" on the facts	Counsel is misstating the testimony of Mr. Witness, or the facts, and in so is misleading and/or confusing this witness and the jury. I ask that the jury be instructed to disregard that last statement from counsel, and to rely on their own recollection of what the evidence was, and counsel be instructed to not misstate the facts

7.6.7   *Beyond the Scope*

Beyond the scope	
Problem testimony	**What to argue**
On re-direct examination, opposing counsel asking questions about irrelevant issues not addressed on cross examination	The question goes beyond the scope of what was asked on cross examination, and the door has not been opened for this line of questioning

7.6.8   *Compound Question*

Compound question	
Problem testimony	**What to argue**
Listen for compound questions that ask for multiple facts or different answers or discussion of different topics	Counsel is asking for two separate factual answers, and in so is misleading and/or confusing the jury

7.6.9   *"You'd Agree with Me" or "Isn't It True"*

"You'd agree with me" or "Isn't it true"	
Problem testimony	**What to argue**
Any phrase that essentially asks the witness to agree or concede to opposing counsel's version of the facts	Counsel is attempted to have this witness agree with his or her own personal opinions of this case, which are irrelevant, and this line of questioning is entirely improper

7.6.10   *Asked and Answered*

Asked and answered	
Problem testimony	**What to argue**
The same question over and over, even in slightly various incarnations	Counsel has asked for a fact, and a fact was given. Asking for the same fact over and over is improper, cumulative

To control opposing counsel, you must listen carefully to the questions and be ready to object at the exact moment the question is finished but *before* the witness has a chance to answer it. The timing is important, as the judge cannot rule on the question until it is formed. Premature objections will draw an admonition from the judge to let counsel finish the question. For instance:

Q   *Ms. Witness, as you were in your yard, what did your neighbor—?*

OBJ *Objection, Your Honor, calls for hearsay.*

J   *Well, let me hear the question first.*

You have not only highlighted the testimony, you have lost the objection you likely would have won had it been a hearsay question (thus either confusing the jury or simply having them think you are incompetent), and opposing counsel gets another stab at getting out the hearsay statement. This is assuming, of course, that the statement is in fact hearsay and there is no valid exception under the rules. Or, that the question was going to be "what did your neighbor *do*?" which does not call for hearsay.

Otherwise, get your timing down by being on your toes:

Q   *Ms. Witness, as you were in your yard, what did your neighbor say to you about the prior owners of the property?*

OBJ Objection, Your Honor, calls for hearsay.

J   Sustained.

The witness has no time to answer before your valid objection is interposed. You have stopped your opponent's attempt to circumvent the rules.

In the event you miss the objection, and the hearsay or other inadmissible evidence comes out, interject over and interrupt the witness. Try to cut it off. If all of the hearsay comes out before you can make the objection, and your objection is sustained, consider asking for a curative instruction to disregard, to strike the hearsay, and an admonishment to the witness not to do that again. As always, *keep objecting.*

7.7 Being on the End of a Sustained Objection

There will be those times where you get shut down—rightfully, or maybe not so rightfully. We all ask just bad questions from time to time.

Don't just give up—try again. Think about where you are and what you are doing. There should be no surprises in your examinations, as you will have thought through your themes, topics, and target questions. You should not have any issues come up that you have not anticipated and are prepared.

If, however, you do find yourself in a jam, do the following:

Never, never, never lose your cool. Stay professional. Stay focused on why you are there—the client—and what your story is, and what your goals are in the courtroom. Judges have seen too many attorneys roll eyes, blow out huffy frustrated sighs, and some even accuse the judge and opposing counsel of somehow ganging up on the attorney. Just stay calm and *think.* Think before you speak.

Ask for a moment. When the objection comes, stop and think about the objection, and if there is any ruling, what it was. Does it apply—is the judge right or wrong? It is better to take a second to recompose, than to continue to ask the bad question over and over.

Confer with co-counsel. You should have a trial partner, who should be paying attention. When you ask the judge for a moment (which you may even phrase as, "Your Honor, may I have a moment to confer with co-counsel?"), purposefully walk to your counsel table, and have a discreet conversation with your partner.

Re-phrase the question. Take another stab at it, and carefully reword your question to narrow it to the exact and precise. If you need a second, take it. Jot down the question so you do not trip up again.

Ask to approach. If you think the objection was improvidently sustained against, you, ask to approach or for a sidebar. Or ask, "may I be heard?" Whatever the custom in your locale, be sure to get the judge's attention so you can expand your legal argument outside the earshot of the jury.

Make a record. Sometimes the judge is just wrong and will not entertain any of your attempts to be heard. At the next break, when the jury is not in the room, ask to be heard again. If the judge still refuses, ask that you be able to proffer the question and answer for the record. Some judges will let you, some won't (those that won't must not mind being reversed on appeal!). If that does not work, then make careful notes and file the appropriate post-trial motions (just in case you do not win your trial).

When to give up. You must know when you are beat, and make a professional and dignified retreat. As stated above, there are times when the judge is just going to have to make your life miserable and not budge. If you continue to fight in front of the jury, it's *you* who looks bad—not the judge. Be respectful, make your record, and move on. You might be able to recall the witness as your own, so at the end of the cross examination and re-direct examination, ask the judge to have the witness remain.

7.8 Making a Record (Proffers, Court Exhibits)

If you have a line of questioning that the judge will not permit, you must preserve it and your objection/motion for review on appeal (just in case).

A proffer is merely a prevention, or offer, of proof that is made on and for the record but is outside the purvey of the trier of fact. A proffer gets the information into the record when that information is otherwise not in evidence.

You cannot forget to make a necessary proffer, nor can you leave before putting something on the record. If you do not make a record, then the appellate court has no idea what the issue was and cannot make a ruling. On the other hand, if you have made an objection, or tried to present some evidence that the judge has excluded, and you have a full record of what the missing testimony or evidence is, then the appeals court may be able to bail you out in the even you lost the trial.

7.8.1   *Example of a Proffer*

Virtually any situation in cross examination may be subject to a judge intervening and closing down the questioning. Some are truly collateral or irrelevant—if you properly prepared, you should not encounter that problem.

When faced with a judge excluding critical questioning, be sure to get the questions on the record. Take this cross examination, for example:

Q   *Mr. Witness, have you ever been convicted of a felony?*

OBJ   *Objection, relevance and improper impeachment.*

J   *Sustained.*

Q   *Your Honor, may we approach the bench for a sidebar?*

J   *Yes, please approach.*

[SIDEBAR]

Q   *Judge, impeachment with prior convictions is permitted under Federal Rule of Evidence 610, and the credibility of this witness is a critical component of this cross examination in the defense of my client.*

A   *Judge, this is a minor witness in comparison to the others, so his criminal record is of no relevance.*

J   *I agree, I do not see why we have to embarrass this witness.*

Q   *Your Honor, this is the accuser, the victim—there could not be a more important witness. He is claiming my client stole from him—I have the right to challenge his credibility under the rules.*

J   *No, I don't see why this poor victim has to be put through any further discomfort. Sustained.*

Q   *Your Honor, may I quickly proffer what the anticipated testimony would be?*

J   *Quickly.*

Q   *My question would be, "have you ever been convicted of a felony?", and I anticipate the response would be yes. In fact, Mr. Witness has three separate prior convictions for fraud. Those convictions were in 2010, 2012, and 2016—all of*

*which involved convictions. And for the last
conviction he has been on probation on the entire
time from when the allegations in this case occurred
until now.*

J   *Opposing counsel, do you agree with that?*

A   *Oh, clearly, judge, Mr. Witness has those three
convictions.*

J   *OK. I'll maintain my prior ruling, and sustain the
objection. You have made your record, and the
appellate court will decide if I have made the right
call. Please step back, and move on to your next
question.*

This situation may not be as absurd as you would think, as there
are times when the judge may just make a mistake. You cannot
compound the matter by making the additional mistake of *not*
making a complete and accurate record. In this example, if you lose
the trial, the appellate court now has a complete picture of what
happened, and why the error is reversible.

7.8.2   *Making a Court Exhibit*

If the excluded evidence is in the form of a document, or other
tangible piece of evidence (an audio or video recording, a photo,
etc.), then you should include it in the record for appellate review.

Take the example above, of the bench conference (sidebar)
about the witness' prior conviction If someone has been convicted
of a crime, there will be a court document memorializing that
conviction. In fact, most jurisdictions will not let you even ask the
question unless you have the good faith to ask it based on having
possession of a certified copy of a judgment of conviction. *See*
5.8.1.2 for how to do an impeachment with prior convictions.

Here is how you would make a proffer of the documents:

Q   *My question would be, "have you ever been convicted of a felony?", and I anticipate the response would be yes. In fact, Mr. Witness has three separate prior convictions for fraud. Those convictions were in 2010, 2012, and 2016—all of which involved convictions. And for the last conviction he has been on probation on the entire time from when the allegations in this case occurred until now.*

J   *Opposing counsel, do you agree with that?*

A   *Oh, clearly, judge, Mr. Witness has those three convictions.*

J   *OK. I'll maintain my prior ruling, and sustain the objection. You have made your record, and the appellate court will decide if I have made the right call. Please step back, and move on to your next question.*

Q   *Yes, Your Honor. I have certified copies of the judgment of conviction in each of those cases, and I would like to have it included in the record as a court exhibit.*

J   *The court will receive as Court's Exhibit 1A, 1B, and 1C the certified copies that counsel has just handed to me. I will give those to the clerk for inclusion in the record, but direct that they not go back with the jury in deliberations. They are not evidence in this trial at this time. Both counsel will refrain from making reference to them before this jury.*

Q   *Yes, Your Honor.*

A   *Yes, Your Honor.*

It's that simple. Remember, in the event that the judge does not permit you to proffer the documents at that time, do it at the first recess outside the presence of the jury. If the judge will not hear that, then do a separate *Notice of Filing* and file them with the clerk, making note as to why they are being included.

Again, do not give up. If you don't win at trial, your success on appeal could depend on making a complete and accurate record for the appellate court to review.

7.9 Checklists

7.9.1   *Admissibility Checklist*

Is this piece of evidence or testimony objectionable?	
If so, what is the objection?	
Is this piece of evidence or testimony critical and material?	
Is the issue clear on its fact, such that can be argued on the face of the rule?	
If the issue so complicated that it requires case law authority in order to properly argue it?	
Should a motion *in limine* be filed?	

Should a bench brief be prepared?	
What is the proper legal objection to be contemporaneously made in trial?	

7.9.2   To Object or Not to Object?

	Does the item or testimony "hop the bar"? (*See* BARHOP, above)
	Is the evidence violating a pretrial order?
	Is the substance of the evidence hurting you (on the ultimate issue or witness credibility)?
	Does the objection need to be made for control purposes?
	Should an objection be made to assist the jury in knowing what the other side is doing?
	Do you need to make the contemporaneous objection to preserve for appeal a pre-trial motion you filed that was denied?

7.9.3   Making a Record (Proffer)

	Ask your question on direct or cross
	If objection made and overruled, move on (you won)
	If objection made and sustained without argument, ask to approach the bench or for a sidebar conference • If not allowed to approach, ask "may I make a proffer?" • If not permitted, move on; wait until jury is out of courtroom and make proffer on the record

•	If allowed to make a proffer, ask to approach, and state into the record your question and the anticipated testimony
	Offer proffered document/evidence in as a court exhibit (that does not go back to jury)
	Re-raise issue in post-trial motions if necessary (i.e. you lose the case)
	IF ALL FAILS: Do not argue with the court in front of the jury, or discuss the proffered testimony in front of the jury; do it outside the hearing of the jury and in post-trial motions (if necessary)

7.9.4   *Objections Rulings List*

No one wants to lose a trial, but you must be prepared to lose. That means taking precautions such as making proffers (discussed above) and contemporaneous objections. If you lose, you may want to file any post-trial motions available to you under the rules.

For a post-trial motion to be effective, it needs to cite back to the trial specifically. A way to help you preserve any issues in your mind is to use an Objections Rulings List. This takes no particular form, and can be something as simple as a sheet of paper kept next to your Center Sheet (see section 1.8). Here is an example:

Day of trial; time	Part of trial*	Wit; Item	Issue	Obj	Ruling	Proffer (y/n)

* Examples of notations and abbreviations: P in-chief; D rebutt., etc.

This item of work product can save you a lot of time trying to remember everything. Hopefully, you won't need it and you'll win your case?

CHAPTER 8

Post-Trial Issues and Evaluation

> **OBJECTIVES:** When the trial is over, the heavy-lifting is over—mostly. There are still important tasks at hand. For this chapter, we are going to cover the most important basics of wrapping the case up, post-trial issues, and self-evaluation.

Win or lose, the verdict does not mark the end of your work as a trial lawyer. You have to tie-up the loose ends, and reflect on the whole thing.

8.1 Case-Related "to Dos"

Post-trial motions. Consult with applicable rules and statutes, and consult with your client. Are there authorized post-trial motions that you should consider filing? Is there a judgment to collect? Start the process. Do you have to appeal? Timely file a notice of appeal. Be mindful of deadlines.

Appeal issues. Again, consult with your client, and note the conversations. In civil cases, the client will continue to pay fees for the appeal. A very real conversation must be had. Perhaps there is negotiation to be done with the other side to resolve the case without even more litigation. In a criminal case, you may have to file the appeal even if the client does not have any viable issues—it is the right of the defendant. File the notice of appeal, followed by a motion to withdraw as counsel (and possibly appoint counsel for indigent clients). At a minimum, you *must* file the notice of appeal if directed by the client.

Return of evidence. Evidence that is no longer needed can be released by the clerk (except, of course, illegal drugs or pornography, etc.). But just about anything else. If you don't need it, let the clerk dispose of it. If you need it, check local rules and laws for the procedure to move for its release.

Closing the file. Organize and archive your file. Converting paper to digital is *highly recommended*. It can be stored for years to come, and accessed quickly if needed. The cost to digitally store a file is small; renting a storage unit for old files, or paying to store them at a commercial document storage facility is costly. *NOTE: if you have any originals that belong to the client, now is the time to return them.

8.2 Personal Review, Evaluation, and Analysis

A lawyer never stops learning. No matter how many trials or hearings you do, you can always learn something. Consider keeping a journal of your trials and hearings. First and foremost, you can record things while they are fresh and analyze how you did and what you need to work on in future trials. Second, over a long career, you will forget things. It is always fun and interesting to revisit old cases. You can think about how you did things *then* as opposed to how you do them *now* (after reading this book!).

The final words in this book are about your mental well-being. Being a trial lawyer is incredibly rewarding. You can attain prestige and wealth. You can also make yourself sick and cause your relationships to suffer. *Take the time to decompress. Take the time to be yourself and do the things you like to do. Take time for your family and friends.* Work to live—don't live to work.

If you have issues, turn to the American Bar Association or your local bar association's lawyer assistance programs. Go to a counselor. Your client's future, and your future, are dependent on having the best version of you at the trial.

Pretrial Practice

Describe your preparation.

Do you feel you were totally prepared?

What could you have done to better prepare?

What was your level of confidence going into the trial?

Whether you thought you were going to win or not, did you feel like you were ready?

How did you go through the analysis of facts and witnesses? Were you right?

Did you take effective discovery?

Did you conduct effective depositions?

Could your outcome at trial be attributed to your pretrial preparation?

Motion Hearings

Did you file any pretrial motions?

How did the hearings go?

Could you have filed motions that you did not file? Why/why not?

Did your pretrial litigation impact the case at trial? How or how not?

Voir Dire and Jury Selection

Describe your preparation.

Do you feel you were totally prepared?

What was your ideal juror? Did you get "ideal jurors"?

What things did you cover with the venire?

How did the prospective jurors respond to you?

Did you get feedback from them, beyond their words (eye contact, body language)?

Were you able to get them talking?

What tools did you use to try to get the potential jurors to open up?

Did you have any problems?

Overall, did you get a good jury for your case?

What will you or could you do differently next time?

Opening Statement

How did it go?

Did you use the structure of rivet phrase-mini stories-intro law- "the ask?"

Why or why not? If not, could you have?

Was there anything you wanted to include but didn't? Why (not sure would be admitted, etc.)?

Did you mention anything that ultimately was not admitted at trial or testified about?

How did you avoid arguing?

Did you use demonstrative or any items of evidence?

How did you introduce the law to the jury?

Did you draw any objections in your opening? Ruling? What could you have done better?

Did you get feedback from the jury?

What was different between your opening's style and content and that of opposing counsel?

Direct Examinations

Describe your preparation.

Do you feel you were totally prepared?

What was your structure?

Did you prepare your witnesses? Did they perform accordingly?

Did the jurors seem to like and/or respond well to them?

What problems did you encounter?

What could you do differently next time?

Did you get any feedback from the jurors during your direct exams?

Mid-trial motions

Did you make any mid-trial motions?

Did you make a record or do any proffers to preserve the record?

Cross Examinations

How did it go?

Overall, do you feel like you told your story through your cross examination?

How did you prepare for cross—list of questions, or Cross Sheets?

Why did you use the list or Cross Sheets (as opposed to the other)?

Did you structure your overall cross with theme-topic-target fact?

Did you have any issues with the witness? What happened?

Where you able to control the witness? Why or why not? What control tools did you try?

Did you get any feedback from the jury during your cross?

Did you make any adjustments during cross based on what you saw from the jurors?

What problems did you have?

If you had these crosses to do over, what would you do differently?

What will you do differently next time?

Closing Arguments

How did it go?

When did you begin preparation for closing?

What was your structure? Did it work? How could you have done it differently?

What were you able to use from opening?

How much adjusting did you have to do from what happened in trial?

Did you have to abandon any arguments you initially made or intended to use?

What specific argument tools did you use (word, phrases)?

How was your confidence with your case going into closing?

Did your level of confidence impact what/how you argued?

Were you able to connect with the jurors?

How did you connect? Eye contact? Conversational tone? Movements?

Did you get any feedback from the jurors while closing (nods, smiles, etc.)?

Did you use evidence or demonstratives?

Did you use the jury instructions? How?

How did you use counterarguments?

What was "The Ask?" How did you go about "The Ask"?

Overall, how do you feel about your closing as opposed to the other side's closing?

What was stylistically different between you and the other side, apart from the argument?

Style

What is your style of advocacy?

Have you modeled your style from another attorney?

What about that attorney is admirable and what you are trying to adopt?

Did the judge seem OK with your style?

How did the jurors react to you?

How were you different from opposing counsel or co-counsel?

What did you do better? What did opposing counsel do better?

What main emotions for feelings were you trying to convey (anger, fairness, etc.)?

How did you do that?

Did it work?

Did you win the trial?

Why or why not?

What could have changed the verdict?

If this was a "slam dunk" for or against you, how did you perform in spite of that?

Did anyone (judge, jurors, client, opposing counsel) comment on your performance?

If you had it all to do over again, what would you do differently, and why?

Impact of this case on you and your client

How long did the case take, from initial intake to post-verdict?

Could you have moved it along any faster? Would that have made a difference?

How did the case impact your client?

What was your relationship with your client throughout?

How did you do on the money—did you make money or lose money on the case?

How much did you put into the case, and was it worth it based on the verdict?

How was your mental well-being pretrial and in trial?

If you had issues, how did you deal with it?

Did you seek any professional help with your personal or mental health issues?

If you had it to do again, what would you do differently?